NGOs and the Millennium Development Goals

NGOs and the Millennium Development Goals

Citizen Action to Reduce Poverty

Edited by
Jennifer M. Brinkerhoff, Stephen C. Smith,
and Hildy Teegen

NGOs AND THE MILLENNIUM DEVELOPMENT GOALS

First published in 2007 by
PALGRAVE MACMILLAN™
175 Fifth Avenue, New York, N.Y. 10010 and
Houndmills, Basingstoke, Hampshire, England RG21 6XS.
Companies and representatives throughout the world.

PALGRAVE MACMILLAN is the global academic imprint of the Palgrave Macmillan division of St. Martin's Press, LLC and of Palgrave Macmillan Ltd. Macmillan® is a registered trademark in the United States, United Kingdom and other countries. Palgrave is a registered trademark in the European Union and other countries.

ISBN-13: 978-1-4039-7974-2
ISBN-10: 1-4039-7974-X

Library of Congress Cataloging-in-Publication Data

NGOs and the Millennium Development Goals : citizen action to reduce poverty/edited by Jennifer M. Brinkerhoff, Stephen C. Smith, and Hildy Teegen.
     p. cm.
  ISBN 1-4039-7974-X (alk. paper)
  1. Economic assistance–Developing countries–International cooperation.
  2. Non-governmental organizations–Developing countries. 3. UN Millennium Project. 4. Poverty–Developing countries. I. Brinkerhoff, Jennifer M., 1965- II. Smith, Stephen C., 1955- III. Teegen, Hildy.
  HC60.N499 2007
  362.5'57091724–dc22

                                                                2006037222

A catalogue record for this book is available from the British Library.

Design by Macmillan India Ltd.

First edition: July 2007

10 9 8 7 6 5 4 3 2 1

Printed in the United States of America.

Contents

List of Figures

List of Tables

List of Contributors

The George Washington University International NGO Team (GW-INGOT)

GW-INGOT brings together faculty, researchers, and graduate students with a primary focus on discussing and promoting research related to international development and NGOs, from a broad range of disciplinary perspectives. GW-INGOT works with individuals and organizations from outside GW that share our focus on international development and NGOs.

GW-INGOT was founded by the co-editors of this volume—three professors who share a research focus, an educational mission, and a commitment to development and to poverty alleviation, particularly through the enhanced effectiveness of NGOs:

- **Jennifer M. Brinkerhoff**, Associate Professor of Public Administration and International Affairs, The George Washington University. Brinkerhoff is the author of *Partnership for International Development: Rhetoric or Results* (Lynne Rienner Publishers, 2002) and co-author (with Derick W. Brinkerhoff) of *Working for Change: Making a Career in International Public Service* (Kumarian Press, 2005).

- **Stephen C. Smith**, Professor of Economics and International Affairs, The George Washington University. Smith is the author of *Ending Global Poverty: A Guide to What Works* (Palgrave Macmillan, 2005) and coauthor (with Michael Todaro) of *Economic Development* (9th ed. Addison-Wesley, 2005).

- **Hildy Teegen**, Professor of International Business and International Affairs, The George Washington University. Teegen is Director of GW's Center for International Business Education and Research and co-editor (with Jonathan P. Doh) of *Globalization and NGOs: Transforming Business, Governments and Society* (Praeger Books, 2003).

The collaboration among the three founders and other members of the Team is indicative of trends in academe that have gained momentum over the past few years. Given the complexity of the problems we face in our global society, it is essential that the intellectual capital available in all relevant disciplines be involved in developing solutions. The barriers between disciplines are disintegrating, and GW-INGOT provides an exemplary model of the multidisciplinary approach. Like many of the NGOs that the Team studies, GW-INGOT is working both within and outside traditional disciplinary and institutional boundaries. The faculty and graduate students involved in GW-INGOT represent areas including international education, public health, international affairs, political science, public administration, business, and economics. Many of these Team members served as discussants for the GW-INGOT conference panels that gave rise to this volume.

A second important trend that has been emerging over time is greater collaboration among those in academe, and those dedicated to making and implementing policy. GW-INGOT works closely with NGO practitioners, policy makers, donors, consultants, academics, and graduate students from within and outside GW, in the area of international development.

The collective strength represented in INGOT is a critical component of the effort to help improve the capacity of the NGO sector to develop innovative ideas, plan strategically, and then design—and rigorously evaluate—poverty and related development programs.

Additional Chapter Contributors

Derick W. Brinkerhoff is Senior Fellow in International Public Management at RTI International (Research Triangle Institute) and an associate faculty member of the School of Public Policy and Public Administration, The George Washington University.

William Drayton is CEO and chair and founder of Ashoka Innovators for the Public.

Michael Edwards is the director of the Governance and Civil Society Unit at the Ford Foundation.

Martha Finnemore is Professor of Political Science and International Affairs at The George Washington University.

Jan Vandemoortele is the United Nations Development Programme (UNDP) Resident Representative of Pakistan and formerly Principal Advisor of the Bureau for Development Policy, part of the UNDP.

Carol Welch is the U.S. campaign coordinator of the Millennium Development Goals Campaign.

1

Introduction

Jennifer M. Brinkerhoff, Stephen C. Smith,
and Hildy Teegen

The imperative to end extreme poverty has risen to the top of the global policy agenda as never before. In July 2005, the Group of Eight (G8) summit focused on poverty in Africa; despite the catastrophic bombings in London, leaders never lost sight of this as a priority. There is also probably greater awareness than ever before in government and business circles, and among the general public, concerning problems of extreme poverty.

In September 2005, the world's leaders met at the UN to review progress, and in some cases lack of progress, toward international poverty goals. In September 2000, the 189 member states of the UN adopted the UN Millennium Declaration, which includes eight Millennium Development Goals (MDGs) to address development and make substantial progress toward the eradication of poverty by 2015 (see Figure 1.1). Many of these goals refer to actions that poor states must take to impact poverty; the last goal addresses the contributions needed from the rich countries to support these efforts within the developing world. Despite some controversy about whether the United States had agreed to the specific goals and targets of the MDGs, by the end of the conference all member countries renewed their commitment to them. The MDGs have now become widely accepted in the international community. But many countries are behind schedule, and indeed many of the poorest countries have been losing ground.

Given the inability or unwillingness of some public-sector actors to fulfill poverty goals, despite their local and public good character citizen interests are increasingly being reflected, promoted, and organized within nongovernmental organizations (NGOs) (Teegen 2003; Kaul 2001). But while Kofi Annan, the former UN Secretary-General, and others have noted in general terms that there is an important role for NGOs in promoting development, and NGOs receive brief mentions in UN documents such as those prepared in January 2005 by the Millennium Project, NGOs' specific roles in achieving the MDGs have so far gone largely unaddressed.

Moreover, despite this lip service, the focus of official development assistance is, if anything, moving *away* from embracing a larger NGO role. Multilateral donors led by the World Bank, along with bilateral donors such as U. S. Agency for International Development (USAID) and the Department for International Development, U.K. (DFID), are increasingly emphasizing direct support for government budgets in African nations and low-income countries elsewhere. The influential Africa Commission report released in June 2005 stressed the need for such direct support of government budgets. It noted that creation of separate accounts and government entities to administer new initiatives draws away the best staff from regular government departments and generally detracts from their capacity-building efforts. While this is a valid point, the supplemental role of NGOs was all but ignored, except for describing positively civil society's role in acting as advocate and watchdog and making minor mentions of their possible service-delivery roles in some cases. The otherwise comprehensive January 2005 report of the UN Millennium Project gives very little weight to NGOs.

NGOs working to end poverty are a diverse group of organizations and include some relatively ineffective groups. But the best of them make up for lack of heft with deftness, flexibility, innovativeness, specialized expertise, cross-national sharing of lessons learned, closeness to and trust by local communities and marginalized groups of the poor, and credibility with a wide range of domestic and international actors. It simply does not make sense that the renewed commitment to ending global poverty has included so little focus on the past, current, and potential contributions of NGOs.

To respond to this huge gap in knowledge, a major conference was held at George Washington University in Washington, D.C., in May–June 2004 to address the role of NGOs in achieving the MDGs (see the appendix to this chapter). Over 300 participants discussed NGOs' role in addressing extreme poverty and the needs of the poor in health, nutrition, education, gender equity, and environmental sustainability, as well as in promoting partnerships for development across developed and developing worlds. This book is a product of that conference.

The MDGs: A Global Initiative for Poverty Reduction and Human Development

The UN Millennium Declaration featured eight MDGs to address development and the eradication of poverty by 2015. The MDGs represent an unprecedented commitment to global poverty reduction and quality-of-life issues. Since their adoption, all major bilateral and multilateral donors have incorporated the MDGs into their humanitarian assistance, development, and lending programs.Figure 1.1 outlines the eight MDGs and their associated targets. The Millennium Development Compact, a detailed action plan for meeting the goals, was published in the July 2003 *Human Development Report* (United Nations 2003) as an important follow-on to the initial statement titled *Goals, Targets, and Indicators* outlined in September 2000.

The MDGs represent a unique approach to global development for a number of reasons. First, their development was undertaken in direct consultation with the poor countries that are the focus of development. This is in stark contrast to similar exercises in the past initiated by the rich countries. For example, initiatives undertaken by member countries of the Organisation of Economic Co-operation and Development (OECD) under Development Assistance Cooperation (DAC) were criticized by poor countries on grounds that they did not directly solicit or necessarily incorporate the most pressing concerns of poor nations. Second, by jointly signing the Millennium Declaration, all the key multilateral institutions—including the UN, the World Bank, the International Monetary Fund (IMF), the OECD, and the World Trade Organization (WTO)—now share a policy commitment to a people-centered approach to alleviating poverty. The publicly cooperative relationship among these agencies, signaled by their joint adherence to the eighth goal, fills a key institutional policy alignment gap in many previous development efforts (WFUNA 2002). Clear and tangible support for the MDGs has been offered since the signing of the Declaration. The Zedillo Report, which originated from the (UN) High-Level Panel on Financing for Development (Zedillo 2002), details the financial requirements of the MDGs; the tenets of the MDGs were endorsed at the 2002 World Summit on Sustainable Development; and the G8 nations reaffirmed support for the MDGs at their meeting in France in spring 2003 and emphasized support for Africa, which has been falling behind on the goal schedule, in July 2005.

Third, given their breadth, the MDGs hold promise for acting upon synergies among development targets. On the one hand, the MDGs are sufficiently broad to incorporate many other existing development initiatives and, as such, will serve to reinforce and potentially revitalize these parallel efforts. On the other hand, the MDGs implicitly recognize the potential synergies and positive externalities (including "strong complementarities") inherent in development (Todaro and Smith 2005). Similarly, poverty traps often include vicious cycles in which deficiencies in one sector reinforce deficiencies in other sectors, and so an integrated approach may be needed in poverty programs (Smith 2002, 2005). By including a wide range of poverty and development issues, the MDGs may

1. **Eradicate extreme poverty and hunger**
Target for 2015:   Halve the proportion of people living on less than a dollar a day and those who suffer from hunger.

2. **Achieve universal primary education**
Target for 2015:   Ensure that all boys and girls complete primary school.

3. **Promote gender equality and empower women**
Targets for 2005:   Eliminate gender disparities in primary and secondary education (preferred).
Targets for 2015:   Eliminate gender disparities at all levels.

4. **Reduce child mortality**
Target for 2015:   Reduce by two-thirds the mortality rate among children under five.

5. **Improve maternal health**
Target for 2015:   Reduce by three-quarters the ratio of women dying in childbirth.

6. **Combat HIV/AIDS, malaria, and other diseases**
Target for 2015:   Halt and begin to reverse the spread of HIV/AIDS and the incidence of malaria and other major diseases.

7. **Ensure environmental sustainability**
General target: Integrate the principles of sustainable development into country policies and programs and reverse the loss of environmental resources.
Target for 2015:   Reduce by half the proportion of people without access to safe drinking water.
Target for 2020:   Achieve significant improvement in the lives of at least 100 million slum dwellers.

8. **Develop a global partnership for development**
Targets:
- Develop further an open trading and financial system that includes a commitment to good governance, development, and poverty reduction—nationally and internationally.

- Address the least-developed countries' special needs, and the special needs of landlocked and small-island developing states.

- Deal comprehensively with developing countries' debt problems.

- Develop decent and productive work for youth.

- In cooperation with pharmaceutical companies, provide access to affordable essential drugs in developing countries.

- In cooperation with the private sector, make available the benefits of new technologies, especially information and communications technologies.

Figure 1.1   Millennium Development Goals: Themes and targets

Source: United Nations Development Programme (UNDP), http://www.undp.org/mdg/

promote solutions that leverage possible joint gains across the goals and targets.

Fourth, the MDGs indicate specific roles and responsibilities for the rich countries in promoting development among the world's poor, including increased economic assistance, removal of trade and investment barriers that inhibit poor countries' growth prospects, and reduction or elimination of unsustainable debts of the poor countries. In this way, all of the UN member countries are held responsible for promoting development. The inclusion of the rich countries as responsible parties is related to the direct and intentional mapping of the MDGs to universal human rights as originally detailed in the Universal Declaration of Human Rights (articles 22, 24, 25, 26) and other human-rights instruments. Human-rights status for the MDGs imposes an obligation on the part of rich countries to protect and promote the realization of the MDGs (United Nations 2003; Figure 1.1). Of course, beyond this formal rationale, the inclusion of rich-country obligations is widely understood in the developing countries to reflect a historical culpability for the legacy of colonialism.

Finally, the concept of partnership extends beyond the explicit role given to rich countries in support of poor countries' development efforts. Goal 8's explicit recognition that development gains can be promoted through cross-sectoral partnering and interactions significantly broadens the cast of characters who must be drawn upon to achieve the other MDGs. Unique resources brought into play by the various sectors, and in novel combinations of partnering organizations from various sectors, can be applied to promote development (Brinkerhoff 2002; WEFGGI 2003). As Annan put it: "The entire United Nations family of Member States, international organizations, funds, agencies, programmes, the private sector and civil society must join together to meet the lofty commitments that are embodied in the Millennium Declaration" (Annan 2001, 5).

Meetings of official intergovernmental bodies (e.g., the UN and the OECD) and other international bodies (e.g., the WTO) confirm the importance of private-sector participation as well as that of NGOs that have achieved formal consultative status with most multilateral institutions. Nonofficial supranational organizations, such as the World Economic Forum, through their Global Governance Initiative, have been explicitly gauging what civil-society organizations (CSOs) can do to meet the MDGs. This effort is in recognition of the important contributions and new opportunities for progress in global governance afforded by the growing role of civil-society groups (WEFGGI 2003).

In considering the roles of multiple actors in addressing the MDGs, it is important to acknowledge the primacy of their main beneficiaries—poor people themselves. As research at the World Bank and elsewhere has shown, poor communities often have greater capabilities to pursue broad-based development than previously recognized. Importantly, the poor have the strongest incentives to design, adapt, and implement programs that have the best chance to achieve real poverty reduction. Therefore, in considering an MDG role for civil society and for NGOs, we must focus primarily on civil-society institutions *of* the poor, and not on others who would like to work *with* the poor. The 2003 *UN Human Development Report* calls for national ownership of development plans, with action driven not only by government officials and agencies but also by local communities (United Nations 2003, 31). This is what the poor want.

The *Voices of the Poor* study (Narayan et al. 2002) found that the poor everywhere want their own organizations to negotiate with government, with traders, and also with NGOs. The poor want a say in the design, management, and use of funds for poverty programs: they want accountability from NGOs as well as governments. The answers the poor give about their greatest problems sometimes surprise outsiders. The poor may cite certain forms of crime or local corruption, daily and yearly school scheduling, attitudes of health personnel at the local clinic, the experience of being ridiculed in public when they speak up about social conditions that hold them back, or about thefts from wives by husbands (Smith 2005). Adding not just voices but a real say for the poor can more than compensate for organizational complexities by creating vital checks or balances, which can improve overall performance.

MDG Achievements to Date: Progress and Challenges

While some view UN goals such as the MDGs as overly ambitious (Jolly 2002), contrary to popular belief, there was a time when the trajectory of investment and progress would have left their feasibility unquestioned (see Vandemoortele 2002). Unfortunately, progress in the 1990s slowed in most of the targeted areas, either generally or in ways specific to particular countries and regions. The record of achievement since the MDGs' adoption has been mixed when viewed holistically; in this section we highlight some of the gains alongside areas lacking adequate progress.

Detailed expositions concerning the progress made to date for each indicator and target for each of the eight MDGs are presented in, for example, the *UN Human Development Report* (2003), the annual *Reports on Implementation of the UN Millennium Declaration* by the UN Secretary-General, and the detailed examination by Vandemoortele (2002). Regrettably, none of these reports indicates that current efforts are on track for universal achievement of the MDGs by 2015. The challenges to achieving the MDGs are many; to date the demonstrated shortcomings are numerous and widespread. The 2003 *UN Human Development Report* indicates, for instance, that 54 developing countries showed average income declines over the past decade. A full 21 countries declined in terms of the Human Development Index in the 1990s as contrasted with 4 that similarly exhibited declines in the decade earlier (Malloch Brown 2003). And *none* of the 49 least-developed countries were on track to halve extreme poverty by 2015 as stipulated in Goal 1 (WFUNA 2002).

On the other hand, certain countries have made significant progress and are ahead of schedule in meeting a variety of MDG targets. Globally, the effort toward Goal 1/Target 1 of halving by 2015 the proportion of people whose income is less than one dollar a day relative to 1990 levels could be seen as being on track, owing largely to great gains by China and India (see, e.g., Chen and Ravallion 2004), even though the extent of these gains is the subject of some dispute (e.g., Reddy and Pogge 2003). Vandermoortele (2002) argues that the target concerning access to clean water may be achievable based on current rates. These successes provide evidence that achievement is possible—evidence that may serve to spur others' efforts to take the MDGs seriously as feasible goals (Vandermoortele 2002; Millennium Project 2005).

Independent assessments of progress on the MDGs (Black and White 2004) as well as ones undertaken under the auspices of associated organizations such as the OECD (cf. Maddison 2001) have begun to emerge to lend different perspectives on the MDGs and their prospects of achievement. Accurate assessments of MDG progress are hampered by a lack of reliable and consistent data across areas, projects, and time (Vandermoortele 2002). Examples of progress (such as China and India) are typically reported in average or similarly aggregated terms. For example, the gains in China and India with regard to Goal 1/Target 1 mask problems that persist or are worsening in other areas, such as the recent increase in hunger in India (FAO 2003). Within these and most developing countries, important issues concerning the distribution of benefits from development gains loom large. Women, the rural poor, and ethnic minorities continue to be marginalized from much development progress even where indicators for MDG achievement would score (aggregate) gains. Naim (2002) echoes this concern with inequality among the poor. The very choice of the policy target to halve the fraction of the poor living on less than a dollar a day appears to provide a perverse incentive for agents whose performance is judged on this criterion to focus their attention on those earning 95 cents a day rather than those earning 50 cents a day. It requires less extra income to bring them above this poverty line; in addition, those far below the dollar-a-day line are more likely in poverty traps, which present special challenges for policy and poverty programs (see chapter 8).

Progress in achieving the MDGs may be forthcoming along a less direct path than would be indicated by preliminary indicators and targets, however. The MDGs' creation and their widespread adoption by states and influential organizations globally have resulted in a global institutionalization of the MDGs as the accepted development goals. As such, the policy community as a whole and the development community in particular have galvanized their respective development efforts to adhere (precisely, or in adapted form) to the MDGs. SocialWatch (www.socialwatch.org), which was launched as an information-sharing network of CSOs after the Beijing Conference on Women, has member organizations that prepare individual country performance reports that map to the MDGs. The highly publicized Millennium Challenge Account (MCA) of the United States and the World Bank/IMF Poverty Reduction Strategy Papers (PRSPs) encourage country proposals and national strategies that incorporate the MDGs, though the effectiveness of this "encouragement" in actually responding to the MDGs is questionable (see Vandermoortele, chapter 2). The World Economic Forum's Global Governance Initiative project links its governance assessments of international organizations, national governments, private-sector firms, and civil-society actors to the MDGs and other related development indicators (WEFGGI 2003). The degree to which the incorporation of MDGs is substantive rather than pro forma remains unclear, however. For example, the PRSPs themselves—with or without an emphasis on the MDGs—in most cases have minimal impact on actual budgets.

In cases where important development problems have associated MDGs and targets, they enjoy heightened visibility, a previously vetted set of indicators for achievement, and thus some apparent external validity; and this may attract the increased attention of key stakeholders. For instance, the Bill and Melinda Gates Foundation's announcement of a multimillion-dollar gift geared toward the eradication of malaria (MDG 6, Target 8, Indicators 21 and 22), in particular, might stem from such an MDG validation. The MDGs have provided a common language that has achieved a demonstrable level of acceptance by the broad community concerned with development, and focused attention on specific goals for development. Thus, the goals may pave the way for enhanced information sharing, reduce duplication of efforts, and lend insight into complex issues by drawing the attention of many actors to these specific development goals. Jolly (2002) argues that setting goals in and of itself may explain certain gains; by focusing attention on specific targets and indicators, policy makers and others involved in development can marshal resources in ways that may enhance the probability of MDG achievement.

Although embraced by most global institutions and nations, critical stakeholders remain outside the "embrace" of the MDGs. The World

Federation of UN Associations' survey of CSOs in 75 countries reported that nearly one-third of these respondents had not heard of the MDGs; the *UN Human Development Report* cautioned that CSOs are suspicious of the MDGs (United Nations 2003, 32). This same survey indicates very low confidence in governments' (both foreign and domestic) level of MDG implementation: only 5 percent viewed governments' role as positive (Foster 2003). This implies that CSOs believe governments acting alone cannot be trusted to follow through effectively on commitments. These findings do not bode well for ultimate achievement of the MDGs since CSOs are directly involved in the day-to-day management and delivery of development efforts and often rely upon governments' political will to create enabling environments, including the provision of critical resources.

Better integration of development programs is needed to leverage positive externalities among them and to avoid critical insufficiencies in basic social services across the board that lay the necessary foundation for effective follow-up development efforts. Indebtedness and HIV/AIDS, for instance, have pervasive negative consequences on the achievement of other MDGs (United Nations 2003). Increasing aid to $100 billion, enhancing local revenue generation and resource reallocation, and an embedding of MDGs within national development plans are highlighted for improving MDG achievement (ibid.). Targeted, "better" spending of resources and the fostering of improved institutional backdrops are also seen as necessary conditions for MDG achievement (Vandermoortele 2002). NGOs have a critical role to play in promoting, and sometimes embodying, these enabling factors.

Call for NGOs in the MDGs

Annan articulated the now widely accepted view that civil society has an essential role to play in ensuring success in meeting the MDGs. A number of new organizations and NGO networks have been formed by the UN, such as IRENE (the NGO Informal Regional Network), in partnership with entities such as the World Federation of UN Associations (WFUNA) and the Conference of Non-Governmental Organizations (CONGO). NGOs not only work in all of the functional areas of the MDGs, such as health, education, and gender equity, but are also widely understood to play a central role in achieving the eighth goal of effective partnership. Thus, despite their widely recognized moniker that defines them by what they are not rather than by what they do (see chapter 4), NGOs are directly involved in the broad range of important activities associated with development around the world.

It has been argued that NGOs are unique in their strong commitment to and follow through on more appropriate development solutions (see United Nations 1998). The United States, through the MCA, has proposed a new approach to foreign aid in which nongovernmental groups (profit and nonprofit) join recipient governments in proposing projects funded with aid (Radelet and Herring 2003). Moreover, businesses are increasingly pairing with NGOs in implementing "fair trade" and other projects intended to make progress on the MDGs while enhancing their corporate images (Teegen, Doh, and Vachani 2004).

Despite the flurry of activity (official and otherwise) to incorporate NGOs into global development efforts and programs for achieving the MDGs, few studies have systematically reviewed the potential roles that international and local NGOs can play in this process. Most UN documents, including recent human development reports (UNDP 2003), note the importance of civil society in terms of advocacy and member states' accountability in complying with foreign-aid commitments necessary to achieving the MDGs. Other scholars point to NGOs' ability to hold the World Bank accountable for its financed projects (Clark, Fox, and Treakle 2003; see also Fox and Brown 1998). The World Federation of United Nations Associations' report (WFUNA 2002) notes that 90 percent of surveyed CSOs believe the MDGs are relevant to them; yet only 58 percent of these organizations had launched even a single initiative aimed at the implementation of specific MDGs. The report calls for a broad range of roles for NGOs, including developing networks and coalitions in support of implementation; monitoring progress; promoting awareness and disseminating results reports; creating specific proposals for more effective partnerships with the UN; initiating cooperative efforts with governments; and promoting institutional reform to democratize global governance. While this and other reports have offered plausible suggestions, in the absence of a strategic analysis of sector roles it is difficult to assess priorities and implied assignments of responsibility (see chapter 3).

Development NGOs

NGOs are considered a subset of civil society. They are distinguished from CSOs in that they constitute formally registered, legally recognized organizations. Our discussion will examine NGOs generally, as well as the particular roles and comparative advantages of international NGOs (INGOs) and local (indigenous) NGOs. While most of our attention is paid to these more formal organizations, much of the reflection and analysis in this book is applicable to the much wider range of civil-society actors that comprise the citizen sector. These include, for example, citizens' associations (e.g., parent-teacher associations, or PTAs), village organizations and user groups, faith-based institutions, and other "surprises"—novel organizations and initiatives that take shape in civil society and engage in important development work, such as those identified by Edwards (chapter 3).

NGOs can serve as the organizational manifestation of diverse societal interests. These interests are promoted through two distinct vehicles. First, NGOs supply advocacy efforts—offering otherwise excluded publics a voice (Stromquist 1998). Second, NGOs directly provide goods and services that private-sector markets fail to offer (Weisbrod 1975) or that public-sector actors are unable or unwilling to make available to citizens (Meyer 1999). Whereas governments rely on authority to achieve outcomes, and private-sector firms rely on market mechanisms to provide incentives for mutually beneficial exchange, civil-society actors utilize independent voluntary efforts and influence to promote their values and promote aspects of social, economic, and political development (Brown et al. 2000).

The term "NGO" includes a wide range of organizations. In the 1980s, donor organizations began to more formally recognize NGOs as development actors and sought to pay attention to them in donor programming. For example, the World Bank issued an Operational Directive on NGOs in 1989, defining them as "groups and institutions that are entirely or largely independent of government and characterized primarily by humanitarian or cooperative rather than commercial objectives." More recently, the UN (2003) defined NGOs and sought to describe their roles in development as follows:

> [An NGO is] any non-profit, voluntary citizens' group which is organized on a local, national or international level. Task-oriented and driven by people with a common interest, NGOs perform a variety of services and humanitarian functions, bring citizens' concerns to Governments, monitor policies and encourage political participation at the community level. They provide analysis and expertise, serve as early warning mechanisms and help monitor and implement international agreements. Some are organized around specific issues, such as human rights, the environment or health.

The difficulty in conceptualizing NGOs is reflective of the broad and diverse sector these actors have come to constitute. Generally, there is an assumption that these organizations seek to advance some public good, which leads some to describe them as social-benefit organizations. The difficulty with this descriptor is that it still does not distinguish NGOs from governments, nor does it capture the possibility that NGOs can be self-interested—pursuing very particularistic agendas—excluding all but a narrowly defined few.

In order to grasp the diversity of this sector, it is helpful to consider typologies based on structure and activity. NGOs can be distinguished according to their location—do they operate internationally (i.e., crossing national borders), at the national level of a particular country, or are they very local? Each location may offer different advantages for contributing to development objectives. Local organizations are more likely to embody the important comparative advantages of being closer to the people and all the benefits this represents. National NGOs may have easier access to government structures and representatives and may be more sophisticated and established. This is also true of international NGOs, which offer additional advantages of wider access to donor funding and comparative expertise, owing to their multiregional and global engagement.

The quality of NGO contributions may also depend on the NGO's origins: was the NGO initiated by government or is it a private initiative? Is it a direct donor creation, or did it arise in response to contracting opportunities? Or is the NGO in question largely a membership organization? All but (a subset of) the last of these origin types focus on working with the poor, as opposed to being organizations of the poor. These origins are likely to impact the chosen or implicit development strategy of an NGO. Korten (1990) provides a useful typology of development strategies based on his generation model of NGOs. While these generations originally referred to the evolution of the NGO sector as a whole, we now find NGOs undertaking each of these strategies, and some NGOs may embrace more than one strategy, depending on their mission and the needs at hand. Korten delineates NGOs according to whether they pursue a development strategy of relief and welfare (the pure humanitarian-assistance-type NGO), local self-reliance (organizations focusing on community mobilization and capacity building), or sustainable systems development (organizations seeking systems change through advocacy and empowerment, for example). More generally, an NGO may be categorized according to its basic function: is it operational (i.e., providing services), or does it focus on policy influence? And in what sector?

With a plethora of terms and acronyms to describe them—from people's organizations (POs) to "briefcase organizations" or nongovernmental individuals (NGIs)—NGOs run the gamut from essentially profit-seeking entrepreneurs to well-intentioned catalytic organizations to professional, streamlined service deliverers. Overall, while many NGOs retain their philanthropic origin and orientation, they have frequently evolved into strategically managed development specialists, treading the fine line between the technical language and processes of the development industry on the one hand, while attempting to maintain responsiveness to developing country clientele and individual contributors on the other (Brinkerhoff 2002).

Despite these conceptual difficulties, civil-society actors such as NGOs have clearly emerged as key players in global affairs. This growing role has been symbolically recognized by their prominent inclusion in both the

World Economic Forum and the World Social Forum in recent years (Naidoo 2003), and through the Nobel Peace Prize, which has been awarded in recent years to NGOs such as the Campaign to Ban Landmines in 1997 and Doctors Without Borders (MSF) in 1999 (other recent recipients have included social entrepreneurs who have founded innovative NGOs, such as the 2004 Nobel Laureate, Wangari Maathai). The growing importance of NGOs is confirmed in their numbers: at least 2,250 NGOs have consultative status with the UN (UN 2003); OECD-nation NGOs alone enjoyed a 50 percent increase in numbers from 1980 –to 1990 (van Tuijl 1999), and nearly three-quarters of all World Bank projects involve NGOs (Gibbs et al. 1999). INGOs grew 20 percent in the 1990s (United Nations 2001) and twentyfold from 1964 to 1998 (Raymond 2003). The dramatic growth of the citizen sector is chronicled by Bill Drayton in the final chapter of this volume. Today, many NGOs are large, far-flung multinational organizations, managing significant budgets and intricate organizational structures spanning national boundaries. The potential impact of the sector in terms of overall numbers is paralleled by their kaleidoscopic range of activities and issue areas, and by their size as measured by number of members, contributors, and employees, as well as in terms of budgets—Conservation International alone operates under an annual budget of nearly $100 million (Conservation International 2005).

The emergence and growth of NGOs can be traced to the greater reliance on nonpublic entities for goods and services (Ramia 2003); the persistence of poverty, which remains unaddressed by governments and firms (Hodess 2002), and enhanced mechanisms for collective action, including global communications infrastructure advancement (Salamon 1994), among other trends. To some extent the degree to which the NGO role has expanded may prove to be temporary, as government and business play catch-up on technical and social innovations that may assist the poor (see Prahalad 2004). However, as outlined later in the book, there are also reasons to expect that the expansion of the NGO sector relative to government and business may represent a permanent shift in this sector's importance.

Outline of the Book

The remainder of the book further explores NGOs' potential contribution, specifically to achieving the MDGs; it is organized in three parts. Part 1 introduces the MDGs, NGOs, and theoretical perspectives on NGOs' potential roles. Jan Vandermoortele sets the stage in chapter 2, exploring the question, Can the MDGs foster a new partnership for pro-poor policies? After a brief review of the evolution and progress on the MDGs through the 1990s, and prospects for achieving the MDGs by 2015,

Vandermoortele examines the appropriateness of broader policy frameworks and outlines seven parameters for effective pro-poor policies. He then focuses on the role of external actors and identifies three additional "tips" for designing pro-poor policies. Drawing on previous experiences with global targets, he concludes with seven recommendations for operationalizing the MDGs. Vandermoortele presents a cautiously optimistic perspective, emphasizing the context of the MDGs and their implementation, and highlighting the role of domestic revenue generation and political will, and revealing the dynamics of what he calls the "development coin" and the need to turn it from "money changing hands" to "ideas changing minds."

In chapter 3, Michael Edwards provides a broader context for exploring NGOs and their role in achieving the MDGs. In this original and thought-provoking essay, Edwards argues that the premise that the NGO sector is an important actor and resource for achieving the MDGs is based on a series of assumptions, and that to truly assess NGOs' potential role, these assumptions must be examined critically. Among the complexities to be considered, Edwards identifies a broader range of civil-society actors who potentially contribute and highlights common Western biases in interpreting the relevance and effectiveness of particular types of actors, noting the varied experience and outcomes across countries and regions. Edwards concludes that expanded activities of NGOs—and even civil society more broadly—must be understood as complementary to, and not as a substitute for, democratic state building and pro-poor market reform, and that NGOs must neither be given a privileged place on ideological grounds nor be instrumentalized. Instead, in identifying potential aid-recipients we must examine "the entire ecosystem to identify gaps, disconnections and areas of oversupply."

In chapter 4 we develop our theoretical framework for considering the potential roles of NGOs in achieving the MDGs. Building on a typology often used in economics (stressing degrees of excludability and rivalry among different goods or services), we review the generally accepted roles of government, the private sector, and NGOs based on associated comparative advantages. Then, drawing from sector failure models (including "voluntary failure" in the NGO sector, as well as market and government failure), we propose a framework for NGO MDG roles, measures, and contingency factors that encapsulates our hypotheses.

Part 2 outlines the context for achieving the MDGs, focusing on actions governments can take to enable effective NGO roles (D. Brinkerhoff, chapter 5); the general political context of MDG achievement, particularly with respect to Goal 8 (Finnemore, chapter 6), and the efforts of the Millennium Campaign to inspire political will (Welch, chapter 7).

Part 3 applies the theoretical framework (from chapter 4), first with reference to the core MDG 1 and to general efforts to eradicate poverty and hunger (Smith, chapter 8). In chapter 9, we examine NGOs' role in achieving the health, education, environment, and gender goals, building on the respective contributions to the May–June 2004 conference by speakers including Salehuddin Ahmed, Mushtaque Chowdhury, Chris Dunford, Kek Galabru, Michael Gibbons, Caren Grown, Ruth Levine, Frank Method, Marc Levy, Carolyne Odhiambo, Marie Price, Yolanda Richardson, James Williams, and Sharon Wolchik. We present conclusions and policy implications in chapter 10, and the volume concludes with an Afterword by Bill Drayton, the founder of Ashoka.

References

Annan, Kofi. *Road Map Towards the Implementation of the United Nations Millennium Declaration: Report of the Secretary General.* UN Doc A/56/326. New York: United Nations General Assembly, September 6, 2001.

Black, Richard, and Howard White. *Targeting Development: Critical Perspectives on the Millennium Development Goals.* London: Routledge, 2004.

Brinkerhoff, Jennifer M. *Partnership for Development: Rhetoric or Results?* Boulder, CO: Lynne Rienner., 2002.

Brown, David L., S. Khagram, M.H. Moore, and P. Frumkin. "Globalization, NGOs and Multisectoral Relations." In *Governance in a Globalizing World,* ed. Joseph S. Nye and J. Donahue. Washington, D.C.: Brookings Institution Press, 2000: 271–286.

Chen, Shaohua, and Martin Ravallion. "How Have the World's Poorest Fared Since the Early 1980s?" World Bank Policy Research Working Paper No. 3341, June 10, 2004.

Clark, Dana, Jonathan A. Fox, and Kay Treakle, eds. *Demanding Accountability: Civil Society Claims and the World Bank Inspection Panel.* Lanham, MD: Rowman and Littlefield, 2003.

Conservation International. Web page. http://www.conservation.org/xp/CIWEB/about/annualreport.xml (accessed December 3, 2005).

Food and Agriculture Organization (FAO). *The State of Food Insecurity in the World.* Rome: FAO, November 2003.

Foster, John W. "The Millennium Declaration: Mobilising Civil Society Organisations." *UNDP Development Policy Journal* 3 (April 2003). www.undp.org/dpa/publications/DPJ3Final1.pdf (accessed September 20, 2003).

Fox, Jonathan A., and L. David Brown. *The Struggle for Accountability: The World Bank, NGOs and Grassroots Movements.* Cambridge, MA: MIT Press, 1998.

Gibbs, Christopher, Claudia Fumo, and Thomas Kuby. *Nongovernmental Organizations in World Bank-Supported Projects: A Review.* Washington, D.C.: World Bank Operations Evaluation Department, 1999.

Hodess, Robin. "The Contested Competence of NGOs and Business in Public Life." In *The Market or the Public Domain,* ed. D. Drache. New York: Routledge, 2002.

Jolly, Richard, ed. *Jim Grant: UNICEF Visionary.* Florence, Italy: United Nations Children's Fund, Innocenti Research Center, 2002.

Kaul, Inge. Global Public Goods: What Role for Civil Society? *Nonprofit and Voluntary Sector Quarterly* 30(3): 588-602, 2001.

Korten, David C. *Getting to the 21st Century: Voluntary Action and the Global Agenda.* West Hartford, CT: Kumarian Press, 1990.

Maddison, Angus. *The World Economy in the Millennium Perspective.* Paris: OECD, 2001.

Malloch Brown, Marc. Quoted in "Human Development Index Reveals Debt Crisis." http://www.undp.org/hdr2003 (accessed September 20, 2003).

Meyer, Carrie A. *The Economics and Politics of NGOs in Latin America.* Westport, CT: Praeger, 1999.

Millennium Project. *Investing in Development: A Practical Plan to Achieve the Millennium Development Goals.* New York: UNDP, 2005.

Naidoo, Kumi. "Civil Society, Governance and Globalization." World Bank Presidential Fellows Lecture (monograph), Washington, D.C., February 10, 2003.

Naim, Moises. Panelist comments at the World Bank Poverty Day conference, Washington, DC: The World Bank, October 17, 2002. http://www.world bank.org/wbi/B-SPAN/sub_poverty_day_2_2002.htm (audio transcript accessed September 20, 2003).

Narayan, Deepa, et al., eds. *Voices of the Poor: From Many Lands.* New York: Oxford University Press for the World Bank, 2002.

Prahalad, C. K. *The Fortune at the Bottom of the Pyramid: Eradicating Poverty through Profits.* Upper Saddle River, NJ: Wharton School Publishing, 2004.

Radelet, Stephen, and Sheila Herring. "The Millennium Challenge Account: Soft Power or Collateral Damage?" *Center for Global Development Brief* 2(2): 1–7, 2003.

Ramia, Gaby. "Global Governance, Social Policy and Management in International NGOs: A Theoretical and Empirical Analysis." Paper presented at the Policy and Politics International conference on "Policy and Politics in a Globalising World," Bristol, U.K., July 24–26, 2003.

Raymond, S. "The Non-Profit Piece of the Global Puzzle." http://www.onphilan-thropy.com/op2001-10-15.html (accessed February 7, 2003).

Reddy, Sanjay G., and Thomas W. Pogge. "How Not to Count the Poor." Working Paper, Columbia University, 2003.

Salamon, L.M. The Rise of the Nonprofit Sector. *Foreign Affairs,* 73(4): 109–22, 1994.

Smith, Stephen C. *Ending Global Poverty: A Guide to What Works.* New York: Palgrave Macmillan, 2005.

Smith, Stephen C. Village Banking and Maternal and Child Health: Evidence from Ecuador and Honduras. *World Development* 30(4): 707–723, 2002.

Stromquist, N. P. "NGOs in a New Paradigm of Civil Society." *Current Issues in Comparative Education* 1(1): 1–5, 1998.

Teegen, Hildy. "International NGOs as Global Institutions: Using Social Capital to Impact Multinational Enterprises and Governments." *Journal of International Management* 9(September): 271-285, 2003.

Teegen, Hildy, Jonathan P. Doh, and Sushil Vachani. "The Importance of Nongovernmental Organizations (NGOs) in Global Governance and Value

Creation: An International Business Research Agenda." *Journal of International Business Studies* 35(6): 463–483, 2004.

Todaro, Michael, and Stephen C. Smith. *Economic Development,* 8th ed., Reading, MA: Addison-Wesley, 2005.

United Nations. "Arrangements and Practices for the Interaction of Non-Governmental Organizations in All Activities of the United Nations System." *Report of the Secretary-General.* United Nations, New York, 1998.

United Nations Development Programme. *Human Development Report.* New York: United Nations. http://www.undp.org/hdr2001/.

———. *Human Development Report.* New York: United Nations. http://www.www.undp.org/hdr2003/.

Van Tuijl, P. "NGOs and Human Rights: Sources of Justice and Democracy." *Journal of International Affairs* 52(2): 493–512.

Vandemoortele, Jan. *Are the MDGs Feasible?* Report. New York: United Nations Development Program, Bureau for Development Policy, July 2002.

Weisbrod, Burton A. "Toward a Theory of the Voluntary Non-Profit Sector in a Three-Sector Economy." In *Altruism, Morality, and Economic Theory,* ed. Edmund S. Phelps. New York: Russell Sage Foundation, 1975: 197–223.

World Economic Forum Global Governance Initiative (WEFGGI). http://www.brook.edu/gs/research/projects/globalgovernance/ggi_aboutus.htm) accessed September 1, 2003).

World Federation of United Nations Associations (WFUNA). *We the Peoples . . . A Call to Action for the UN Millennium Declaration.* New York: WFUNA, 2002. www.wfuna.org (accessed June 16, 2003).

Zedillo, Ernesto. "Report of the High-Level Panel on Financing for Development." From the Monterey conference on financing for development. http://www.un.org/reports/financing/2002.

Appendix : Conference Contributions

The MDGs and Requirements for Pro-Poor Policies

- *Jan Vandemoortele,* Principal Advisor, Bureau for Development Policy, United Nations Development Program

Perspectives on NGOs

- *Michael Edwards,* Director, Governance and Civil Society Unit, Ford Foundation

- *Salehuddin Ahmed,* Deputy Executive Director, BRAC (Bangladesh)

The Enabling Environment for MDG Success

- *Derick W. Brinkerhoff,* Senior Fellow in International Public Management, RTI International (Research Triangle Institute)

Assessing Effectiveness

- Economic Perspective
  Martin Ravallion, Research Manager, Poverty Development Research Group, World Bank

- Public Administration Perspective
  Philip Joyce, Professor of Public Administration, George Washington University

- NGO Experience
  Jim Rugh, Director of Evaluation, CARE

Global Partnership

- Presenter: *Lael Brainard,* Senior Fellow, Economics and Foreign Policy, Brookings Institution

- NGO respondent: *Nancy Alexander,* Director, Citizens Network for Essential Services

- Discussant: *Martha Finnemore,* Associate Professor of Political Science and International Affairs, George Washington University

Alleviating Poverty and Hunger

- Presenter: *Stephen C. Smith,* Professor of Economics and International Affairs, George Washington University

- NGO respondent: *Christopher Dunford,* President, Freedom from Hunger

- Discussant: *Shahe Emran,* Assistant Professor of Economics and International Affairs, George Washington University

Achieving Universal Primary Education

- Presenter: *Frank Method,* Director, International Education Program, RTI International (Research Triangle Institute)
- NGO respondent: *Michael Gibbons,* Associate Director, Banyan Tree Foundation
- Discussant: *James Williams,* Associate Professor of International Education and International Affairs, George Washington University

Achieving Health MDGs

- Session Chair: *Muhiuddin Haider,* Senior Associate for the Center for Global Health and Assistant Professor, School of Public Health and International Affairs, George Washington University
- Presenter: *Ruth Levine,* Director of Programs and Senior Fellow, Global Health and Social Policy, Center for Global Development
- NGO respondent: *Mushtaque Chowdhury,* Director of Research and Evaluation, BRAC (Bangladesh)
- Discussant: *Tom Merrick,* Adjunct Faculty, Center for Global Health, School of Public Health, George Washington University

Achieving Environmental Sustainability

- Presenter: *Marc Levy,* Group Head, Science and Applications Group—CIESIN and SIPA, Columbia University
- NGO Respondent: *Carolyne Odhiambo,* Kenyan NGO practitioner
- Discussant: *Marie Price,* Associate Professor of Geography and International Affairs, George Washington University

Achieving Gender Equality

- **Caren Grown,** Director, Poverty Reduction and Economic Governance, International Center for Research on Women
- **Kek Galabru,** Founder and President, LICADHO; Founder and Chair, Committee for Free and Fair Elections in Cambodia; Founder and Chair, Cambodian Committee for Women
- **Yolonda Richardson,** President and Chief Executive Officer of the Centre for Development and Population Activities

(Continued)

- **Sharon Wolchik,** Director of the Russian and East European Studies Program and Director, Masters of International Policy and Practice Program, George Washington University

Integrative Plenary/The Road Ahead

- **UN Respondent**
  Carol Welch, U.S. Campaign Coordinator, Millennium Development Goals Campaign

- **Democracy and Global Governance**
  Ann Florini, Senior Fellow, Governance Studies, Brookings Institution

- **Closing Keynote: The Power of Individuals**
  William Drayton, CEO, Chair and Founder, Ashoka

Part I

The MDGs and NGO Potential Roles

2

Can the MDGs Foster a New Partnership for Pro-Poor Policies?

Jan Vandemoortele

There are times when the enunciation of even the most elementary common sense has an aspect of eccentricity, irrationality, even mild insanity.

—*J. K. Galbraith*

The partnership between rich and poor countries takes many forms, but its most explicit expression is embodied in foreign aid—formally known as official development assistance, or ODA. Foreign aid is a coin with two faces: one side deals with issues associated with "money changing hands"; the other side addresses the aspects of "ideas changing minds."

The former covers the important aspects of budgeting, accountability, and transparency. It addresses the questions of where to spend aid money—geographically and sectorally—and how to spend it: direct budget support versus technical assistance; bilateral versus multilateral channels; government versus nongovernmental organizations; development versus humanitarian programs; project versus program aid, etc. Concerns about procurement, accounting, and reporting are important, but they tend to overshadow the debate about the objective of aid. In essence, this side of the coin represents a one-way street focused on money matters, often leading to micromanagement at the expense of the larger question about the ultimate purpose of development assistance.

When the partnership is too focused on money issues, little time and energy are devoted to the crucial dimension of "ideas changing minds."

Once money is put on the table, the nature of the partnership between poor and rich countries changes radically. However, it is only when the ultimate purpose of foreign aid is made clear and agreed upon between the recipient and the donor beforehand—mostly through active listening on the part of the latter—that its effectiveness and efficiency will measurably improve. Indeed, the issues related to "ideas changing minds" involve two-way traffic for advancing a genuine partnership, based on the principles of equality, mutual respect, and national ownership.

In this chapter, I focus on the dimension of "ideas changing minds." I ask whether the MDGs have created opportunities for enlarging pro-poor policy choices at the country level, especially through the PRSPs. I examine whether policy frameworks are becoming MDG-friendly, and I look into the potential role of external partners in engendering pro-poor policies. I highlight three "don'ts" when making the policy framework pro-poor. The chapter concludes by asking whether global targets can really make a difference.

Before examining these central questions, I describe some of the differences in perception that surround the MDGs; review some of the main issues concerning the MDG indicators as they relate to MDG progress; and summarize the progress made toward the targets in the 1990s.

Are the MDGs a Step Forward, Sideways, or Backwards?

The MDGs are subject to different perceptions. Some see them as a major step forward because they represent an internationally agreed agenda for development, something that has eluded the international community so far. Others see the MDGs as a step sideways because they represent a familiar agenda that is rather minimal in scope. Still others see them as a step backwards because the quantitative and time-bound targets do not explicitly cover human rights, reproductive health, jobs, governance, or the role of the private sector. Neither do they adequately address concerns about gender equality and environmental sustainability.

Thus, the MDGs can be seen as either an agreed agenda, a minimalist agenda, or an incomplete agenda for human development. Given these profound differences in perceptions, it might be useful to paraphrase John F. Kennedy in that we should not ask what we can do for the MDGs but what the MDGs can do for us or for our cause. This approach is likely to broaden the constituency in favor of the MDGs. The MDGs were not developed from scratch; they resulted from an incremental, and sometimes piecemeal, process of generating a political consensus on the major elements of the development agenda—mostly through a series of world summits and international conferences of the 1990s.

The MDGs are also seen to project different paradigms of development. Some consider them as a new global compact between rich and poor countries, while others see them as an old paradigm of welfare entitlements or North-South recriminations. Those who take the latter position often view the "new" paradigm as development that is driven by good governance and the private sector. Different views also exist as to the relevance of MDGs. Some people limit their relevance to low-income countries or even the least-developed countries while others see them as essential for addressing poverty in all developing countries, including in middle-income countries where pockets of deep poverty persist.

Finally, the way the global MDGs were formulated may not be conducive to success because the HIV pandemic was acknowledged but not really internalized. By and large, global MDG targets were set on the premise that the global trends observed in the 1970s and 1980s would continue until 2015—i.e., during the lifetime of one generation. While a separate target for halting and reversing HIV was inserted in the Millennium Declaration, the quantitative targets for health, water, education, income poverty, and hunger were set as if no HIV pandemic existed—thereby ignoring the undeniable fact that HIV is slowing down global progress in health and beyond.

Can all MDG Indicators Be Taken at Face Value?

Before assessing MDG progress, I want to point out that not all indicators offer equally good gauges of reality. All economic and social indicators are based on two ingredients—observation and construction—but not all use these ingredients in the same proportion. The reliability of an indicator tends to decline as more construction is involved because construction is based on assumptions. Statistics on water, for instance, frequently overstate access in urban areas because they report that all residents within 100 meters of a public supply point as adequately covered, based on the assumption that one single pump or tap can cover the needs of 500 or 1,000 residents within that radius—always assuming that the tap or pump is actually in good working order.

In education, it is easier to observe whether a child is enrolled in school than to estimate whether she will complete primary education because of the possibility of repetition, dropout, reentry, and ultimate dropout. Hence, the indicator called "completion rate" is more problematic than the "enrolment ratio" because the former needs more construction. Similarly, it is not possible to visit a village or a slum and observe whether someone earns less than $1 per day, whereas it is possible to observe whether a child survived her fifth birthday or whether she is malnourished. As income poverty cannot be readily observed, it needs a large set of information and a complex process of construction, which creates many occasions for errors and omissions to occur.

The world reportedly made impressive progress in the fight against income poverty during the 1990s. The proportion of the population in developing countries below $1 per day is estimated to have declined from about one-third in 1990 to less than one-quarter in 2000. But the poverty data produced by the World Bank show that the global trend is heavily influenced by two countries—China and India. When they are excluded, the global poverty performance during the 1990s becomes one of stagnation, even regression—not of remarkable progress. This illustrates how the level of aggregation can influence claims about MDG trends. What is valid at one level of aggregation is not necessarily valid at another level.

The same is true for the choice of the indicators. What is valid based on one indicator is not always valid for another indicator. After reviewing four different definitions and measurements of poverty, Laderchi et al. (2003) concluded, "What is striking is that low levels of poverty according to one measure are compatible with high levels of poverty according to another." Therefore, one always needs to be aware and to beware. The choice of the indicator and the level of aggregation at which the analysis is done invariably influence the claims and conclusions made in social sciences.

Another factor that can influence the interpretation of data is the time horizon. While it is true, for instance, that the reduction in the under-five mortality rate in developing countries—from an average of 223 per 1,000 live births in 1960 to 91 in 2000—has been impressive, it is equally true that the progress made in the 1990s was much slower than that witnessed in the 1970s and 1980s—about one-third. Data are sometimes used as a fig leaf to hide the lack of progress in recent years behind rapid progress of earlier decades. Hence, the choice of the time horizon can shape the claims and conclusions about MDG progress or lack thereof.

In short, all indicators are imperfect, but some are more imperfect than others. Among the most frequently used MDG indicators, I prefer the following top five for their reliability, coverage, and relevance: (1) under-five mortality rate, (2) underweight among children, (3) net enrollment ratio in primary education, (4) ratio of girls to boys in primary and secondary schools, and (5) the proportion of births attended by skilled health personnel. On the other hand, the five I consider most problematic include: (1) proportion of the population below $1 per day, (2) proportion of the population below a minimum level of dietary energy consumption, (3) primary school completion rate, (4) maternal mortality ratio, and (5) the proportion of the population with access to safe drinking water. These indicators involve a high dose of construction, which can easily lead to esoteric statistics.

Are We on Track to Meeting the MDGs by 2015?

The MDGs are morally imperative and legally binding—they are embedded in human rights treaties. They are technically feasible and financially affordable. They also make good economic sense. Yet, all is not well with the MDGs. Although all member states of the United Nations pledged to "spare no effort to free our fellow men, women and children from the abject and dehumanizing conditions of extreme poverty" (United Nations 2000), global progress towards the MDGs has been slow and very uneven.

Without denying the great diversity in performance across countries, the story of the 1990s can be summarized in three main points. First, progress was made, but it was too slow for reaching the agreed targets by 2015. Second, in many cases less progress was made in the 1990s than in the 1970s and 1980s. Third, much of the modest progress bypassed the poor. The countries and the people who most needed to see progress frequently saw the least of it.

Indeed, the 1990s were characterized by an unprecedented number of cases where human development stagnated or reversed. The number of countries that saw a decline in their human development index rose to 21 in the 1990s, from only four during the 1980s (UNDP 2003a). Most of the reversals stemmed from the HIV/AIDS pandemic and economic crises, particularly in sub-Saharan Africa and in the transition economies. Nevertheless, it remains an enigma why the global prosperity of the past decade did not lead to faster and more robust progress in terms of human development. After all, the "roaring" 1990s were associated with booming foreign direct investment and soaring trade flows—all part of the phenomenon of globalization.

As of 2000, the world was reportedly on track for only two targets—income poverty and access to safe water. Both, however, have serious measurement problems and might be on "statistical steroids." Global poverty trends that are based on the metric of $1 per day cannot be considered a robust source of information.

Regrettably, a dollar per day does not keep poverty at bay. A growing number of analysts argue that the international poverty line of $1 or $2 per day is not a good gauge (Reddy and Pogge 2003). After examining cross-country data on underweight and income poverty—using both national and international poverty lines—Morrisson (2002) concluded, "The number of malnourished children is correlated to the number of poor individuals if we use the national poverty line; they are less satisfactory, however, when we use the measure of $1 per day." Indeed, many analysts agree that the use of a national poverty line is preferable to the use of the international poverty line of $1 per day. The inherent disadvantage of a fixed international poverty line, combined with inaccurate conversion rates into purchasing power parity, argues for an extremely cautious interpretation of these data.

With respect to other targets, for water the picture is also clouded by measurement problems and by the fact that much of the progress of the 1990s may not be sustainable as many parts of the world face growing water shortages. During the 1990s, most targets for hunger, health, education, and gender equality witnessed about half the progress they should have seen in order to reach their agreed goalposts by 2015. For HIV/AIDS, little or no progress was achieved apart from a few countries. Progress toward building a global partnership for human development—the so-called MDG 8 in terms of aid, trade, and debt relief—was also disheartening.

Perhaps most disappointing of all is the situation vis-à-vis primary education. An estimated 115 million children are "out of school," and perhaps three times as many are "out of education"—in the sense that they do not acquire basic literacy and numeracy. There is no good reason to explain this sorry state of affairs today. The cost of universal primary education is perfectly affordable (Delamonica et al. 2004); no new technologies are needed to make it a reality; everyone agrees that it makes good economic sense; and basic education is universally seen as a basic human right. If these arguments do not convince policy makers about the absolute necessity of reaching the education goal, then we can only wonder what it will take to meet the other MDGs. Sadly, the failure to keep the education promise will undermine the chances of reaching the other targets because of its high instrumental value. New HIV infections, for instance, are disproportionately concentrated among young illiterate women, which indicates the existence of an "education vaccine" against HIV (Vandemoortele and Delamonica 2000).

The above picture does not get any brighter when we look beyond global and national averages. Not only was progress inadequate in most countries during the 1990s, much of it bypassed the poorest countries and the poorest people. The least progress occurred where most progress was needed—both across and within countries. Slow "average" progress was frequently compounded by limited progress for the poorest and most disadvantaged groups within countries. Quantitative targets are primarily meant to help improve the situation of poor people, not only that of better-off and privileged people. Unfortunately, the poor have benefited proportionately little from "average" progress, as evidenced by widening disparities within countries in terms of education, nutrition, and health (Minujin and Delamonica 2003).

In sum, the world is not on track to meet the global MDG targets by 2015; it is even difficult to argue that the glass is half full. While progress was made in the 1990s it was slower than that observed in the 1970s and 1980s, and too much of it bypassed the countries and the people who were most in need of it.

Yet, the MDGs are not "mission impossible"; they remain doable propositions. While the 1990s failed to generate the desired progress, it is not too late to avoid the legacy of this generation becoming a series of broken promises. Experience shows that determined leadership and awakened public interest can put the world back on the MDG track. This is exactly what happened in the 1960s when the U.S. Administration decided to send a man to the moon. At the time, nobody knew how to realize that technological feat, let alone how much it would cost; yet it was turned into a practical reality. The same can be achieved for the MDGs—given strong political leadership and deliberate public advocacy for the MDG targets at the local, national, and global levels.

Are Policy Frameworks MDG-Friendly?

Poverty reduction strategies continue to look strikingly similar, even for countries that face very different challenges. If they were genuinely home-grown, it would not be unreasonable to expect that antipoverty strategies would be much more diverse. Actually, most of them are little different from the policy framework prescribed during the era of structural adjustment of the 1980s, apart from the important fact that they now make a stronger case for pro-poor public expenditure. Growth continues to be seen as the panacea, and macroeconomic stability, financial deregulation, and trade liberalization as its prerequisites. But not everybody shares the same faith in the power of economic growth for reducing poverty.

China, for instance, is frequently looked at with admiration and awe as rapid growth reportedly led to a steep reduction in income poverty. Between 1981 and 2001, nearly 400 million people are estimated to have escaped poverty (World Bank 2004). Yet, the link between growth and poverty remains a mystery. Over the last five years of that period, for example, the Chinese economy expanded by about one-half; yet the number of poor people (i.e., those with an income of below $1 per day) remained unchanged. It is a moot question why such impressive growth between 1996 and 2001 failed to make a difference for the estimated 212 million people who struggled to survive on less than $1 a day in that country.

The centennial anniversary of the invention of flying offers an interesting analogy. The main protagonists in designing the first flying machine in the early 1900s were Samuel Langley and the Wright Brothers. With generous support from the War Department, Langley's strategy was to use brute power to get his theoretically stable machine aloft. The Wright Brothers, on the other hand, developed an engine that was less powerful, because they understood that moderate power combined with smart design would be sufficient to get their craft airborne. There is an analogy to be made to the different paradigms of those who believe in the overwhelming power of economic growth to reduce human poverty, and those who argue that the pattern of growth and the design of pro-poor policies are at least as important as the rate of economic growth.

In practice, few of the macroeconomic policy reforms explicitly consider their impact on the poor. A recent IMF review, for instance, concluded that none of the documents that supported the poverty reduction and growth facility (PRGF) "present a rigorous study assessing poverty and social impact" (Inchauste 2002). A strong commitment to the MDGs would imply that the objective of reducing human poverty drives the policy framework, not the other way round.

Most PRSPs have generated more inclusive public debates and policy dialogues, but participation by itself does not guarantee pro-poor outcomes. An evaluation commissioned by the UNDP (2003c) regarding its role in the PRSP process found little or no correlation between the breadth of participation and the policy content of the PRSP. Stewart and Wang (2003) also concluded, "PRSPs do not significantly empower poor countries." An Oxfam paper (2004) reports that out of 20 countries, 16 had an agreed PRGF prior to the completion of the PRSP—thereby severely limiting the influence of national stakeholders over macroeconomic target setting. Representatives from government ministries, trade unions, civil society, and academia are beginning to feel that they are involved in a process of "choiceless" participation; all sense severe limitations for generating homegrown strategies.

Although the significance of basic services is now recognized more broadly, few poverty-reduction strategies explicitly align their policy framework with the MDGs. The IMF (2003) reported, for instance, that low-income countries cut inflation and import tariffs by half over the past decade, reduced their budget deficits, and improved their foreign exchange reserves; yet, by its own admission, these countries made little progress in terms of income growth and poverty reduction. Nonetheless, the validity of the standard macroeconomic framework is not called into question. Instead, the tendency is to add new elements to the policy matrix in terms of structural reforms, improvements in the rule of law, enforcement of property rights, and civil service reform. A more ambitious and accommodating policy framework focused on the MDGs is seldom considered.

Most poverty-reduction strategies fail to translate the concept of "pro-poor growth" in specific and practical policy measures. An independent evaluation of the impact of the International Development Association (IDA)—the window of concessional lending at the World Bank—on poverty concluded, "The development outcomes of IDA programs have been partially satisfactory" (World Bank 2001). The evaluation confirmed that while macroeconomic stability improved and many economic distortions were removed, no strong evidence emerged as to whether the poor saw their incomes increase and their job opportunities improve. It proved difficult to come up with practical policies to achieve not just growth but equitable growth. Concrete measures to transmit the benefits of policy reforms to the poor were usually missing.

The good news is that pro-poor growth is perfectly possible, as has been shown by the case of the Republic of Korea. After studying five Asian countries, Pernia (2003) concluded that Lao People's Democratic Republic was the longest distance away from generating pro-poor growth in the (precrisis) 1990s, followed by Thailand, the Philippines, and Vietnam, with the latter two coming close to achieving pro-poor growth. But the Republic of Korea was the only one that saw the income of the poor grow proportionately faster than the average income. This country also confirms that initial conditions of equity—through successful land reform and deliberate health and education policies—do matter a great deal for reducing poverty in a sustainable manner.

What are Pro-Poor Policies?

Although increasingly used, the term "pro-poor growth" remains vague and general. Growth is pro-poor, it is argued, if it uses the assets that the poor own, if it favors the sectors where the poor work, and if it occurs in areas where the poor live. These obvious points, however, are seldom decoded into detailed reforms that make policy frameworks pro-poor in practice, not just in theory. As is often the case, the devil is in the details. Once the objective of reducing human poverty is taken beyond the abstract level, it usually ceases to look like a "universal good." An honest search for real solutions to poverty invariably leads to hard trade-offs and tough policy choices—hence the tendency of many to play it safe by sticking to conventional wisdom and generalities, even platitudes.

Pro-poor policies imply that the social and economic indicators for the disadvantaged people improve more rapidly than those for the rest of society. It is not sufficient that the indicators for the poor improve; they have to improve at a faster pace than for the nonpoor because absolute poverty always has a relative dimension. Therefore, before being called "pro-poor," the policy framework needs a thorough examination.

We examine whether the standard elements of the policy framework are really pro-poor and whether it can be claimed that existing frameworks will meet the MDGs. Seven elements are highlighted, including fiscal, monetary, and trade policies. They draw from lessons identified by the UNDP's review of how macroeconomic policies incorporate—or fail to incorporate—the objective of poverty reduction in a number of Asian countries (McKinley 2003).

1. Avoid a Dogmatic View of the "Small Government" Paradigm

The first element covers fiscal policy. A policy framework that is focused on poverty reduction and on the MDGs must accommodate a more expansionary fiscal stance. The introduction of the PRSPs and the PRGF are an implicit admission that reducing poverty has to go hand in hand with increased public spending and more flexible macroeconomic policies; yet their policy framework seldom goes beyond the paradigm of fiscal conservatism and monetary orthodoxy. The standard framework proposed by the international financial institutions seldom makes a strong case for increased taxation, although an overall tax rate of 10–12 per cent of national income is woefully inadequate for a low-income country to keep its MDG promise.

The standard macroeconomic framework is premised on keeping the size of the public sector to a strict minimum, based on the assumption that low taxes and limited regulation will stimulate investment and generate economic growth, which in turn will reduce poverty. Public-investment programs are often kept to a minimum, based on the argument that they crowd out private investment. This, however, is at odds with empirical evidence. Public investment in sectors such as energy, rural roads, irrigation, and primary schools often stimulates private investment. Public investment was a key instrument for fostering growth and reducing human poverty in the Republic of Korea and still plays that role in China and Vietnam—two top performers vis-à-vis the MDG targets.

But many governments lack public revenue to invest in growth and to fight poverty. Thus, government needs to raise more money, besides allocating it better. While most poverty-reduction strategies now devote more attention to directing scarce budgetary resources to pro-poor public expenditure, few address the issue of raising more domestic revenue in a progressive way. Public revenue that accounts for 15 per cent or less of national income is grossly insufficient for reducing human poverty. In most developing countries, domestically raised revenue is too small, not too big. Trevor Manuel (2003), South Africa's Finance Minister, has stated, "Most African states need to expand, not contract, their public sector."

The tax systems in developing countries often make the poor pay proportionately more than the nonpoor. The Inter-American Development Bank (1999), for instance, documents the regressive nature of the tax incidence for several Latin American countries. In the 1990s, trade liberalization reduced the significance of taxes on imports and exports as a source of public revenue. In many low-income countries, they were replaced by taxes on consumption, which tend to be more regressive than direct taxes. The lure of the value added tax (VAT) proved particularly irresistible.

According to IMF data, the number of developing countries that adopted VAT more than doubled—to 73 in 2001 from 30 in 1989. By contrast, taxes on income and wealth remained low or benefited from generous loopholes and lax enforcement. The evidence clearly shows that the tax system in many countries has become less equitable and less pro-poor. Reforms are urgently needed in direct and indirect tax policies to generate more domestic resources for the MDGs and do so in a more progressive way.

Winning the battle on pro-poor public expenditure was the result, at least in part, of the UN's advocacy and analytical work (UNICEF 1987; UNDP 1990), which crystallized in the form of the 20/20 initiative. Endorsed at the 1995 Social Summit in Copenhagen, it calls for the allocation of an indicative 20 per cent of the national budget and 20 per cent of ODA to basic social services—basic education, primary health, reproductive health, water and sanitation, and nutrition. The actual shares —as estimated for the mid-1990s—were both about 12 per cent (UNICEF and UNDP 1998). While both have shown a tendency to increase, faster progress from a 12/12 ratio to a 20/20 compact will be essential for reaching the MDGs.

Thus, the next battle will focus on pro-poor public revenue. It would be incorrect to assume that most of the MDG funding gap will be financed from external sources. This would be an untenable proposition from an economic, financial, and political perspective. While more—and better— foreign aid will be part of the solution, aid cannot be viewed as the principal source for funding priority spending at the country level.

2. Use Cost Recovery Sparingly

When the policy framework is driven by low taxation, an alternative way of generating budgetary resources is through user fees. The merits of user financing will depend on the type of services. Charging fees for nonbasic services is very different from charging for basic services. Since basic services are public goods with strong synergies and positive externalities, they should be either free or heavily subsidized—regardless of whether they are provided by public, private, or nongovernmental agencies.

A dozen countries in sub-Saharan Africa, for example, currently charge fees for basic education. Fees are often justified on the ground of pragmatism. To reject them on the basis of principle, the argument goes, is to leave large segments of the population unserved for the foreseeable future. A review of experiences leads to a more cautious stance vis-à-vis user fees for basic social services (Reddy and Vandemoortele 1996).

Despite the very modest amount of money they generate, user fees invariably lead to a reduction in the demand for services, particularly among the poor. Attempts to protect the poor—through exemptions or waivers—are seldom effective and often expensive. The introduction of user fees also tends to aggravate gender discrimination.

Whenever the option of cost sharing is contemplated, special attention needs to be paid to important details such as retaining the bulk of the revenue and its spending authority at the local level; ensuring that users will see an immediate improvement in the quality of the service (by using the extra money for inputs such as essential medicines, textbooks, and spare parts for water pumps); accepting different types of contributions (in cash, in kind, or in labor); implementing an exemption scheme that is based on measurable criteria agreed by the community; using graduated fees whenever possible to promote cross-subsidization; and conducting regular monitoring to adjust and improve the scheme—relying heavily on community participation. It is critical to demonstrate that user fees do not substitute for existing budgetary allocations. In the interest of both the users and the providers of services, it is important to maintain adequate regulation and oversight because self-policing has proved inadequate and ineffective, both for public agencies and private companies.

Since the mid-1990s, school fees have been abolished in Malawi and Uganda and more recently in Kenya. This pro-poor policy was followed by a surge in enrollment in all three countries—with girls being the prime beneficiaries. These positive experiences illustrate that even a small nominal fee can be a formidable obstacle for poor families. Nevertheless, the skeptics argue that such measures generated short-lived gains. As enrollment increased, they claim, the quality of education dropped precipitously so that pupils and parents lost interest in primary schooling. They argue that the surge in enrollment was soon followed by a surge in dropout—nullifying most of the initial gains. While it is true that the initial spike in enrollment leveled off in subsequent years, it cannot be denied that the enrollment ratio stabilized at a level that was considerably higher than the one that prevailed prior to the policy reform. Claiming that such policy reforms are ineffective for reducing human poverty is tantamount to making the perfect the enemy of the good.

3. Use Narrow Targeting with Caution

Given severe fiscal constraints and limited options for user financing, most poverty-reduction strategies recommend targeted interventions on narrowly defined social groups or geographical areas. Narrowly targeted programs are increasingly prescribed for reasons of efficiency and cost savings—for, they claim to minimize leakage to the nonpoor. Obviously, the merits of targeting depend on what is being targeted. Targeting fertilizer subsidies or micro-credit, for instance, is very different from targeting vouchers for primary education or antimalarial bednets.

As far as basic services are concerned, narrow targeting can have huge hidden costs. They result from the fact that it is often difficult to identify the poor and to reach them because the nonpoor—most of whom remain "near-poor"—seldom fail to capture a large part of subsidies destined for more destitute people. Also, administering narrowly targeted programs is at least twice as costly as running untargeted ones. In addition, the poor must frequently document eligibility, which involves expenses such as bus fares, apart from the social stigma they generate. Such out-of-pocket costs can be a real obstacle. Most importantly, however, is the fact that once the nonpoor cease to have a stake in narrowly targeted programs, the political commitment to sustain their scope and quality is at risk. The voice of the poor alone is usually too weak to maintain strong public support. This is why programs meant to benefit exclusively the poor frequently end up as "poor" programs.

As part of narrow targeting, many countries have launched social investment funds or social action programs; but few of them have been institutionalized. They mostly remain under the political patronage of the president or the first lady. Although social-safety nets can lead to rapid responses in situations of crisis and emergency, they are seldom effective. Even if they are cost efficient, they are not necessarily effective because they are usually underfunded and seldom reach beyond an insignificant proportion of the poor.

While narrow targeting, user fees, and social investment funds can play a role, they can never be the mainstay of a country's antipoverty strategy. In most contexts, they are likely to yield savings that are penny-wise but pound-foolish. High-achieving areas in terms of human development, such as Costa Rica, the state of Kerala (India), the Republic of Korea, and Mauritius, all applied broad targeting; none of them relied on shortcuts through user fees, narrowly targeted programs, or social investment funds (UNICEF 1995).

There is no doubt that public spending on basic services includes wastage, but those who argue that existing budgets have to be used more efficiently before more public money can be invested fail to see that insufficiencies can—and often do— aggravate inefficiencies. In many instances, inefficiencies in public administration and governance result from a lack of adequate public resources to fund basic services. Indeed, inefficiencies and insufficiencies are not independent but very much interdependent. For example, when 98 per cent of the budget for primary education is needed to pay teacher salaries—a basic expense—there is little scope for improving the quality of education without raising the budgetary envelop first. In such cases, extra resources will be a prerequisite for enhancing the efficiency of public spending.

4. Set Inflation Targets That Are Not Too Tight

McKinley (2003) and others have argued that tight inflation targets can hurt the poor. Out of 20 low-income countries reviewed by Oxfam (2003), 16 had an inflation rate of less than 5 per cent per year. The standard argument is that inflation is particularly bad for poor people because they cannot maintain their level of consumption by drawing from savings. Therefore, stringent fiscal and monetary policies to achieve macroeconomic stability are assumed to be pro-poor, virtually by definition. However, the case that the poor are the prime victims of inflation is not a solid one. If the poor consume more self-produced goods and services than the nonpoor—as is confirmed by numerous household studies—then they will be less affected by inflation because their consumption basket is less monetized. If anything, the experience in Latin America has shown that middle-class families are most vulnerable in situations of high inflation—mostly because they are unable to protect their modest assets against monetary erosion.

What has been established is that moderate inflation is not damaging, neither for growth nor for the poor. Studies define moderate inflation within the range of 5–30 per cent per year; mostly clustered around 10–15 per cent. Ultimately, the optimal rate of inflation will change in space and in time, and will be positively correlated with the rate of economic growth. While some will interpret this as a license for big spending, huge deficits, and hyperinflation, I simply point out that there is no strong evidence in support of the argument that very low inflation is either pro-growth or pro-poor. Actually, too low an inflation rate can be as harmful to the poor as too high a rate of inflation.

All observers agree that hyperinflation and macroeconomic instability hurts the poor as well as the economy at large; but the objective of poverty reduction cannot be considered an automatic by-product of macroeconomic stability. It cannot be assumed that any set of policies aimed at achieving price stability will always be pro-growth, pro-jobs, and pro-poor. That would be an act of faith. It often reflects the false logic of opposites, whereby it is often assumed—either consciously or unconsciously—that when something does not work, its opposite will work. For instance, if high inflation is bad for the poor, then low inflation will always be good for the poor; if large budget deficits are bad for the economy, then a budget surplus will always be good for economic growth; if autarchy is bad for the economy, then free trade will always be good for the poor. Such thinking reduces the policy framework to rather simplistic "either-or" options. At most, they set up straw men that fail to reflect the complexities and many nuances encountered in real situations. Moreover, straw men often prove highly flammable in policy debates.

5. Deregulate Financial Markets with Great Care

The record of financial liberalization has been neither pro-poor nor pro-growth. It has often destabilized the economy and denied access of poor people to credit. Real interest rates have tended to rise, and the spread between the deposit and lending rates has widened, both undercutting jobs and growth. Farm and nonfarm enterprises often lost access to credit as banks focused on short-term lending for consumer durables in urban areas. Banks and corporations have frequently resorted to short-term external borrowing, making the country vulnerable to capital flight and wreaking havoc in times of crisis, as was the case in East Asia in 1997. After reviewing Latin America's experience in recent years, Birdsall (2002) wrote, "The 'villains' among the reforms have not been trade liberalization or privatization, but financial sector reforms and the opening of the capital account." Yet, financial liberalization continues to be part of many so-called poverty-reduction strategies.

6. Liberalize Trade Cautiously

Similarly, trade must be liberalized cautiously. Surging imports have had destabilizing effects in many countries. The benefits from trade are often concentrated in enclaves or benefit people with skills or capital that are beyond the scope of the poor. Also, heavily subsided exports from rich countries, such as sugar, cotton, fruit, corn, meat, and dairy products, have played havoc with the livelihood of millions of smallholders in poor nations. A study by Carnegie (2003) concluded that the North American Free Trade Agreement (NAFTA) has hurt subsistence farmers in Mexico and that the expected gain in jobs did not materialize; neither did it prevent real wages from declining and income disparities from rising. The study stated, "Trade agreements do not need to result in this kind of hardship for the world's rural poor." The study reconfirms that it is incorrect to assume that trade liberalization will automatically yield outcomes that are pro-poor, pro-jobs, and pro-growth.

UNDP (2003b) reviewed how the global trading system can help or hurt the prospects for human development in low-income countries. It supports the argument that open trade is more a result of development than a prerequisite for it. As countries grow richer, they gradually take advantage of new opportunities offered by global trade. Trade follows development; it seldom leads development. While recognizing that no country has ever developed by keeping its borders closed, it is equally true that no country has developed by throwing open its borders to foreign trade. Current rules no longer allow countries to follow an export-led development strategy similar to that experienced by the so-called East Asian tigers in the 1970s and 1980s, because global trading rules have narrowed the policy space for individual countries to use selective export subsidies and import tariffs.

The potential impact of trade on human poverty has also been affected by the entry into force of intellectual property rights. The Trade-Related Intellectual Property Rights (TRIPS) agreement has gained public attention as patents have barred access to antiretroviral medicines for millions of HIV-positive people in low-income countries. The rules regarding intellectual property rights have to balance the dual objective of serving as an incentive for innovation and of guaranteeing fair access to its results for poor countries and poor people. On balance, the TRIPS agreement has erred in favor of the former. Moreover, there is no evidence that stronger patent protection has led to more research and innovation vis-à-vis tropical diseases. In sum, the days are gone when a pharmaceutical company gave away a profitable patent based on the conviction of its CEO that "medicine is for people not for profit"—a position taken by George W. Merck some 50 years ago when his company released its hold on the exclusive rights to the first antibiotic against tuberculosis.

7. Bring Equity Concerns into the Policy Debate

After reviewing the growth literature, Temple (1999) concluded, "It has become extremely difficult to build a case that inequality is good for growth." Persson and Tabellini (1994) stated, "Inequality is harmful for growth." Ravallion (2000) wrote, "On balance, the existing evidence […] appears to offer more support for the view that inequality is harmful to growth." A study by the Economic Commission for Latin America and the Caribbean (ECLAC), the Institute for Applied Economic Research (IPEA) and UNDP (2002) concluded, "There is every reason to suspect that some amount of redistribution […] might in fact contribute to more economic growth." Williamson (2003) admitted that if anything was omitted from his original ten-point reform agenda that came to be known as the "Washington Consensus," it was the need for "correcting the appallingly unequal income distributions that afflict the region [Latin America]."

Nevertheless, most poverty-reduction strategies overlook equity concerns. At best, the existence of inequalities is recognized, but concrete policies to reduce them remain absent. This is exemplified by gender equality, which continues to get scant attention in most antipoverty plans, although gender equality is at the very heart of achieving the MDGs. A review by the World Bank (2003a) of 27 PRSPs reported that as many as ten failed to include even the slightest recognition of the gender goal.

It is incorrect to assume that higher "average" income will automatically lead to less poverty; economic analyses raise the specter of reasonable doubt. Research has documented the link between high inequality and slow economic growth. High inequality is not only harmful for the poor; it also inhibits economic growth, delays policy reforms, and entrenches special interests. Thus, equity is good for the poor because it is good for growth. Growth alone is not the answer; only when the poor participate in, contribute to, and benefit from economic growth will it make a measurable and lasting dent on human poverty. A little equity will go a long way toward reducing poverty.

Our concern about equity is not solely driven by noble ideals and compassion; it is primarily motivated by the need for laying the foundation of a strong economy. A just society can only emerge when there is a level playing field at the starting line. Only when people are given the means to become agents of their own development, rather than recipients of aid or handouts, will poverty reduction be rapid and sustainable.

Universal coverage of basic social services is key to ensuring equitable growth. Without their universal coverage, the virtuous circle of social and economic development will remain elusive. Once access to an integrated package of basic social services of good quality becomes universal, social progress and economic growth can be rapid and sustainable.

Can External Partners Play a Role in Enlarging Pro-Poor Policies?

It cannot be denied that foreign aid has made a difference in the past. Alongside fairer trade and steeper debt relief, more and more effective ODA will be indispensable for reaching the MDGs by 2015, particularly—but not exclusively—in the least-developed and low-income countries. But let there be no doubt: the bulk of the extra investment in basic services and antipoverty programs will have to come from domestic resources, not from external sources. However, this requirement does not diminish the marginal value of ODA. Indeed, foreign aid can play a critical role in overcoming obstacles in the transitory phase toward pro-poor policies since the latter are bound to meet stiff resistance from several quarters. Budget restructuring, for instance, is never an easy task.

Regrettably, the adoption of noble goals and targets at world summits and international conferences of the 1990s did not prevent aid efforts from declining by one-third. Initiatives such as the Fast Track for Education-for-All; the Global Fund for AIDS, Tuberculosis, and Malaria; the Rollback Malaria initiative; and the HIPC Trust Fund have all been severely hampered by inadequate funding. It remains to be seen whether the Monterrey Consensus will reverse the trend. While early indications show a hesitant recovery, most observers agree that foreign aid is unlikely to recover the ground lost during the 1990s because the fiscal position has worsened in several donor countries since the promises for more aid were made. Also, as we move closer to 2015, foreign aid will increasingly compete with the rising costs of public health care and social security for the aging population in Europe, Japan, and North America. Hence, the sooner we see a major increase in aid, the better it will be for both rich and poor countries—for keeping the promise in the former and for reaching the MDGs in the latter.

Showing that foreign aid can help improve the access of people to primary health care, basic education, and safe water will make it easier to convince parliamentarians and the public in donor countries that aid has a tangible impact on the lives of poor people. A greater focus on basic social services, therefore, will help reverse the decline in ODA that was observed in the 1990s.

As ODA has fallen, concerns about its effectiveness have risen. Greater scrutiny regarding aid's effectiveness is welcome; areas that have seen progress in recent years include the untying of aid, directing it to activities that are likely to benefit the poor, and the pooling of donor resources. Donors increasingly agree to simplify and harmonize their rules, procedures, and procurement so as to lower the transaction cost for the recipient country. Indeed, foreign aid can be very expensive for recipients—although this may seem like an oxymoron. Nonetheless, improvements regarding the issues of "money changing hands" cannot substitute for greater attention to be paid to the aspects related to "ideas changing minds."

A series of influential studies claim that aid is most effective when allocated to countries with good policies. Collier and Dollar (1999), for instance, argued that a diversion of aid to countries where the poverty problem is soluble, owing to "good policies," could lift 82 million people out of poverty each year—against 30 million with the present pattern of aid allocation. In terms of absorptive capacity, Devarajan et al. (2002) calculated, "For countries which have policies and institutions that are among the best … the point beyond which the growth impact is zero is reached when aid is around 30 percent of GDP. By contrast, the saturation point for countries with extremely weak policies and institutions is calculated to be around six percent of GDP." A document to the Development Committee of the World Bank and IMF (World Bank 2003b) uses the concept of "good policies" to identify 18 priority countries for additional aid allocations—ranging from 20 to 100 per cent increases in current ODA levels.

Not only do such studies stretch the reliability of the data—as they are often influenced by faulty indicators, inaccurate data, and omitted variables—they also tend to mask the extent of judgment and subjectivity involved. The definition of "good policies" is frequently based on the country policy and institutional assessment (CPIA) index for which the World Bank country team assigns a value of between one and six for 20 different aspects of the economy. An average score of at least three is required for a country to be classified among those with so-called "good policies."

But several of these dimensions cannot be quantified or assessed objectively. For example, values are given as to whether the country has a distortionary minimum wage, excessive labor-market regulations, or too many public sector workers. It also asks whether the state is able to protect "most of the citizens most of the time." It is obvious that calculating the CPIA index is more an art than a science, likely to be influenced as much by perceptions and prejudice than by facts and figures.

Other studies that used different methods, different indicators, or different levels of aggregation have concluded that aid is effective irrespective of the policy framework. The UNDP's report on development effectiveness (2003d) pointed out that while a good policy environment is important for achieving development results, no single set of policies can guarantee desired outcomes. It stated, "Aid seems to improve social indicators regardless of the type of policy environment." Mosley (1987) called attention to the "micro-macro" paradox whereby the impact of aid is observable when measured at the local level but becomes more difficult to detect at the aggregate level on economic growth.

In short, "good policies" cannot be readily measured, certainly not objectively. Moreover, the idea that there is some form of discontinuity between "good" and "bad" policies is inappropriate (Stewart and Wang 2003). All policy frameworks form a continuum; there is no clear break that can distinguish between "good" and "bad" ones. As beauty, it is in the eye of the beholder. On what basis would one argue, for instance, that Canada has better policies than, say, Germany? Even if it were possible to rank countries according to one specific policy dimension, how could one pretend to be able to do so at the aggregate level and state that a country's policies are better than those of another country? This would be a daring endeavor; yet that is exactly what is being done—without meeting much objection or raising any alarm.

The introduction of the "LICUS," or low-income countries under stress, category is not unrelated to the fact that a strict policy of aid selectivity, based on the criteria of "good" policies, is likely to bypass many of the countries that are most in need of external support. As such, the LICUS concept is an attempt to keep a degree of common sense in the process of aid allocation.

It seems, if anything, that the debate about aid effectiveness—although much welcomed—led several countries to become less generous in the 1990s. Indeed, the skeptics of foreign aid have eagerly used the claims about the importance of "good policies" as a justification to cut ODA, which is unlikely to have helped any poor person in any poor country.

What are the "Don'ts" When Making the Policy Framework Pro-Poor?

We noted that in most countries the policy framework is not yet aligned with the MDGs and the fundamental objective of reducing human poverty. Poverty reduction is seen as an automatic by-product of economic growth and macroeconomic stability. Governments and their partners find it difficult to translate the concept of "pro-poor policies" into practice. Equity continues to be the big absentee in most antipoverty strategies. Although the objective of reducing human poverty features prominently on the international agenda, its actual pursuit remains conventional, unimaginative, and often ineffective. It is a tragedy, in our view, that countries with high HIV prevalence rates have a macroeconomic framework that is not dissimilar from that for countries without HIV/AIDS. The framework for the former should be much more accommodating and expansionary for the foreseeable future if they are to achieve the MDGs and overcome their HIV/AIDS crisis.

The poverty-reduction strategies have to face the MDG challenge more explicitly. This will require a quantum leap in public investment, in domestic resources mobilization, in external assistance and debt relief, as well as in meaningful trade concessions. The era of targeted small-scale antipoverty interventions is over. If small is beautiful, big is now indispensable for reaching the MDGs; if prudence is silver, ambition is golden.

The question whether the MDGs and the PRSPs are enlarging pro-poor policy choices at the country level cannot be answered affirmatively—at least not yet—notwithstanding the overwhelming evidence that business-as-usual will not turn the MDG targets into a practical reality by 2015. Three "don'ts" are to be considered when trying to engender pro-poor policy frameworks.

The first "don't" is not to be statistically illiterate. We saw how the story about MDG performance depends on the choice of the indicator and the level of aggregation, as well as the time horizon used. In order to interpret the validity of the different versions of such stories, the stakeholders and the public at large need to improve their basic statistical literacy to be able to separate false arguments from valid ones—always admitting that any version of the story will inevitably include an element of judgment and subjectivity.

The second "don't" is not to make assumptions about the so-called pro-poor nature of specific policy reforms. It is seldom correct, for instance, to assume that what works for men will work equally well for women. The same applies to macroeconomic policies; many of the alleged pro-poor policies frequently end up bypassing the poor, sometimes hurting them. Policy reforms that are presumed gender-neutral are in fact gender-blind; similarly, many policy reforms are often blind to the realities faced by the poor. Thus, one is never to be gullible vis-à-vis arguments about the pro-poor nature of macroeconomic stability, financial deregulation, trade liberalization, user fees, narrow targeting, and aid selectivity. They must always be interpreted with caution. Just as the goldsmith handles gold—by rubbing, cutting, and melting it—so must the validity of the pro-poor nature of reforms and investments be analyzed within their specific context and circumstances.

The third "don't" is not to focus too narrowly on short-term results but to seek sustained partnerships—based on the principles of equality, mutual respect, and national ownership. The drive to improve aid efficiency is certainly welcome but should not blind external partners to the reality that reaching the MDGs will require prolonged efforts. Success in the fight against river blindness and polio, for instance, did not occur overnight. External partners have to accept that over such prolonged periods of time some policy changes will inevitably be imperfect and that progress will not always be linear. There will be instances of events or reforms being perceived as setbacks or as "bad" policies, which have traditionally triggered a suspension in aid flows. But such drastic measures inherently contradict the pursuit for equal partnership and national ownership. Greater understanding and more flexibility on the part of external partners is therefore sine qua non for sustained partnerships. For many donors—bilateral as well as multilateral—this will require more active listening. Turning the development coin will change the way foreign aid is managed from a one-way street centered on "money changing hands" to a two-way exchange of "ideas changing minds."

Can Global Targets Make a Difference?

After several false dawns and missed opportunities, it might be tempting to dismiss the MDGs as targets that are "easily set but never met." But this would be incorrect; global targets have made a difference in the past (Jolly 2003).

Success stories with a target-driven approach to development—such as those against smallpox and polio, for iodized salt, or increased access to safe water—indicate that they have seven elements in common. The seven "do's" for operationalizing the MDGs follow.

First, do express the vision of development in an inspiring but measurable way. Fuzzily formulated targets are as unhelpful as they are unmeasurable. Targets for reducing human poverty must be specific; they cannot rely on vague assumptions, faulty indicators, or inaccurate data.

Second, do make sure that the targets are well known; they must reach the kitchen table. Targets must be addressed in parliament, from the pulpit, and in the press, as well as in the pub—involving presidents, prime ministers, preachers, and primary school teachers. Public interest must be awakened and nurtured, ambition stirred, and expectation aroused. The media has a critical role to play in keeping the eyes of the public on the prize.

Third, do tailor the targets to the national context and local priorities. Targets must strike a judicious balance between ambition and realism. Overambitious targets are unlikely to trigger action; underambitious targets are unlikely to mobilize people and resources. The MDGs encourage all stakeholders to think globally but to act locally. Targets must be tailored and customized through an inclusive dialogue because only genuine participation will result in a consensus centered on a pro-poor development agenda. At the same time, tailored targets cannot turn into an escape clause, whereby the government hides inadequate political commitment behind targets that lack any sense of ambition or urgency.

Fourth, do formulate intermediate targets. Long-term goals will not guarantee immediate action because they are not on the watch of today's political leadership. Targets must be broken down in actionable propositions that can be achieved within the lifetime of the current government. Such intermediate targets must drive the shorter-term policy framework, budgetary priorities and decisions about aid allocations, debt relief, and trade reforms. A target-driven approach that pays insufficient attention to the immediate realities is likely to lead to a situation of "meeting the target but missing the point."

Fifth, do constant monitoring. A journey to an agreed destination requires a map. If we are to reach the MDGs by 2015, good statistics are needed to document progress, to mobilize people, and to design pro-poor policies based on hard evidence—not only on economic theory. Monitoring must use a few solid but easy-to-grasp indicators. It cannot be confined to specialists and experts alone; it must inform political leaders, parliamentarians, journalists, NGO activists, and the general public. Monitoring must go beyond averages and aggregates. Data must be broken down according to gender, age, geographical location, and socioeconomic groups. Comparing the performance of neighboring localities and communities can be a catalyst for change.

Sixth, do provide leadership. Targets that fostered success often had strong leadership behind them, frequently in the form of a public-private partnership, such as the Rotary Club against polio and the Carter Center against guinea worm. These actors constantly nag policy makers—both globally and locally—to stay focused on the target. They also bring technical expertise and good campaign tactics.

Seventh, do remember that nothing speaks louder than financial commitments. A balance must be kept between output and input targets. Results do not come for free; they carry a price tag. Two global input targets are the 20/20 target for the national budget and the aid target of 0.7 percent of rich countries' income. Another relevant indicator is how much of the money budgeted for basic services actually reaches the unit of service delivery, such as a primary school or a rural health center. The latter can serve as a proxy indicator of good governance.

These seven steps apply to both developing and developed countries, albeit in different ways. In the latter, for instance, opinion polls show similar levels of public support for foreign aid, irrespective of the country's actual aid effort. Countries where such efforts are low register equally high levels of public support for foreign aid than countries that exceed the 0.7 per cent aid target—the so-called G7 members. Differences in actual aid efforts often stem from a series of deliberate actions within donor countries, such as regular briefing of parliamentarians and journalists, a focus on success stories rather than on failures, setting time-bound targets for ODA, explicit monitoring of aid levels when the national budget is submitted for a vote, and the strong involvement of politicians, community, or religious leaders, and celebrities in making the case for foreign aid.

The seventh step closes the circle by turning the "development coin" from the side of "ideas changing minds" to the side of "money changing hands." But that step should never come first—as is often the case in practice—because real change is ultimately an act of freedom; it is never an act of compliance with rules and conditionalities associated with "money changing hands."

The periodic consultations between a developing country and its external partners provide an opportunity for substantive discussions about the national development strategy. However, these events frequently turn into a ritual of compliance with the rules and conditionalities associated with "money changing hands," which overshadows the dimension of "ideas changing minds." I propose a *peer and partner review* to make such consultations less asymmetric and more substantive. The current mode whereby a developing country faces 20–30 bilateral donors and multilateral institutions is not always conducive for an equal exchange and a frank debate. *A peer and partner review* would involve peer countries and a more select group of external partners to review the antipoverty strategy, programs, and financing plans. When Lesotho, for instance, meets with its external partners, it could be joined by Mozambique, South Africa, Zambia, and perhaps another landlocked country, such as Bolivia or Nepal. A person of distinction could also join the consultative process to help maintain the high moral ground. A *peer and partner review* could combine existing mechanisms such as the peer review within New Partnership for African Development (NEPAD) and the Development Assistance Committee (DAC) of the Organisation of Economic Co-operation and Development.

References

Birdsall, N. 2002. From social policy to an open-economy social contract in Latin America. Working Paper No. 21, Center for Global Development, Washington, D.C.

Carnegie Endowment for International Peace. 2003. Lessons from Mexico for the hemisphere. *NAFTA's promise and reality.* Washington, D.C. (http://www.ceip.org/files/publications/NAFTA_Report_full.asp)

Collier, P., and D. Dollar. 1999. Aid allocation and poverty reduction. Policy Research Working Paper No. 2041, World Bank, Washington, D.C.

Delamonica, E., S. Malhotra, and J. Vandemoortele.2004. Education for all: How much will it cost? *Development and Change* 35(1): 3–30.

Devarajan, S., M. Miller, and E. Swanson. 2002. Goals for development: History, prospects, and costs. Policy Research Working Paper No. 2819, World Bank, Washington, D.C.

ECLAC, IPEA, and UNDP. 2002. *Meeting the millennium poverty reduction targets in Latin America and the Caribbean.* Santiago: United Nations.

Inchauste, G. 2002. *Poverty and social impact analysis of PRGF supported programs.* Washington, D.C.: IMF.

Inter-American Development Bank. 1999. *Facing up to inequality in Latin America. Economic and social progress in Latin America.* Washington, D.C.: IDB.

International Monetary Fund. 2003. Role of the fund in low-income member countries over the medium term. Issues paper for discussion, Policy Development and Review Department, IMF, Washington, D.C.

Jolly, R. 2003. Global goals—the UN experience. Background paper for the Human Development Report 2003. New York: UNDP (mimeographed).

Laderchi, C., R. Saith, and F. Stewart. 2003. Does it matter that we don't agree on the definition of poverty?—A comparison of four approaches. Working Paper No. 107, University of Oxford, Queen Elizabeth House.

Manuel, T. 2003. Finding the right part—Africa and the Washington consensus. *Finance and Development,* September, 18–20. Washington, D.C.: IMF.

McKinley, T. 2003. The macroeconomics of poverty reduction. Initial findings of the UNDP Asia-Pacific regional program. New York: UNDP's Poverty Group (mimeographed).

Minujin, A., and E. Delamonica. 2003. Equality matters for a world fit for children. Lessons from the 1990s. Staff Working Paper, Division for Policy and Planning, UNICEF, New York.

Morrisson, C. 2002. Health, Education, and Poverty Reduction. Policy Brief No. 19, OECD Development Centre, Paris.

Mosley, P. 1987. *Overseas aid: Its defence and reform.* Brighton, U.K.: Wheatsheaf.

Nebie, G. 2003. Analysis of the macroeconomic policies in the first three final PRSPs in Central and Eastern Africa, UNDP's Poverty Group, Addis Ababa (mimeographed).

Oxfam. 2003. The IMF and the millennium goals. Oxfam Briefing Paper No. 54, Oxfam International.

———. 2004. From 'donorship' to ownership. Moving towards PRSP round two, Oxfam Briefing Paper No. 51, Oxfam International.

Pernia E. 2003. Pro-poor growth: What is it and how is it important? ERD Policy Brief No. 17, Asian Development Bank, Manila.

Persson, T., and G. Tabellini.1994. Is Inequality Harmful for Growth? *The American Economic Review* 84(3): 600–621.

Ravallion, M. 2000. *Growth, inequality and poverty: Looking beyond averages.* Development Research Group. Washington, D.C.: World Bank.

Reddy, S., and J. Vandemoortele. 1996. User financing of basic social services: A review of theoretical arguments and empirical evidence. Staff Working Paper No. 6, Evaluation Policy and Planning Division, UNICEF, New York.

Reddy, S., and T. Pogge. 2003. *How not to count the poor.* New York: Columbia University. http://www.socialanalysis.org.

Stewart, F., and M. Wang. 2003. Do PRSPs empower poor countries and disempower the World Bank, or is it the other way round? Working Paper No. 108, University of Oxford, Queen Elizabeth House.

Temple, J. 1999. "The New Growth Evidence." *Journal of Economic Literature* 37(1): 112–156.

United Nations. 2000. *Millennium Declaration.* New York: United Nations.

UNICEF. 1987. *Adjustment with a Human Face: Protecting the Vulnerable and Promoting Growth*, ed. G. A. Cornia, R. Jolly and F. Stewart. Oxford: Clarendon Press.

———. 1995. *Profiles in success. People's progress in Africa, Asia and Latin America.* New York: UNICEF.

UNICEF and UNDP. 1998. Country experiences in assessing the adequacy, equity, and efficiency of public spending on basic social services. Document prepared for the Hanoi meeting on the 20/20 Initiative with contributions from the World Bank and the UNFPA. New York: UNICEF.

UNDP. 1990. *Human development report.* New York: Oxford University Press.

———. 2003a. Millennium Development Goals: A Compact among Nations to End Human Poverty. *Human development report* 2003. New York: Oxford University Press.

————. 2003b. *Making global trade work for people.* Cosponsored by four private foundations. London: Earthscan.

————. 2003c. *Evaluation of UNDP's role in the PRSP process.* Evaluation Office. New York: UNDP.

————. 2003d. *Development effectiveness report 2003.* Partnership for results. Evaluation Office. New York: UNDP.

Vandemoortele, J., and E. Delamonica. 2000. The "education vaccine" against HIV. *Current Issues in Comparative Education* 3(1). http://www.tc.columbia.edu/cice.

Williamson J. 2003. From reform agenda to damaged brand name—a short history of the Washington Consensus and suggestions for what to do next. *Finance and Development,* September, 11–13. Washington, D.C.: IMF.

World Bank. 2001. *IDA's partnership for poverty reduction (TY94–TY00). An independent evaluation.* Operations Evaluation Department. Washington, D.C.: World Bank.

————. 2003a. *Getting serious about meeting the Millennium Development Goals. A CDF progress report.* Washington, D.C.: World Bank.

————. 2003b. Supporting sound policies with adequate and appropriate financing. Paper submitted to Development Committee. Washington, D.C.: World Bank.

————. 2004. Global poverty down by half since 1981 but progress uneven as economic growth eludes many countries. News release no. 2004/309/S, April 23, 2004. Washington, D.C.: World Bank.

3

Some Practical Limits of the NGO Role: A Critical Perspective

Michael Edwards

A Pavlovian reaction to the title I was given ("who are the NGOs") would have me regaling you with reams of statistics about trends in the nongovernmental organization (NGO) universe that would reveal little of consequence in terms of the relationships between nonstate action and achieving the Millennium Development Goals (MDGs), for reasons that I hope will become clear. Instead, I want to challenge some of the conventional wisdom about NGOs and relocate this debate in the much broader terrain of critical thinking about civil society.

Now, what is this "conventional wisdom" that I have the temerity to question? In Chapter 4, it runs something like this: achieving the MDGs requires particular, though shifting, combinations of public, private, and NGO action, with NGOs addressing instances of state and market failure in the provision of certain goods through direct delivery or indirect "leverage" (advocacy, etc.). NGOs also have weaknesses (what the chapter calls "voluntary failures"), and these set up an agenda, or a series of entry points, for capacity building and other interventions such as strengthening accountability that are deemed necessary for NGOs to take responsible advantage of spaces for participation in the MDG process. Yes, questions remain, but in general terms we have this sorted out—the more NGOs we have, the stronger they are, and the more they participate, the closer we will get to achieving the Goals. We know what to do—just do it!

There is a lot of good sense in this account, but it is partial and unsatisfactory, and based on a set of assumptions that need to be carefully scrutinized.

We need to add another six or seven layers of complexity to the argument in order to have a sensible conversation. Why? Because:

- NGOs (even by a relatively broad definition) are a poor proxy for the richness of associational life and the dynamics of citizen action that characterize most societies;
- The assumptions we make about different associations and their effects are often untested, or are found to be unreliable when they are;
- In any case, we lack the kind of systematic comparative evidence that would enable us to test the transmission mechanisms involved across a sufficient number of different settings;
- When we *do* carry out research we use liberal democratic templates about collective action that often make little sense in non-Western contexts; and
- Overall, we've become obsessed with one particular interpretation of civil society that crowds out other, equally important interpretations.

This is not surprising, since the view that civil society is a *part* of society—the world of voluntary associations—has become almost completely dominant, and the earlier and later traditions that have just as much to offer have been forgotten. It was Alexis de Tocqueville who started this craze on his visits across the Atlantic in the 1830s. He saw America's rich tapestry of associational life as the key to its emerging democracy. NGOs are obviously one category of associational life whose popularity and profile have increased so much that this may deter us from appreciating the complex "ecosystems" that people create when they associate with one another in different ways for different purposes, a point I will return to.

Originally, however, civil society, from Aristotle to Thomas Hobbes, represented a *kind* of society that was identified with certain ideals. And in modern societies, realizing these ideals, such as political equality or peaceful coexistence, requires action across many different institutions, not just voluntary associations. The MDGs serve as an international bureaucratic proxy for the goals of "a civil society" in this normative sense. Most recently, philosophers have developed a new set of theories about civil society as the "public sphere"—the places where citizens argue with one another about the great questions of the day and negotiate a constantly evolving sense of the "common" or "public" interest. The current enthusiasm for Poverty Reduction Strategy Papers, negotiated Country Strategies, and so on is a variant of this theme.

We could have a whole conference on the comparative utility of these different schools of thought, but for the moment what is important is the overall question they raise, which is this: what are the transmission mechanisms between the shape and structure of the associational ecosystem, the health of the public sphere, and the achievement of the good society (or the MDGs), and can one generalize about these relationships from one context or time period to another? We may think we know the answer—start and strengthen as many NGOs as possible—but in reality the answers are much less predictable. Compare the following cases:

- Lebanon, Rwanda, and the Weimar Republic: a dense network of voluntary associations but poor results in terms of democracy and peaceful coexistence;
- India or Brazil: a dense network with good results in democratic participation but poor results in terms of poverty reduction;
- Bangladesh: an increasing number of very large NGOs but highly disputed impacts, at least in terms of institutional reform;
- Spain, Botswana, and Hungary: all have achieved good economic and social results but with a low density of NGOs;
- China and the East Asian tigers: they have achieved, over time, good economic results with an increasing number of associations but few NGOs in the accepted sense (organizations independent of government, as Western theory would have us believe); and
- The United States, the context where we have most evidence and analysis: there is no consensus on these questions at all.

Some scholars, such as Robert Putnam, see associational life in general as the driving force behind the positive social norms on which the good society is founded—things like cooperation, trust, and reciprocity, or *social capital*, to use his language. So, the logical policy is to encourage as much volunteering and voluntary action as possible even if some of it is used for nefarious purposes. Somewhat magically, in my view, these differences will, Putnam argues, work themselves out in the general scheme of things.

Other scholars, such as Theda Skocpol, see particular configurations of associational life as the key to securing the public policy reforms the good society requires—the nationally federated mass-membership, cross-class groups such as PTAs, labor unions, elks, and other forest creatures, which have declined so much over the last 50 years and which used to provide strong bridges between citizens and government that led to reforms such as the GI Bill of 1944. And, of course, there are the skeptics such as Nancy Rosenblum who don't see any reliable link between the structure of civil society and its achievements. If such arguments rage in the United States where the literature is very rich, wouldn't the same be true, or even more so, in settings where cultures of association and collective action grow from very different roots?

Where does this brief excursion into civil society theory lead us in relation to the more limited set of questions on the table for this particular research effort?

- Civil society as the good society encourages us to see NGOs as complementary to, not as a substitute for, the demands of democratic state building and pro-poor market reform. Instrumentalizing NGOs or privileging them on ideological grounds—to deliver the MDGs or any other magic formula for development—should be resisted.
- Civil society as the public sphere encourages us to bring politics back into the equation and ask ourselves how the MDGs are going to obtain the political purchase required for structural reform, something that must grow from deep within society. This means exploring the neglected links between civil and political society, examining whether NGOs are sufficiently connected to prepolitical publics, and exploring support for independent media groups that foster public deliberation.
- Civil society as associational life encourages us to look at the entire ecosystem to identify gaps, disconnections, and areas of oversupply rather than jump to conclusions about which NGOs to support and what capacities they need— usually advocacy groups in capital cities or intermediaries with a large absorptive capacity for foreign aid. We need to make room for surprises (such as mosque associations in Lebanon, for example, or burial societies in South Africa), hybrids that mix delivery and leverage, and organizations with different characteristics that play different but complementary roles—innovation (social entrepreneurs?), facilitation/bridge building (relationship skills), counterweights (watchdogs, advocates, movements), and representation (member controlled).

To conclude, am I attacking a straw man here? Not if you look at actual patterns of donor assistance and the crude conceptual models that underpin them. We need to ask ourselves whether "NGO" is a meaningful or useful analytical category any more, and whether the relationship between NGOs and the MDGs is therefore the right question, or at least the most useful way to frame the question. More useful, in my view, is to ask what the transmission mechanisms are in different contexts between the shape of associational life, the character of politics and the public sphere, and the achievement of good-society goals. And if that is what we mean by this debate, then let us be clear and rigorous with ourselves about it. Specifying the debate in this way implies a much deeper conversation and a much more sophisticated strategy for NGO support.

4

Beyond the "Non": The Strategic Space for NGOs in Development

Jennifer M. Brinkerhoff, Stephen C. Smith, and Hildy Teegen

Citizen-sector agents in the fields of development and poverty reduction are more often labeled by what they are not—"nongovernmental" or "nonprofit" organizations—than by what they are. Although, indeed, nongovernmental organizations (NGOs) do not fit comfortably within either the public or the private sector, the terminology reflects the broader problem that development scholars and practitioners have rarely been particularly clear about the citizen sector's own inherent comparative advantages. Of course, sometimes NGOs must fill in where government and firms fail to fulfill their roles; but is there also a more fundamental NGO role? In this chapter, we examine the *strategic* function of NGOs in development.

The nature of NGOs raises key questions with respect to their effectiveness and potential contributions to meeting the Millennium Development Goals (MDGs). Connections between management practices of international nongovernmental organizations (INGOs) and effective delivery of social programs are in need of detailed assessment (see, for example, Ramia 2003). Beyond this and the questions Michael Edwards raises in chapter 3, other questions remain regarding NGOs and the MDGs: are NGOs too small and insignificant to produce the scale of results necessary? Are they too diverse and unreliable? Can they be made sufficiently transparent and accountable, and if so, to whom? We discuss possible, or ideal, roles for NGOs in achieving the MDGs by way of a more general discussion of roles for the three principal sectors—private sector, governments, and NGOs—in development.

In examining potential MDG roles for NGOs, we begin with general theoretical considerations and then account for likely contingencies encountered in practice, taking into account political and marketplace realities. Potential NGO roles in the MDGs span both advocacy and implementation activities, and NGOs work both independently and in partnership with other actors. We review the respective roles and comparative advantages of governments, the private sector, and NGOs (as a subset of civil society) for a clearer understanding of NGOs' full potential contribution to the MDGs. As implied by the questions above, NGOs are not always the appropriate actors for making progress on the MDGs or related objectives; their presumed comparative advantages are based on theoretically possible, though not necessarily probable, characteristics of individual organizations.

The chapter is organized as follows: we first briefly introduce a typology of goods and services that sets the stage conceptually for sector role designation and an examination of sector failures. We then address government and private-sector roles in implementing the MDGs, noting where sector failure may occur when these actors engage in development activities. Next, we extend the notion of sector failure to more specifically consider NGOs in terms of their potential roles and comparative advantages in light of government and market failures, as well as NGOs' own limitations, termed voluntary-sector failure. Pulling these analyses together, we propose a set of roles for NGOs in support of the MDGs, along with corresponding achievement measures and contingency factors. We argue that careful assessment of NGO activities is critical for identifying viable and efficient roles for NGOs in achieving the MDGs. The evidence provided in subsequent chapters will offer an initial appraisal on the basis of NGO activities as they pertain globally to each MDG. In chapter 8, Smith applies our framework using these indications to MDG1; in chapter 9 we apply it more broadly. We conclude by providing policy prescriptions (chapter 10). Our goal is to gain insight into the strategic space that NGOs can, or should, occupy as essential players for achieving the MDGs.

Typology of Goods and Services

There are a number of ways to differentiate the types of goods and services produced and delivered by firms, governments, and NGOs (or the third sector). One of the simplest and most readily applicable schemas is found in the distinctions based on excludability and rivalry (Musgrave 1969). *Excludability* refers to the degree to which benefits conferred on a given individual or segment of society can be effectively denied (at less than prohibitive cost) to others. Situations characterized by high *rivalry* are those in which one person's or group's consumption (or enjoyment) of a particular good or benefit inherently limits another person's or group's consumption of the same good or benefit.

In common practice, and consistent with the basic theory of welfare economics, goods that are more excludable and more rival are normally left to the private sector (*private goods*), as decentralized, profit-making activities can lead to their efficient provision. A government role is more common for goods that are less excludable and less rival—*public goods.* Public goods are associated with important societal needs, yet profit opportunities to provide them at socially efficient levels are lacking. Solving this problem generally requires that governments provide some of these goods (when the state is concerned with societal needs and does not require profitable returns on its investments). Figure 4.1 illustrates key (pure type) goods as arrayed within this framework.

The gray diagonal indicates the area of primary NGO roles, at least with respect to these two characteristics of goods and services, based on natural comparative advantages (as discussed later in this chapter). Examples of *common-pool goods* are natural resources such as fisheries, pastures, and forests, with open access (often termed common-property resources). Because NGOs are organizations based more on trust than on coercion (government) or individual self-interest (market), third-sector actors may

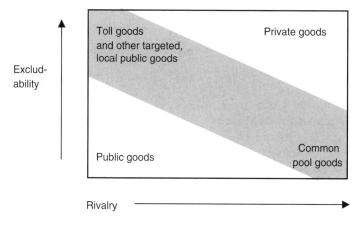

Figure 4.1   Typology of goods

be able to arrive at efficient and socially acceptable allocations of common-pool resources at relatively low (transaction) costs.

Toll goods and other targeted, local public goods are typically assigned to government-regulated private sector or civil society actors (see Ostrom and Ostrom 1977; Weimar and Vining 1992). For example, toll roads may be operated by either public departments or private firms; productive ideas are often developed by universities in the nonprofit sector, and technology transfer is often undertaken by specialized NGOs (such as Technoserve) or nonprofit industry associations or consortia.

Under some circumstances, NGOs can effectively engage in service and goods provision outside the gray area of figure 4.1 that indicates their primary-role designation. Local conditions (such as government failure or extremely small market size) may result in situations where NGOs are in an advantaged position to supply public or private goods (at a lower price or of higher quality, in a more timely fashion, or in a more reliable manner, etc.) vis-à-vis actors in other sectors. In these cases, NGOs may productively expand into these areas as well.

In the MDG context, where the goals themselves may be conceptualized as public goods whose delivery requires contributions from all sectors, the designation of sector roles and responsibilities *solely* on the basis of this sort of typology is insufficient. Indeed, *complementary* provision of all types of goods—public, private, common pool, and toll goods—may be required for achievement of the MDGs. By means of illustration, average incomes cannot be increased society-wide without private-sector firms profitably employing workers in the provision of private goods. Neither firms nor NGOs can achieve efficiency if government fails to provide essential infrastructure and other public goods. Similarly, watersheds, forests, clean air, and fisheries are examples of common-pool goods that must be well managed to meet the sustainability goal. Resource scarcity, and unequal use of goods across members in a society, may call for the provision of toll goods such as tuition fees for informal high school schemes in order to meet goals related to education and gender equity.

Ideally, role designation is based upon the relative strengths of each available actor, including those strengths that derive from their corresponding sector, as well as contingencies specific to those individual actors, sectors, and the environments in which they operate. Even so, when activities are complementary, coordination of actors across the three sectors (Todaro and Smith 2003, chapter 5) may be required. To develop the typology further in the MDG context, we first turn to the roles and comparative advantages of government and the private sector.

Roles of Governments and the Private Sector: A Brief Review

The Role of Government

In principle, governments, through national institutions, work to protect public welfare interests. In exchange for the provision of security, economic promotion, and other public goods, citizens transfer their sovereignty to the national government (i.e., the social contract). A government, therefore, is presumed to be accountable to its citizens, who depend upon it and who judge it based on its performance in providing for social and economic welfare. Governments hold the central role in international relations as the ultimate representative of their citizens. In governing and providing public goods, there is a broad, eclectic role for government in providing[1]

- A stable macro environment;
- Infrastructure (social and physical), though in fewer sectors than thought necessary in the past;
- Public health;
- Education and training;
- Technology transfer (and, for advanced developing countries, the beginnings of original research and development);
- Incentives and regulation for ensuring environmentally sustainable development and ecological protection;
- Export incentives;
- Support to the private sector to overcome coordination failures;
- Frameworks to ensure "shared growth," acting to reduce poverty and inequality and ensure that as the economy grows, the poor share substantially in the benefits;
- Prudential regulation and supervision in financial sectors; and
- Fundamental public goods, such as legal infrastructure including the protection of property rights.

The effectiveness of governments in these roles derives, in part, from the public sector's particular comparative advantages owing to specialized skills, experience/institutional memory, and relationships resident in their bureaucracy. Their relatively larger scale and the resources they control provide additional sources of strength and capability to governments.

In the MDG context, governments can establish the MDGs as a national agenda and support their achievement by providing essential financial and material resources and key services, including administrative, supervisory/oversight, coercion, information and research, technical assistance, training, and promotion. Their scale, institutional longevity, and broad responsibility in society offer the potential for expanding, sustaining, and replicating implementation efforts. Governments can provide checks on elite control, as well as support equity objectives. Finally, governments have the ability and authority to convene diverse actors for the purpose of policy deliberation and consultation, and can heavily influence other key stakeholders by, for example, providing fora for their coordination and promoting the participation of various actors and the inclusion of diverse perspectives (see Clark 1997). At their discretion, governments can engage citizens and other stakeholders in participatory processes; local governments in particular can motivate and facilitate citizen participation (USAID 1995a). Indeed, government alone represents all citizens, at least as an ideal. Thus, governments can and do contribute in significant ways to achieving the MDGs.

The Private Sector

The private sector has a central role to play in economic life and hence in broader social aims generally and for the MDGs in particular (Teegen 2005). Private-sector firms engage with citizens via market mechanisms, trading goods and services produced for valuable monetary and nonmonetary compensation. Owing to the pressures of a competitive marketplace, firms are held accountable to customer demands as expressed by their patronage of a given firm. Multinational enterprises (MNEs) are firms active across nation-state boundaries that seek to reap competitive advantage by uniquely configuring and coordinating their activities to access, transform, and deploy valuable and scarce resources in responding to customer needs globally. Ultimately, the MNE is responsible for maximizing the value created for its shareholders.

Yet firms also play a potentially important, albeit less direct, role in providing for social welfare. As employers, investors, infrastructure providers, and producers, firms provide vehicles for individual incomes and economies to grow, with positive impacts on poverty reduction. When incomes grow, and where private sector activities promote a more equitable income distribution, social and political stability may result.[2] In their commercial pursuits, firms can provide an important demonstration of initiative, entrepreneurship, and responsibility. Firm activities that may also contribute positively to human development include philanthropy under the broad rubric of corporate social responsibility initiatives and promotion of improved institutional environments (Nelson 1996). In many cases these roles are carried out in consortia including industry associations and chambers of commerce.

Thus, the private sector has an important role to play in supporting the MDGs both indirectly, through its contributions to economic growth and other spillover effects of its pursuit of profit (e.g., infrastructure investment), and also through advocacy and partnership, such as through corporate social responsibility. The International Business Leaders Forum (Nelson and Prescott 2003) outlines three spheres in which businesses can contribute to the MDGs, through: (1) their core business activities as they relate to each of the MDGs (e.g., in the selection and production of products and services, and related policies and practice); (2) social investment and philanthropic activities in support of each of the MDGs (with special attention to the implications and potential contributions of firms' people, profits, products, premises, purchasing, power, and promotions through social marketing); and (3) engagement in policy dialogue and advocacy activities—both through leadership in promoting one or more NGOs through public platforms, and through participating in collective action and dialogue with government and civil society to set rules, norms, and standards in support of the MDGs.

Government Failures and Market Failures

The public sector in many developing countries lacks the resources, expertise, and/or political will to provide critical public goods or services to all or a subset of the nation's citizens. Public-sector resource impediments include high debt burdens, the dual financial drains of healthcare provision, and productivity declines due to pandemics such as HIV/AIDS and low effective tax capacity. Inexperienced bureaucracies resulting from age-structure imbalances and legacies of underinvestment in human capital contribute to expertise limitations. Corruption, elitism, cronyism, political patronage, and pervasive institutional weakness are manifest in certain of these political systems and can systematically preclude development benefits from reaching certain segments of society. In these instances, the public sector fails to address the needs of citizens and prevents widespread and sustainable human development from taking place. This is a case of "political failure," where government agents are unable or unwilling to adequately respond to societal needs and desires (Brinkerhoff and Brinkerhoff 2002).

For their part, private-sector firms will be inherently less responsive to citizen needs in their commercial activities when they enjoy monopolistic advantages and market power due to extreme firm concentration, institutional arrangements that do not protect against firm collusion, and government protection of certain firms or industries against competitive threats. Business groups founded by historically powerful families or other groups control resource access and raise entry barriers to newcomers, further exacerbating limits to competition in these markets.

There are three general forms in which market failure can be observed:[3] the market cannot function properly or no market exists; the market exists but produces an economically inefficient allocation of resources; or the market produces undesirable results as measured by certain social objectives. Market failures can occur in situations in which social costs or benefits differ from the private costs or benefits of firms or consumers as in situations concerning public goods, externalities, and (abuses of) market power. With public goods, free riders cannot be excluded from benefits except at high cost. With externalities, consumers or firms do not have to pay all the costs of their activities or are unable to receive all the benefits. Coordination failures occur when agents would be better off if they could cooperate on actions if all or most agents participate, but worse off taking the action if too few participate. These failures differ from the familiar prisoners' dilemma model, in which there is an incentive to defect after coordination is achieved. With organization failures, activities carried out in a less costly fashion within firms rather than across markets are nonetheless subject to inefficiencies made possible by the joint presence of firm-specific investments (asset idiosyncrasy) and opportunism. Market power occurs when firms can influence price by restricting quantity.

Market failure is also linked more specifically to public goods. A more equal distribution of income itself can be considered a public good, when it is an agreed social objective. This can also reflect the well-being of future generations, who cannot participate in today's economic or political markets. Agreed merit goods, such as health, education, and basic welfare, can be considered public goods or as social entitlements guaranteed by government.

Under such conditions, where the narrow, particular interests of a given firm diverge from that of society-wide objectives such as poverty reduction, firm activities may do little to further human development. However, industry groupings, such as chambers of commerce, or sector associations that are genuinely accessible and affordable to the private sector as a whole (versus a few entrenched elite companies) might provide a vehicle for integrating private sector and societal interests. The very yardsticks used to gauge performance in the private sector may effectively preclude these firms from knowing how to contribute meaningfully to human development in the nations where they conduct business (Hodess 2002). This suggests a role for social entrepreneurship, both in the NGO sector and in the overlapping spaces between the sectors (to be discussed later in this chapter).

The case of MNEs is particularly thorny with regard to national development concerns. The essence of multinational firm advantage resides in ownership, location, and internalization advantages (Caves 1982; Dunning 1979). The ability to trade off benefits to one nation against benefits elsewhere is part and parcel to the MNE competitive milieu. MNEs' potential to have a sustainable role in any nation's development efforts (actual or perceived) is constrained by lack of loyalty to the citizens of any one nation[4] and demonstrated evidence of MNEs subverting national interests when they run counter to the firm's pursuit of shareholder-value maximization.

Many development concerns cannot be contained within national boundaries, such as the case of reducing/reversing global warming, or infectious disease prevention. Where a public-sector entity bears the costs of providing these goods or services, limiting access to the benefits is difficult or impossible. In these cases, national governments encounter problems of free riding when the goods or services in question extend extranational benefits. National governments are understandably reluctant to expend their public resources for providing a good that benefits "foreign" publics. In these cases, where the benefits of the good extend beyond state boundaries and where private-sector actors are not given sufficient incentive to provide the good profitably, a sector failure results owing to the fact that the predominant institutions residing in the private sector and the public sector cannot satisfy all needs adequately.

NGOs: Responding to Sector Failures, with Failures of their Own

NGO Roles and Comparative Advantages

Where, then, do NGOs fit in? What are their roles independent of, and in conjunction with, these other actors? There is a broad literature—from practitioners, scholars, and NGO advocates—enumerating a range of purported NGO roles and comparative advantages. In response to earlier treatments of the subject, the literature now has evolved to include skeptical and contingency perspectives.

Theoretically, NGOs' presumed comparative advantages derive in large part from their capacity to respond to a series of government and market failures, filling gaps left by standardized service packages (Brinkerhoff and Brinkerhoff 2002). This leads to greater diversity and customization of services (Weisbrod 1975), increased competition, and, hence, greater efficiency (Hansmann 1987). To the extent that they are generally viewed as being more trustworthy, NGOs can also be seen to respond to contract failures (Mansbridge 1998; Douglas 1987; Lipsky and Smith 1989–1990).

The private sector and NGOs are viewed as more efficient and effective service deliverers than government. This assumption derives from these actors' flexibility in facing fewer equity and accountability requirements than governments (see Douglas 1987). Accordingly, NGOs are presumed to be more efficient, flexible, personal, and higher quality, more holistic service providers (Brinkerhoff and Brinkerhoff 2002). INGOs are particularly well suited to overcome limits in global public goods provision (Teegen 2003). They are not constrained by national borders and owe less allegiance to a particular nation's citizens than do states (Hodess 2002), yet they may be willing and able to provide nonexcludable goods and services despite the lack of profit incentive that would condition a MNE's engagement.

By working more closely with individuals and communities, NGOs may be able to aggregate preferences of community members where public and community (or common-pool resources) goods are concerned. Whether or not they are membership organizations, NGOs are frequently in direct communication with community members, and in many of the best cases are themselves drawn from the community they serve. NGOs may be able to coordinate actions of the community, overcoming coordination failure by leveraging social capital within a community in ways that have proven difficult for either firms or governments to achieve. In this sense they are often well-suited to provide local public goods, or at least to demand an appropriate mix of public goods from other sectors. Through their advocacy efforts and delivery of specialized goods and services, NGOs fill gaps in governments' and firms' ability to fully respond to citizens. NGOs can also be seen to respond to failures beyond service delivery. They can, for example, represent weak and marginalized groups, such as the poor and socially excluded, and they can build the capacity of these groups to more powerfully engage with actors from the other sectors.

Government and market failure models shed light on the extent of such potential NGO comparative advantages. The literature is diverse but often insubstantial, making it difficult to gauge the extent to which the promoted perspective emerges from actual experience or partisan views, and the degree to which the identified comparative advantages apply to a range of circumstances and actors. NGOs' identified roles include those of service provider and potential innovator, agent of accountability, organizer of demand, political agent engaging in mobilization and advocacy, and promoter of democracy and civil society (Brinkerhoff 2002). NGOs may have a role to play in the development of the for-profit business sector, including microenterprises, small and medium enterprises, and networks of these businesses, as seen in activities of NGOs as diverse as Building

Resources Across the Countries (BRAC), Self-Employed Women's Association (SEWA), and Endeavor (Smith 2005). Certainly, the state and the market may also have roles to play, but due to sector failures, a large(r) role may remain for NGOs.

Both local (indigenous) NGOs and INGOs are praised for their comparative advantages in relating to and reaching target beneficiaries, notably the poor and those residing in remote areas. This relationship with "the people" is seen to attribute to NGOs a greater public legitimacy (Hulme and Edwards 1997a) both in terms of moral value as well as effectiveness in actually reaching these populations (see, for example, Fiszbein and Lowden 1998). It has been argued that these attributes tend to produce strong commitment to and follow through on more situationally appropriate solutions (United Nations 1998).

NGOs have been lauded for their intermediary abilities, brokering interactions between and among local communities, other NGOs and civil society actors, governments, donors, and the private sector (Teegen 2003). They also have accumulated experience working with these diverse actors and can bring a broader understanding of various perspectives and operating procedures. NGOs can provide the external support that local communities may need in forming and managing their own representative bodies. Their "in-betweenness" permits them to engage with both governments and firms by using social capital to bridge and bond members of those sectors—permitting interactions that otherwise would be precluded (Teegen 2003).

Local NGOs can no longer be discounted as ineffectual and insignificant, nor can they be viewed merely as implementers for their international counterparts and partners (see Broadhead 1987). They may offer more specific comparative advantages (Brinkerhoff 2002). These include managing local conflicts and fostering joint learning (Brown and Ashman 1996). When they are well developed, local NGOs are sometimes viewed as being more accountable and more effective than INGOs (Beckmann 1991; Bebbington and Riddell 1997). Some analyses of the impressive successes in poverty reduction in Bangladesh have attributed a large part of these gains to the role of major indigenous NGOs such as Grameen, Association for Social Advancement (ASA), and BRAC. Some donors have found that the active involvement of local NGOs is decisive in ensuring benefits reach poorer citizens (see, for example, USAID 1995b). Whether at their own initiative or at the behest of donors, INGOs increasingly partner with local NGOs and community-based organizations (CBOs).[5] Unfortunately, sub-Saharan Africa, the region most offtrack in the achievement of MDGs, is also the region with the least-developed indigenous NGO capacity.

To some degree, local NGOs have become the direct recipients of foreign aid, eliminating the role of INGOs as intermediaries and enhancing the expectation and pressure that INGOs should engage in policy and advocacy as opposed to operational work (see, for example, Korten 1987; Fowler 1997), except, perhaps, in the area of emergency relief (Lindenberg and Bryant 2002). The United States Agency for International Development (USAID) developed the NGO Sector Strengthening Program and the Capable Partners Program that is aimed at developing the program capacity of local NGOs and having them, rather than INGOs, carry out development programs.[6] However, many INGOs retain an operational role, some exclusively, others selectively. Conditions that favor such a role include those requiring initial high visibility and credibility, when tension between government and local NGOs precludes the latter's participation in development projects, and when local NGOs do not yet have sufficient capacity to effectively partner with INGOs (Mawer 1997). In practice, the direct INGO role has remained particularly active in Africa.

Ramia (2003) argues that INGOs seek to parallel the transnational strategy pursued by some MNEs in order to balance pressures for local adaptation with those favoring cost and other advantages stemming from global standardization. Some INGOs may wish to retain direct management of programs for similar reasons. Partnering with local NGOs may be carried out for the same reasons that joint ventures are often established between MNEs and local business partners: either because this is the most beneficial strategy for the objectives of the firms (ultimately profit maximization), or because such partnerships are required or strongly incentivized by local governments.

Regarding policies related to the MDGs (Brinkerhoff 2002), NGOs may have on-the-ground contacts that enable an accurate understanding of the development context, and they can bring this in-depth understanding into the policy process. NGOs contribute to policy change via the introduction of additional and specialized knowledge to the decision-making process, the raising of issues and concerns that might otherwise be neglected, the provision of technical advice, and consensus building (based on trust) essential to ensure commitment of all actors. NGOs can also enlarge the transparency of decision-making fora and the accountability of actors involved, and cultivate and provide an interested and informed constituency (including community-based organizations) to later facilitate implementation and the monitoring of results.

More generally, NGOs can potentially demonstrate successful approaches in addressing the MDGs, educate and empower particular constituencies, represent constituencies in the design and implementation of MDG programs, build capacity for more effective programs, and more directly influence development policies of governments and international institutions in support of the goals. NGOs can act as interlocutors and facilitators of public consultations, catalyzing public debate. Where smaller and less bureaucratic than public- or private-sector counterparts, NGO organizations can respond more quickly to emerging needs. Hence, it is much easier for them to foster social innovation than governments, and NGOs can respond to a wider range of social needs than the private sector, which must maintain an overall focus on profits.

In sum, NGOs have some apparent natural advantages in development-related activities, especially where there is a high need for flexibility in the design and implementation of services, in managing common-pool resources, in communication within and across interest groups, and more generally, in advocacy.

Voluntary Failure: The Limits of NGOs

NGOs are very heterogeneous, perhaps more so than governments at local and national levels or firms in the private sector. Although sector models describe the vast potential for NGOs in promoting achievement of the MDGs, this potential must be tempered by acknowledging the real limits to NGOs in this regard—reflecting potential failure of the NGO sector.

Clearly, the theoretically based comparative advantages examined earlier do not universally hold for all NGOs in all places. In fact, the potential scope of voluntary failure suggests that NGOs are not panaceas for failures of the public and private sectors.[7] Two frameworks outline the voluntary failure model. Kramer (1981, 265) identifies four characteristic vulnerabilities: (1) institutionalization, or "a process of creeping formalization"; (2) goal deflection, or the displacement of ends by means, such as fund-raising; (3) minority rule, in which NGOs reflect their philanthropic origins (i.e., funders) rather than their clientele; and (4) ineffectuality. Salamon (1987) outlines four similar voluntary failures: (1) philanthropic insufficiency, rooted in NGOs' limited scale and resources; (2) philanthropic particularism, reflecting NGOs' choice of clientele and projects; (3) philanthropic paternalism, where those who control the most resources are able to control community priorities; and (4) philanthropic amateurism. In other words, rather than efficiently pursuing their comparative advantages, NGOs may instead be insignificant, owing to their small scale and reach, may be selective and exclusionary, elitist, ineffective, and unaccountable to important constituencies.

NGOs generally have multiple stakeholders who have to be considered. This is both a source of strength and weakness. For developing-country

NGOs, stakeholders may include the overseas INGO partner, indirect funders (including foundations), local and national government, local elites, NGO employees, and the clients/participants/beneficiaries. When NGO management is responsible to several stakeholders, the practical result can be a loss of control over management. Moreover, when objectives differ and translation of objectives into a common unit such as money is difficult, transaction costs in bargaining among stakeholders can be high. Having multiple stakeholders can result in other types of goal deflection as well. Managers are tempted by possible gains from opportunistic acts and may place individual goals, including private gain, over those of the organization. Working with governments and donors in particular can result in "sector blurring," where NGOs increasingly resemble their primary funder and lose many of their comparative advantages over time (see, for example, Hulme and Edwards 1997b). Case-study evidence suggests that in major programmatic decisions, funders tend to hold the decisive influence.[8] This is not inherently negative, but does suggest that the rhetoric of client-driven programs is exaggerated.

Unlike democratic governments, NGOs are not elected. They are not necessarily created out of a presumed social contract, but may reflect priorities of well-funded interest groups. As noted above, access to benefits provided by a given NGO is not guaranteed for all. (Indeed, one advantage of NGOs is their potential ability to better target services to those in extreme poverty.) Limited formal accountability beyond the value and subsequent constraint provided by a reputation for credibility may ultimately limit broad societal gains from NGO activities (Hodess 2002).

Moreover, NGOs do not receive the immediate feedback from the market that private firms receive (whether the product is selling, and at what price, quality, and timing). A potential source of inefficiency lies in the lack of an analogue to the market for mergers and corporate control in the private sector (Smith 2003; Teegen, Doh, and Vachani 2004). Managers, particularly founders, may remain entrenched despite ineffective or duplicative activities. Funding may remain stable despite inefficiency, especially when drawn from endowments, personal relationships with foundation officials, or affiliation with religious bodies or other intrinsic (or "built-in") donor constituency bases.

NGO analysts such as Fowler (1997) argue that INGOs should emphasize their comparative advantages, particularly as intermediaries. When downplaying an advocacy role in favor of meeting immediate service needs, some scholars note that there is a risk that NGOs may inadvertently promote the very systems they profess they are working to change by ameliorating the effects of these systems on their constituents (see, for example, Commins 1999). This possibility has been noted, for example, in environmental partnerships (Murphy and Bendell 1997) and with respect to foreign investment and structural adjustment (Shaw 1990). More subtly, some scholars warn that the mere participation of NGOs in the "New Policy Agenda," wherein foreign aid bypasses national governments, can continue to erode the capacity of the state and its citizens' choices, propagating a myth about how progress can be achieved (Hulme and Edwards 1997b; see also Pearce 1997). INGO decisions to retain an active role in the direct production and delivery of local services could reflect their objective of poverty alleviation, when they determine that active engagement remains the most effective way to achieve this goal. However, it could also reflect a more self-interested form of organizational behavior: retaining control of budgets, building larger organizations, controlling sources of fund-raising, and being able to continue to take organizational credit for the achievement of poverty goals.

The Need to Assess Contingencies

Like the public sector in developing countries, both INGOs and domestic NGOs have been undertaking significant reforms. Arguably, NGOs' increasing sophistication and capacity, as well as their improving internal democratization and increased client-focus, make some of the criticisms of the voluntary failure model decreasingly applicable. For example, NGOs in Latin America and South Asia have attained a new presence and legitimacy as potential partners with the capacity to feasibly work with other groups (see, for example, Fiszbein and Lowden 1998). This is in stark contrast to previous assumptions that NGOs were either insignificant due to limited scale and capacity, or politically problematic as potential partners in development. More generally, NGOs have come a long way in professionalizing and enhancing their capacity, supporting the hope that they will deliver services at private-sector levels of cost control and efficiency (Hulme and Edwards 1997b). Others maintain that the labor-intensive nature of most NGO services preclude unit cost savings (Dichter 1991; Smith 1987).

The NGO sector as a whole exhibits a great deal of churning, particularly at local levels; organizations come and go, and those that participate in the "alms bazaar" (Smillie and Helmich 1993) (i.e., the market for development funding) may change their priorities from one year to the next. The sheer volume and diversity of NGOs make selection of "good" NGOs problematic (see United Nations 1998); and the dynamics of competition and associated marketing within a particular NGO sector further exacerbates a neutral understanding of respective strengths and weaknesses (see Beckmann 1991; see also Bush 1992). However, as we argue in the next section, the identification and assessment of relevant contingencies provide more cogent guidance as to appropriate NGO roles in achieving the MDGs.

Framework for NGO MDG Roles, Measures, and Contingency Factors

Sector Overlap and Extension

As discussed above, government, the private sector, and NGOs each deliver some goods and services in any given society, and, in so doing, their actual roles are likely to overlap (see figure 4.2).

Sometimes there is less genuine overlap than meets the eye. Services that appear identical in fact have important differences of quality, recipient group, longevity of contract or of the period of service delivery, uniformity and flexibility, and so forth. NGOs may specialize in fast response and flexibility, governments in longer term but uniform service delivery. Thus, in many cases, organizational comparative advantage can be identified only with the use of finer gradations of quality and other characteristics than are apparent from the broad categories examined here. By analogy, it often appears that conventional firms and (nonprofit) cooperatives compete in the same industry, but the latter may specialize in higher-quality production (Smith 1994).

In addition to responding to generic sector failures, when market and policy failure result from or are exacerbated by lack of capacity and/or political will, the role of NGOs is likely to extend into these domains, as depicted in figure 4.3. For example, in Bangladesh, in the face of what appears to be government corruption and poor private-sector management, a leading local NGO (BRAC) has produced what are normally thought of as natural government and private-sector goods and services, including the operation

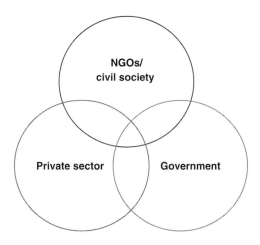

Figure 4.2   Sector overlap: Zones of uncertainty on comparative advantage

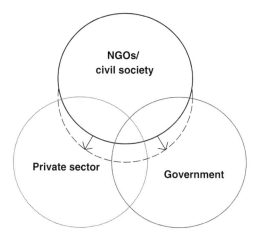

Figure 4.3   Sector overlap extension: Contingency-based shifts in comparative advantage

of primary schools and for-profit production of items such as seeds, chalk, and sanitary napkins.

As a working hypothesis we may expect that, particularly in sector extension, other comparative advantage areas for NGOs are likely to include nontradables over tradable goods, necessities over luxuries, activities involving human and social capital over physical capital, and goods and services associated with nonseparable factor markets over separable ones. On the other hand, sector overlap can also occur when one sector engages or co-opts organizations in another sector to carry out activities in markets for which it is for some reason unsuited, unwilling, or unable to enter.

Table 4.1 summarizes the roles of the three sectors and identifies contingencies that may lead to an at least temporarily efficient role for one of the other sectors. The appropriate NGO role emerges when advocacy efforts are called for, and also when targeted benefits provision is significant, but government and the private sector provide them poorly for the case in question.

Framework for NGO Roles in Achieving the MDGs

Building from this general framework, we can now specifically assess the possible roles for NGOs in achieving the MDGs, relative to other actors involved directly and indirectly in development efforts in local, national, regional, and global settings. Our assessment framework is summarized in table 4.2. We propose this framework as a summary of hypotheses

Table 4.1 Roles of the NGO sector as conditioned by private and public sectors

Sector	Socioeconomic role(s)	Contingency	Observed/potential response of other sectors
Government	General public goods provision; and supply of merit goods, including income distribution	Uncertainty of voter/citizen preferences	NGOs may offer alternative mechanism of preference aggregation, or at least greater knowledge of target populations
		Legitimacy	NGOs may have greater capacity for community mobilization, and credibility, e.g., as good faith broker, especially with marginalized groups
		Corruption	NGOs may offer less corrupt service delivery and advocate to expose problems of corruption by other sectors
		Poor administration	NGO management may be superior or less subject to bureaucratic obstacles and advocate to expose administrative inefficiencies
		Low capacity	NGOs may help build government capacity and fill missing functions and locations
		Resource constraints	NGOs may be able to access resources from sources unavailable to government
		Limited cross-border reach and responsibility	INGOs may have multinational reach, as may MNEs
Private	Private goods provision;	Missing markets	Government acts to overcome coordination failures, or to create markets (e.g., financial markets) NGOs provide for unmet demand and serve to bridge/provide institutions needed to reduce high market creation costs

Sector	Goods / area	Issue	Description
	Toll goods and other targeted, local public goods (an area of sector overlap)	Market failures	Government regulation, procurement (e.g. from NGOs), or (temporary) provision; and NGO-supported service provision
		Poor management or low profit margin	Government and NGOs producing toll goods. NGO-run firms producing private goods, e.g., BRAC. Technology transfer and R&D undertaken by NGOs and government
		Poor institutional environment	NGOs may advocate institutional reforms, or (temporarily) supply valued goods in lieu of the private sector
Third/NGO	Targeted/ specialized public good provision Common pool goods	Resource constraints	Government or private sector may control or have access to greater resources (even if less efficient)
		Competency	The other sectors may exhibit less reliance on unskilled volunteers and traditional society organization
		Government legal and institutional constraints	Government may prevent "competition" from the NGO sector with a variety of constraints, but NGOs may find creative ways of circumventing these restrictions
	Advocacy	Legitimacy issues; accountability	Government may have higher credibility, especially in a democracy; private sector at least subject to market discipline Donors may withhold funds when accountability issues are present

Table 4.2 NGO MDG roles, achievement measures, effectiveness contingencies

Possible MDG-related role(s)	Typical achievement measures regarding MDGs	Key NGO effectiveness contingency factors
NGOs Generally		
Provide services	"Reach" of service provision Results of rigorous impact assessment, including key human development gains Activities improving the capacity of other actors	Lack of onerous reporting and accountability requirements Not constrained by limiting national agendas (i.e., by donor country foreign assistance agendas, and by host country national agendas)
Advocate/influence policy processes	MDG supportive policies, responsiveness to the needs of the poor, and facilitation of the participation of a broad range of actors in meeting the MDGs Establishment and utilization of bridging/influencing mechanisms Participation in formal consultations and decision-making fora	Existence of participation mechanisms and personal relationships Credibility vis-à-vis the targeted government or institution Enabling legal frameworks and structures, including absence of risk for local NGOs Relevant technical expertise
Aggregate and represent interests	Number and scope of communities represented Representation of or quality of links with socially excluded communities Breadth and depth of reach with respect to service delivery and inclusive MDG-supportive policy frameworks	Recognized credibility and legitimacy, both by communities represented and macroactors on the receiving end Local level presence and relationships, with frequent communication Commitment to fully understand the nature of poverty, its causes, and the associated needs of poor communities

Enhance transparency and accountability in decision making	Establishment of conducive rules and procedures, including participation responsiveness, and monitoring mandates, with evaluation of effectiveness	Credibility and access to decision-making bodies Associated mission, beyond self-interest (credible broker) Ethos of democratic practice, accountability, and responsiveness
Monitor other actors' progress on MDG commitments, as well as relevant policies and programs	Progress reports and dissemination plans	NGOs have access to the information needed NGOs have access to information and dissemination networks, nationally and internationally Ethos of responsiveness and potential repercussions for inconsistent action
Demand an appropriate mix of public goods from governments and donors	Examples of effective NGO advocacy in terms of pro-development policy reform	Presumes effective aggregation and representation of community needs Credibility with governments and donors Mechanisms, formal/institutional and personal, for communicating with governments and donors
Intermediate between local communities, other civil society actors, governments, donors, and the private sector	Examples of bridging role, partnership programs, and policy initiatives	Perceived legitimacy by all of these actors Institutional mechanisms and personal relationships that NGOs can capitalize on Experience and an established track record of working with each of these actors Access to verifiable information to inform the policies and programs of these actors Technical expertise pertinent to the policy or program in question

(*Continued*)

Table 4.2 (*Continued*)

Possible MDG-related role(s)	*Typical achievement measures regarding MDGs*	*Key NGO effectiveness contingency factors*
Facilitate public consultations and catalyze public debate	Number of events organized Degree of representation of diverse views, inclusiveness Participation of key actors	Enabling legal framework Limited personal risk to those who might participate Credibility with diverse actors representing a range of perspectives
Cultivate an informed constituency	Degree of mobilization Subsequent participation in monitoring and implementation	Credibility with communities targeted for mobilization
Coordinating communities to identify and respond to needs	Community associations organized, degree of capacity	Community-based mission Trust, prior success, and lengthy relationships with community members
Build the capacity of community groups to interface with government and private sector actors	Capacity-building programs Examples of interface, consultations, partnerships	Stated commitment to capacity building and exit strategy Understanding of political context and actors Understanding of market context and actors Political stability that enables key government actors to be identified and approached Broader, democratic legal frameworks and intentions, e.g., an ethos of citizen responsiveness Socially responsible private sector

International NGO funding to partner with local NGOs and community-based efforts	Examples of partnerships and quality of relationship (partnership versus contracting)	Sufficient access to foreign assistance, with supportive policies (e.g., partnership requirements or absence of prohibitions)
Specific Roles of Local NGOs		
Manage local conflicts and foster joint learning	Examples of NGO mediation	Established presence, trust, and legitimacy vis-à-vis local community Local diversity does not prevent community problem solving
Ensure benefits reach the poorest of the poor	Benefit reach Outcomes monitoring and evaluation	Local knowledge of or experience in the community Stated commitment to and reputation for reaching this population Physical, social, economic, and political barriers
Deliver services	Program reach	Lack of onerous reporting and accountability requirements Not constrained by limiting national agendas (i.e., by donor country foreign assistance agendas, and by host country national agendas) Tension with government does not prevent local NGOs from receiving foreign assistance and participating in partnerships with international NGOs Requisite capacity and resources

concerning NGO roles, associated achievement measures, and effectiveness contingency factors for achieving the MDGs. Subsequent chapters further discuss contingency factors and describe the empirical evidence of NGO contributions to specific MDG areas, providing the basis for testing and refining this framework, the subject of chapters 8 and 9, and generating policy implications (chapter 10).

Conclusion

We believe that a necessary precursor to establishing guidelines on appropriate NGO roles in achieving the MDGs includes careful assessment that reflects the sectoral contingencies present in a given setting (table 4.1) and effectiveness contingencies relevant to the NGO sector in particular (table 4.2). This will allow for an assessment of NGO role viability in given settings relative to other actors. More rigorous evaluation of poverty programs, such as those using randomized trials when feasible, will be an essential component of assessment. Role viability must consider a cost-benefit analysis from included/affected actors' perspectives (to include notions of equity, distribution of benefits, and inclusiveness), recognition of stakeholder response and responsiveness within a given program (incorporating participation and ownership of key individuals and groups) (see Kisunko 2002), potential for sustainability in terms of capacity and legitimacy of the effort and the involved actors, and scalability of the effort to extend learning benefits concerning development from one venue to others (see Binswanger 2002; Balcet 2002).

We offer the preliminary conclusion that owing to certain natural advantages, NGOs have an important role to play in working toward achieving social objectives, including the MDGs. These advantages are to be found in the fields of highly targeted public goods provision, especially where there is a high need for flexibility in the design and implementation of services, in common-pool resources, and in advocacy. However, these roles are inherently limited. Comparative advantage is realized when there is an effective division of labor. If NGOs work in conflict with the private sector and government, benefits will be far smaller than under more cooperative arrangements. Indeed, complementary contributions from all three sectors are needed for sustainable achievement of the MDGs, and this may in many cases require active coordination across organizations in all three sectors. To ensure effectiveness we will need much better evaluation at all levels, from evaluation of microlevel projects run by NGOs, to evaluation of the roles of NGOs in the Poverty Reduction Strategies Papers process and careful consideration about how these can be enhanced. Better evaluation will also be needed with respect to government and private-sector roles, and especially in the overlapping areas between the sectors, where two or more sectors are playing an active role. We also need to better understand conditions under which actors from the three sectors work together effectively rather than compete wastefully. This theoretical framework, its elaboration, and its application in this book are an important first step.

Notes

1. This material draws from Todaro and Smith (2003, chapter 16). See also the several contributions to "The State and Economic Development, A Symposium," *Journal of Economic Perspectives* Summer 1990, 3–130.
2. Such advantage most often accrues when businesses partner with government and civil society (Brown and Korten 1991).
3. The following draws from Smith (1995) and Todaro and Smith (2003).
4. Even citizens domiciled in the MNEs' headquarters country may not enjoy the firm's loyalty or benefits from preferential policies (Reich 1991).
5. For example, USAID's Matching Grant Program for U.S. Private Voluntary Organizations required local NGO partners.
6. See http://www.usaid.gov/our_work/cross-cutting_programs/private_voluntary_cooperation/ngo.html and http://www.usaid.gov/our_work/cross-cutting_programs/private_voluntary_cooperation/capobj.html.
7. This discussion draws from Brinkerhoff and Brinkerhoff (2002).
8. For example, in highly recognized African poverty programs (Smith 2003).

References

Balcet, Jean Claude. Panelist comments at the World Bank Poverty Day Conference, Washington, D.C., October 17, 2002. http://www.worldbank.org/wbi/B-SPAN/sub_poverty_day_2_2002.htm (audio transcript accessed September 20, 2003).

Bebbington, Anthony, and Roger Riddell. "Heavy Hands, Hidden Hands, Holding Hands? Donors, Intermediary NGOs and Civil Society Organizations." In *NGOs, States and Donors: Too Close for Comfort?* Ed. David Hulme and Michael Edwards. New York: St. Martin's Press in association with Save the Children Fund, 1997: 107–127.

Beckmann, David. "Recent Experience and Emerging Trends." In *Nongovernmental Organizations and the World Bank: Cooperation for Development*, ed. Samuel Paul and Arturo Israel. Washington, D.C.: World Bank, 1991: 134–154.

Binswanger, Hans. Panelist comments at the World Bank Poverty Day Conference, October 17, 2002. http://www.worldbank.org/wbi/B-SPAN/sub_poverty_day_2_2002.htm (audio transcript accessed September 20, 2003).

Brinkerhoff, Jennifer M. *Partnership for Development: Rhetoric or Results?* Boulder, CO: Lynne Rienner, 2002.

Brinkerhoff, Jennifer M., and Derick W. Brinkerhoff. "Government-Nonprofit Relations in Comparative Perspective: Evolution, Themes, and New Directions." *Public Administration and Development* 22, no. 1 (2002): 3–18.

Broadhead, Tim. NGOs: "In One Year, Out the Other?" *World Development* 15 (Supplement): 1–6, 1987.

Brown, David L., and Darcy Ashman. "Participation, Social Capital, and Intersectoral Problem-solving: African and Asian Cases." *World Development* 24, no. 9 (September 1996): 1467–1479.

Brown, David L., and David C. Korten. "Working More Effectively with Nongovernmental Organizations." In *Nongovernmental Organizations and the World Bank: Cooperation for Development*, ed. Samuel Paul and Arturo Israel. Washington, D.C.: World Bank, 1991: 44–93.

Bush, Richard. "Survival of the Nonprofit Spirit in a For-Profit World." *Nonprofit and Voluntary Sector Quarterly* 12, no. 4 (Winter 1992): 391–410.

Caves, Richard E. *Multinational Enterprise and Economic Analysis.* New York: Cambridge University Press, 1982.

Clark, John. "The State, Popular Participation and the Voluntary Sector." In *NGOs, States and Donors: Too Close for Comfort?* ed. David Hulme and Michael Edwards. New York: St. Martin's Press, in association with Save the Children, 1997: 43–58.

Commins, Stephen. "NGOs: Ladles in the Global Soup Kitchen?" *Development in Practice* 9, no. 5 (1999).

Dichter, Thomas W. "NGOs and the Replication Trap." *Transnational Associations* 4(1991): 190–196.

Douglas, James. "Political Theories of Nonprofit Organization." In *The Nonprofit Sector: A Research Handbook,* ed. Walter W. Powell. New Haven, CT: Yale University Press, 1987: 43–54.

Dunning, John H. "Explaining Changing Patterns of International Production: In Defence of the Eclectic Theory." *Oxford Bulletin of Economics and Statistics* 4 (November 1979): 269–295.

Fiszbein, Ariel, and Pamela Lowden. *Working Together for a Change: Government, Business and Civic Partnerships for Poverty Reduction in LAC.* Washington, D.C.: Economic Development Institute of the World Bank, May 1998.

Fowler, Alan. *Striking a Balance: A Guide to Enhancing the Effectiveness of NGOs in International Development.* London: Earthscan, 1997.

Hansmann, Henry. "Economic Theories of Nonprofit Organization." In *The Nonprofit Sector: A Research Handbook,* ed. Walter W. Powell. New Haven, CT: Yale University Press, 1987: 27–42.

Hodess, Robin. "The Contested Competence of NGOs and Business in Public Life." In *The Market or the Public Domain,* ed. D. Drache. New York: Routledge, 2002.

Hulme, David, and Michael Edwards. "NGOs, States and Donors: An Overview." In *NGOs, States and Donors: Too Close for Comfort?* Ed. David Hulme and Michael Edwards. New York: St. Martin's Press in association with Save the Children, 1997a: 3–22.

———. "Too Close to the Powerful, Too Far from the Powerless?" In *NGOs, States and Donors: Too Close for Comfort?* ed. David Hulme and Michael Edwards. New York: St. Martin's Press, in association with Save the Children, 1997b: 275–284.

Kisunko, Gregory. Panelist comments at the World Bank Poverty Day Conference, October 17, 2002. http://www.worldbank.org/wbi/B-SPAN/ sub_poverty_day_2 _ 2002.htm (audio transcript accessed September 20, 2003).

Korten, David C. "Third Generation NGO Strategies: A Key to People-Centered Development." *World Development* 15 (Supplement), 1987: 145–161.

Kramer, Ralph M. *Voluntary Agencies in the Welfare State.* Berkeley: University of California Press, 1981.

Lindenberg, Marc, and Coralie Bryant. *Going Global: Transforming Relief and Development NGOs.* Bloomfield, CT: Kumarian Press, 2002.

Lipsky, Michael, and Steven Rathgreb Smith. "Nonprofit Organizations, Government, and the Welfare State." *Political Science Quarterly* 104, no. 4 (1989–1990): 625–648.

Mansbridge, Jane. "On the contested nature of the public good." In *Private Action and the Public Good,* ed. Walter W. Powell and Elisabeth S. Clemens. New Haven and London: Yale University Press , 1998: 3–19.

Mawer, Richard. "Mice Among the Tigers: Adding Value in NGO-Government Relations in South East Asia." In *NGOs, States and Donors: Too Close for Comfort?* ed. David Hulme and Michael Edwards. New York: St. Martin's Press, in association with Save the Children, 1997: 243–253.

Murphy, David F., and Jem Bendell. *In the Company of Partners: Business, Environmental Groups and Sustainable Development Post-Rio.* Bristol, England: Policy Press, 1997.

Musgrave, R.A. "Provision for Social Goods." In *Public Economics,* ed. J. Margolis and H. Guitton. London: International Economics Association, 1969: 124–144.

Nelson, Jane. *Business as Partners in Development: Creating Wealth for Countries, Companies, and Communities.* London: Prince of Wales Business Leaders Forum, in collaboration with the World Bank and the United Nations Development Programme, 1996.

Nelson, Jane, and Dave Prescott. *Business and the Millennium Development Goals: A Framework for Action.* London: International Business Leaders Forum, 2003.

Ostrom, Vincent, and Elinor Ostrom. "Public Goods and Public Choice." In *Alternatives for Delivering Public Services,* ed. E. S. Savas. Boulder, CO: Westview Press,1977: 7–49.

Pearce, Jenny. "Between Co-option and Irrelevance? Latin American NGOs in the 1990s." In *NGOs, States and Donors: Too Close for Comfort? ed.* David Hulme and Michael Edwards.New York: St. Martin's Press, in association with Save the Children, 1997: 257–274.

Ramia, Gaby. "Global Governance, Social Policy and Management in International NGOs: A Theoretical and Empirical Analysis." Paper presented at the Policy and Politics International Conference on Policy and Politics in a Globalizing World, Bristol, U.K., July 24–26, 2003.

Reich, Robert. "Who Is Them?" *Harvard Business Review* (March–April 1991), 78–87.

Salamon, Lester M. "Of Market Failure, Voluntary Failure, and Third-Party Government: Toward a Theory of Government-Nonprofit Relations in the Modern Welfare State." *Journal of Voluntary Action Research* 16, nos. 1 and 2 (January–June 1987): 29–49.

Shaw, Timothy M. "Popular Participation in Non-Governmental Structures in Africa: Implications for Democratic Development." *Africa Today* 37, no. 3 (1990): 5–23.

Smillie, Ian, and Henny Helmich, eds. *Non-Governmental Organisations and Governments: Stakeholders for Development.* Paris: Development Centre, Organisation for Economic Co-operation and Development, 1993.

Smith, Brian H. "An Agenda of Future Tasks for International and Indigenous NGOs: Views from the North." *World Development* 15 (1987): 87–93.

Smith, Stephen C. "Innovation and Market Strategy in Italian Industrial Cooperatives: Econometric Evidence on Organizational Comparative Advantage." *Journal of Economic Behavior and Organization* 23, no. 3 (1994): 303–321.

———. Governance of Nongovernmental Organizations: A Framework and Application to Poverty Programs in East Africa. GWU Law School Public Law Journal of the Social Science Research Network (available at http://papers. ssrn.com/sol3/papers.cfm?abstract_id=628684, July 2003).

———. *Ending Global Poverty: A Guide to What Works.* New York: Palgrave Macmillan, 2005.

Teegen, Hildy. "International NGOs as Global Institutions: Using Social Capital to Impact Multinational Enterprises and Governments." *Journal of International Management* 9 (September 2003): 271–285.

———. "Achieving the Millennium Development Goals: Ways for MNCs to Effectively Interface with NGOs." In *Multinational Corporations and Global Poverty Reduction,* ed. Subhash Jain and Sushil Vachani. London: Edward Elgar, 2005.

Teegen, Hildy, Jonathan P. Doh, and Sushil Vachani. "The Importance of Nongovernmental Organizations (NGOs) in Global Governance and Value Creation: An International Business Research Agenda." *Journal of International Business Studies* 35, no. 6 (2004): 463–483.

Todaro, Michael, and Stephen C. Smith. *Economic Development,* 8th ed., Reading, MA: Addison-Wesley, 2003.

U.S. Agency for International Development. *Core Report of the New Partnerships Initiative.* Washington, D.C.: U.S. Agency for International Development, New Partnerships Initiative, 1995a.

———. "New Partnership Initiative: Small Business Partnership." *Core Report of the New Partnerships Initiative.* Washington, D.C.: U.S. Agency for International Development, New Partnership Initiative, 1995b.

United Nations. "Arrangements and Practices for the Interaction of Non-Governmental Organizations in All Activities of the United Nations System." *Report of the Secretary-General.* New York: United Nations, 1998.

Weimar, D.L., and A. R. Vining. *Policy Analysis: Concepts and Practice.* 2nd ed. Englewood Cliffs, NJ: Prentice Hall, 1992.

Weisbrod, Burton A. "Toward a Theory of the Voluntary Non-Profit Sector in a Three-Sector Economy." In *Altruism, Morality, and Economic Theory,* ed. Edmund S. Phelps. New York: Russell Sage Foundation, 1975: 197–223.

Part II

The Context for Achieving the MDGs

5

The Enabling Environment for Achieving the Millennium Development Goals: Government Actions to Support NGOs

Derick W. Brinkerhoff

The United Nations' Millennium Development Goals (MDGs) have focused the attention of the international community on enduring problems of global poverty and attracted broad support. The MDGs establish ambitious targets for promoting economic growth, improving health and education, empowering women, creating sustainable development, and reducing poverty (UNDP 2003). The magnitude of the challenge is captured in one estimate that, given current trends, "33 countries with more than a quarter of the world's people will achieve fewer than half the Millennium Development Goals by 2015" (DFID 2003, 6). Others express similar views, noting the varying prospects for different regions of the world. An African Development Bank report notes that countries in "Asia, Eastern Europe, and Latin America and the Caribbean are on course to fulfill many of the MDGs. But few African countries are likely to meet most of them" (ADB 2002, 1).

What will it take to achieve the MDGs? This question preoccupies international donor agencies, developing country governments, policy think tanks, international and national nongovernmental organizations (NGOs), local communities, and citizens' groups. Actions at all levels, from the global to the local, are called for, and the recommendations for what needs to be done are numerous. Among the prescriptions for MDG achievement that these various actors voice is the need to create an enabling environment to put in place the conditions that will facilitate the efforts of actors in the public, private, NGO/civil-society sectors to take the various steps needed to reach the MDG targets.

A quick scan of printed and electronic sources reveals the ubiquity of the term. Enabling environment is the topic of NGO conferences, World Bank training programs, and the U.S. Agency for International Development (USAID) and other donor-supported technical assistance projects.[1] It appears repeatedly in analytic studies, policy briefs, and reports. However, like much of the vocabulary of international development and assistance discourse, the term exhibits an apparent clarity that masks the complexity inherent in the conceptual territory it subsumes. In some formulations, the enabling environment is defined so expansively that it becomes nearly synonymous with socioeconomic development itself. In others, it is treated so narrowly as to be clearly inadequate to stimulate sufficient response absent the presence of additional factors—for example, considering the enabling environment as consisting primarily of an appropriate regulatory framework.

This chapter seeks to clarify what government can and should do to support and encourage societal partners to pursue actions related to the MDGs. It does not pretend to sort out the definitional complexity or offer a comprehensive tour of the term's contours. In keeping with the theme of this volume, the main focus is on government's role in involving NGOs in reaching the MDGs. Government is not the only actor involved in the MDGs; clearly, all sectors of a society need to engage in order to make progress toward those goals. But government has a primary role in structuring and influencing the contributions of the private and NGO sectors.[2] The chapter begins with a brief discussion of the evolution of attention to environmental factors in socioeconomic development, and then turns to what has commonly been considered government's role in creating an enabling environment. Next, the chapter develops a framework for more precisely characterizing government's role in creating an enabling environment specifically in regard to NGO participation in the production of public goods. This is followed by a discussion of the incentives for government to create such an enabling environment, touching on topics such as the politics of pro-poor reform, accountability, and citizen participation. The chapter closes with a brief investigation of several measurement and implementation issues, and some concluding remarks.

From Sustainability to the Enabling Environment

Those interested in economic development and poverty alleviation, whether academics or practitioners, have long sought to identify what is necessary and what works to address these objectives. For rich countries and international donor agencies, this interest has been driven by the desire to make the best use of foreign-assistance resources. During the 1980s, the donor community engaged in a number of "soul-searching" exercises as evidence of the limited impact of project investments came to light, leading to a focus on *sustainability* (e.g., USAID 1988; World Bank 1985). Among the findings of these and other reviews was the important influence of external factors on the ability of projects and programs to generate long-term benefits. The current attention to the enabling environment emerged from the earlier debate and analysis on what to do in order to make better development-project investments. Calls to improve the enabling environment can be seen as the latest expression of concern for sustainability and aid effectiveness, which derives from the question, what needs to be in place in order for donor interventions to yield lasting results?

This interest in the enabling environment reflects a swing away from a narrow focus on project designs that can "protect" donor interventions from environmental hostility. Donor investments shifted toward targeting the policy environment itself for intervention, aiming at the range of factors that support and encourage actors in developing countries to take actions to promote socioeconomic improvement, and that generate country ownership and commitment. Whereas the sustainability focus of the 1980s led donors to look for ways to adapt their project/program designs and implementation to inhospitable and constraining operating environments, the trend begun in the 1990s and continuing up to the present poses the question, how can environments be made more supportive so that in-country actors can productively use project/program investments? The search for answers to this question has led to significant research and analysis devoted to better mapping and understanding of the environment for international development efforts and institutions (e.g., Brinkerhoff and Goldsmith 1992; Picciotto and Weisner 1998) as well as spawned several generations of policy-based lending and grants.

While this shift in focus may seem subtle, it has led to a dramatic reorientation in the thinking of the development assistance community, with major policy implications. As research findings increasingly demonstrated the links among successful socioeconomic development, the enabling environment, and government capacity coupled with political will, donor agency policymakers—with the World Bank (which has sponsored much of the research) in the lead—began to emphasize targeting grants and loans to countries with demonstrated performance records (see, for example, Dollar and Svensson 1998; Burnside and Dollar 2000). In the World Bank, these findings undergird the latest generation of policy-based lending, in which countries rated as high performers receive loans with fewer conditionalities and more discretion in utilization of the funds compared with previous generations of structural adjustment programs.[3] Among bilateral donors, the U.S. government concretized this emphasis with the Bush administration's creation of the Millennium Challenge Account (MCA), which is designed to reward countries that have put in place the conditions for sustainability that will ensure the effective utilization of foreign assistance dollars. In the context of the MCA, the presence or absence of an enabling environment distinguishes between those countries eligible for funding and those that are excluded. Thus, the enabling environment shares a prominent place in the foreign-assistance policy arena along with the MDGs.

Defining the Enabling Environment

As noted, definitions of the enabling environment are numerous, and range from all-encompassing to narrow. A typical general definition is as follows: "An enabling environment is a set of interrelated conditions—such as legal, bureaucratic, fiscal, informational, political, and cultural—that impact on the capacity of … development actors to engage in development processes in a sustained and effective manner" (Thindwa 2001, 3). To be useful, broad definitions such as this one need to be unpacked. Getting more specific about the enabling environment requires, first, elaborating a comprehensive set of influential environmental factors, and second, clarifying the nature of their impacts on various development actors.[4] There is a vast body of research and experience that offers a wealth of answers, and a comprehensive treatment is beyond the scope of this chapter. Table 5.1 contains a brief summary of commonly agreed-upon features of the enabling environment, divided into five categories of factors: economic, political, administrative, sociocultural, and resources.[5]

This summary of the enabling environment and government actions to support it reveals the breadth and complexity of factors that analysts and practitioners have identified as important to putting in place the conditions that can support socioeconomic development and the MDGs. Government needs to: (a) improve policy, legal, and regulatory frameworks; (b) build institutional capacity across sectors at various levels; (c) seek out and respond to citizens' needs and preferences; (d) establish and maintain a range of oversight, accountability, and feedback mechanisms; and (e) mobilize and allocate public resources and investments. Indeed, many of the items in this table have been formalized in selectivity choices and conditionalities for World Bank loans and in the eligibility criteria for MCA funding. In one sense, then, the criteria for inclusion as an MCA country, or for selection for a World Bank loan, become the defining features of an enabling environment: good governance, investment in health and education, and sound economic policies. Yet, the table also confirms, as

Table 5.1   Key features of the enabling environment

Category of environmental factors	Key enabling features	Illustrative government enabling actions
Economic	Nondistortionary policy framework Encouragement of free markets and open competition Supportive of investment (including physical security) Low transactions costs, credible commitment	Reducing red tape and unnecessary regulation Managing macroeconomic policy to control inflation, deficit spending, and ensure stability Reducing tariffs, barriers to investment ("level playing field") Investing in physical infrastructure (roads, transportation, etc.) Controlling criminality (e.g., mafias) and violence
Political	Democratic system that supports pluralism, accountability, transparency, and responsiveness Processes that encourage participation, social contract, and state legitimacy Rule of law, contract enforcement respect for human rights and property rights	Conducting free and fair elections Making information widely available, promoting free media Devolving power and resources to subnational levels of government Limiting power and influence of interest groups Supporting civil society Assuring judicial independence
Administrative	Efficient service-delivery capacity Low levels of corruption Institutional checks and balances Decentralization Civil service meritocracy	Curbing abuse and corruption Creating incentives for performance Separating service provision from financing Building cross-sectoral partnerships Establishing monitoring and evaluation systems Improving coordination across agencies and sectors
Sociocultural	Presence of social capital and trust Tolerance of diversity Norms of inclusiveness, equity, and fairness Belief in the value and efficacy of individual effort	Supporting marginalized and disadvantaged societal groups— pro-poor affirmative action, need-based subsidies, safety nets, etc. Encouraging civic dialogue, social compacts, and consensus building Discouraging ethnic-based politics and policies Controlling violence (e.g., ethnic cleansing)
Resources	Policies and investments in health, education, workforce development, information technology, science, and research Adequate funding and institutional capacity	-Setting policies and incentives that encourage private investment and corporate social responsibility Allocating public resources to ensure maximization of social and economic potential

others have pointed out, the difficulties poor countries can face in meeting these conditionalities and criteria, and in establishing an environment that enables rather than disables.

The table highlights the extent to which the features of the enabling environment reflect the public-goods-producing function of government, which relates to the basic rationale for public-sector intervention. However, the table also makes clear that government is not the only actor involved in contributing to an enabling environment. As the governance terminology reflects, societal problem-solving, the production of public goods, and social capital formation are not the sole purview of government actors.

Enabling Environment for NGOs

Among the actors involved in governance are NGOs, and the focus here turns toward a framework for examining government's role in an enabling environment for NGO participation. Government-NGO relations are both complex and diverse, reflecting the myriad rationales and modalities for cross-sectoral action. Najam (2000), for example, distinguishes four types of relationships: cooperation, where government and NGOs share similar ends and means; confrontation, where the ends and means of both actors differ; complementarity, where the ends are similar, but the means differ; and co-optation, where the means are similar, but the actors have different ends in mind. Given this diversity and complexity, any effort to characterize an enabling environment will necessarily be oversimplified. The intent here is to develop a broad-brush picture.[6]

Building on Fox et al. (2002), the role of government in fostering an enabling environment can be categorized as consisting of the following actions: mandating, facilitating, resourcing, partnering, and endorsing. Taking the three categories of NGO engagement in the production of public goods (chapter 4, this volume)— (1) service provision, (2) aggregation and representation of interests, (3) policy advocacy/monitoring—and combining them with the classification of government actions yield a framework for clarifying how government can enable NGO engagement in the MDGs, as illustrated in table 5.2.

Mandating refers to the legal and regulatory framework that affects NGOs, all the way from basic constitutional rights that allow citizens to organize independent of state control, to laws governing the creation and operation of foundations, to NGO registration laws.[7] Laws affecting how government entities operate also play an enabling or constraining role— for example: statutes on public hearings, "sunshine" legislation, freedom of information, laws on citizen participation, etc. These statutes open the

Table 5.2 Government's roles in enabling NGO contributions to public goods

NGO functions	Government enabling roles and illustrative actions				
	Mandating	*Facilitating*	*Resourcing*	*Partnering*	*Endorsing*
Service provision	NGO registration and licensing laws Laws permitting contracting out of public services	Contracting rules, set-asides Procurement regulations	Tax and inheritance laws Public funding of service contracts Import duty exemptions	Formation of service delivery partnerships with NGOs Supporting databases to match NGOs with other partners	Publicizing the value of public service, philanthropy, corporate social responsibility Recognizing the contributions of NGO service providers
Interest aggregation and representation	Laws and regulations on right to organize, hold public meetings Procedures mandating citizen participation, sunshine laws, etc.	Building capacity for public officials to foster citizen participation Literacy programs	Grants for citizen participation Establishment of social funds	Supporting creation of NGO associations Involving NGOs in parliamentary committees, blue-ribbon task forces, etc.	Reinforcing societal values of equity, inclusiveness, and justice Promoting civic education
Policy advocacy and monitoring	Laws and regulations for access to information Laws on freedom of expression NGO accountability and reporting requirements (often linked to registration)	Demystifying policies and budgets Translation of public documents into local languages Establishing social accountability mechanisms	Public funding of NGO participation in policy monitoring	Creation of public arenas and forums for shared policy dialogue	Encouragement of media reporting on NGOs' role in advocacy and accountability Support for reporting on NGO policy research results and findings

door for NGOs to discover what government policies and programs exist or are planned, to obtain budget information, to engage with public officials, and so on. Another important element of government mandating has to do with laws and regulations that govern NGO transparency and accountability, which affects both the legitimacy of individual NGOs through assuring fiduciary responsibility and the broader legitimacy of philanthropy and the NGO sector.[8] Clearly, this government role in creating an enabling environment for NGOs relates to the broader features of democratic political structures and economic liberalism, briefly reviewed earlier in this chapter, that support socioeconomic development for all societal actors, not just NGOs.

In its *facilitating* role, government provides incentives for NGOs; for example, for NGO service providers these incentives can include special provisions for contracting, such as set-asides or similar access guarantees. Government can also provide incentives and capacity-building for other actors, public and private, to work with NGOs. Another type of facilitating action is to make information available to NGOs and citizens in readily understandable language and easily accessible formats; this is important to enable NGOs to effectively represent constituencies and to engage in advocacy (see Brinkerhoff and Goldsmith 2003).

Resourcing can involve direct public funding, as in the case of contracts and grants for NGO service providers. In the United States, for example, nonprofit, tax-exempt organizations rely on government resources for about one-third of their revenues (Independent Sector 2001). In the developing world, where governments are poorer, public funding of NGOs is lower, with international donor agencies' resources serving as an important source of funds. However, beyond direct funding, government resourcing also includes the establishment of financial incentives that encourage other actors to provide resources to NGOs, such as tax policy that offers deductibility for contributions from individuals or private firms through donations or bequests.

Partnering is a role that brings government into relationships with NGOs based more on mutual interest and shared benefits that capitalize on the comparative advantages of the partners (see Brinkerhoff 2002). Government can establish mechanisms and procedures that allow public entities to enter into partnership arrangements with NGOs. An example would be where a government agency enables a policy-advocacy NGO to participate in establishing standard-setting and/or in policy-outcomes monitoring. Or in the legislative branch, members of parliament can bring in NGOs to collect data on policy issues, conduct polls of NGOs' membership, and/or participate in committee hearings and deliberations.

Endorsing refers to actions that publicize, praise, and encourage NGOs and civil-society groups. Government's role here relates to reinforcing cultural values and influencing attitudes. Examples include policymakers publicizing the contributions of voluntarism to social-service provision, or promoting philanthropic values; or public-agency sponsorship of forums that bring together NGOs, private businesses, and individual citizens for policy dialogue.

Supply and Demand: Incentives

The above framework seeks to clarify the features of an enabling environment for NGO participation in the MDGs, but it does not address the conditions under which a government would take the actions necessary to create such an enabling environment. What are the incentives for government to foster an enabling environment? Perhaps the strongest drivers derive from service-delivery needs; government can expand service coverage and increase efficiency and effectiveness by accessing NGOs, whether as contractors, so-called "gap fillers" (operating autonomously where government services are unavailable), or full-fledged partners. Governments everywhere, even autocratic ones, face some pressures to open or broaden access to basic services. For the service-delivery function, which relates to several of the MDGs, the instrumental nature of government–NGO interaction establishes clear incentives for government to enable NGO action.

For the interest-aggregation and policy-advocacy functions of NGOs, however, the incentives picture is mixed. These functions can have an impact on service-delivery effectiveness; they also can increase the quality and responsiveness of public policies and programs, reduce the degree of social exclusion of marginalized groups, express public values, and build social capital. These contributions can occur in the context of incremental improvements in specific policy/program interventions, in which case government has some incentives to enable NGOs to fulfill these functions. Such contributions can also lead over time to broader societal change, such as redefinition of state-citizen interaction, opening up of political space, and/or enacting democratic governance and civic values (see, for example, Fisher 1998).

In mature democracies, these NGO functions are part and parcel of state–society relations and are firmly supported in the constitutional framework and the government apparatus that structures accountability, responsiveness, and checks and balances (see Boris and Steuerle 1999). In these societies, the full range of enabling conditions illustrated in table 5.2 is largely in place and operational. Yet, the existence of an enabling environment does not override the realities of differential access to power and influence, the pervasiveness of interest-group politics, and the persistence of a marginalized and relatively impoverished underclass in the democracies of the industrialized world.

For the poor countries of the globe where democratization is nascent, partial, or nonexistent, the incentives for government to enable NGOs' interest-aggregation and policy-advocacy functions are less clear-cut and in some situations are limited or negative.[9] Many developing- and transitioning-country governments view NGOs with suspicion and antagonism, fearful of their potential for fueling political opposition and jealous of their donor funding, even as they turn to NGOs for service delivery. Government often seeks to maintain controls over NGOs through registration, regulation, and, in some cases, repression. In Egypt, for example, where the government seeks to limit Islamic fundamentalist organizations, NGOs must meet strict requirements to organize and are regulated by the Ministry of Social Welfare.

The MDGs targeting poverty reduction, women's empowerment, and environmental sustainability involve much more than incremental tinkering with technical content of socioeconomic policies and programs. Taken to their logical conclusion, they require substantial degrees of social change, accompanied by redistribution of public revenues and expenditures. Thus, as the extensive literature on the political economy of policymaking demonstrates, powerful societal actors often oppose the changes necessary to reach pro-poor goals and exercise a high degree of influence and control over government (see, for example, World Bank 1997; Brinkerhoff and Crosby 2002; Lakshman 2003). Such power dynamics are at play at local as well as national levels. Thus, the existence of a nominally supportive legal framework notwithstanding (the mandating column in table 5.2), government may be unwilling to facilitate, provide resources for, partner with, or endorse NGOs to organize and empower citizens, engage in policy advocacy, and/or exercise monitoring and accountability. All societies and their governments operate with some degree of patronage, both formal and informal, which tends to preserve existing social patterns and power differentials (Brinkerhoff and Goldsmith 2005).

In terms of pro-poor change and involvement of grassroots NGOs, Jenkins and Goetz, writing about relatively democratic India, offer a sobering realism regarding the likelihood that government actors will be open to enabling the poor or their NGO representatives to take a seat at the policy table:

> … changing the elitist culture of the bureaucracy through training and inculcation of new pro-people values … hardly offers a viable replacement for the

inducements bureaucrats earn from looking the other way when regulations are violated and from mediating the access of politicians and local business elites to state funds. It is hard to see how people's knowledge can translate into power without critical engagements with the bureaucracy, or exposure and prosecution of corrupt practices—all supported by a social movement to protect the poor from the inevitable backlash.

(1999, 613–614)

Much of the donor discussion of enabling environments has a dry technocratic tone or a feel-good participatory one. But it should not be forgotten that power and politics drive the incentives that influence actors' behaviors. Business regulatory regimes, for example, emerge not simply from technical discussions of best practices but from bargaining among power brokers inside government and outside, in the firms being regulated. Government cannot be counted on to supply either the features of an enabling environment for socioeconomic transformation (table 5.1) or the more specific enabling conditions for NGOs to engage in social change (table 5.2) absent mobilization of demand and application of political pressure. NGOs have a role to play both in creating their own enabling environment that will foster their participation, and in serving as a source of demand for change related to the broader set of environmental factors that enable transformation in the economic, political, administrative, sociocultural, and resource allocation realms summarized in table 5.1. This latter role is well documented, for example, in areas such as anticorruption efforts judicial and election monitoring, and community organizing, where NGOs have been critical to successfully mobilizing demand and political pressure.

The demand-making and mobilization task can be relatively easy for service delivery, which tends to be noncontroversial and readily accepted as a beneficial public good. Yet, even in cases where the desirability of the service is not at issue, challenges to entrenched interests arise in the course of renegotiating the distribution of service costs, resources, and benefits, as Bloom (2000) points out regarding efforts to increase equity in health services. It can become progressively more difficult for NGOs to influence those components of the enabling environment that support interest aggregation, citizen mobilization, and advocacy. For example, in some countries it can be a major struggle for NGOs simply to gain rights and access to public information (see Jenkins and Goetz 1999).

Addressing the politics of the enabling environment is central to NGOs' fulfilling their potential functions in contributing to the MDGs. This does not mean that NGOs must necessarily sacrifice one function in favor of another; experience shows that they often simultaneously engage in service delivery, policy advocacy, and constituency empowerment (Brinkerhoff and Brinkerhoff 2002). Even in relatively hostile settings, NGOs can on occasion exploit small openings that allow for progress to be made in enhancing their enabling environment. Well-known examples of NGOs that began with a service-delivery focus, but have grown to encompass advocacy and community empowerment, and eventually to influence the extent to which their government operates democratically, are Building Resources Across the Countries (BRAC) and the Grameen Bank in Bangladesh (see Karim 2000). For some NGOs, their mission aims directly at pressuring government actors for change—not simply to create an enabling environment for NGOs, but for promoting socioeconomic development, democracy, and social justice. As these NGOs connect across national boundaries, they contribute to transnational civil society, an increasingly potent force for change around the world, well skilled in the exercise of power politics (see Florini 2000).

As countries democratize and decentralize, the opportunities for government-NGO interactions increase, as do the possibilities for NGOs to engage in demand-making to create a more favorable enabling environment. These arise in response to the incentives for responsiveness and accountability that flow from democratization and decentralization. The exploitation of accountability linkages can enhance the effectiveness of NGO demand-making, such as through political campaigns, lobbying, and public hearings with legislators and policymakers, and in the executive branch through engagement with service delivery agencies in participatory planning exercises, client satisfaction surveys, and so on. The interaction patterns that evolve from this kind of cross-sectoral pushing and pulling result in an iterative process of engagement, exchange, feedback, adjustment, and reengagement. As a result, government-NGO relations and the features of the enabling environment can be highly dynamic (Brinkerhoff and Brinkerhoff 2002).

It should be noted that the accountability linkages in these dynamic interactions go both ways. As NGOs play roles in holding politicians, policymakers, and service deliverers to account, so government's roles in regulating, contracting, and partnering with NGOs serve to increase their accountability and responsiveness as well. In countries where the government does not interact significantly with NGOs, these roles tend to be fulfilled de facto by the international donors who fund NGO service delivery, policy monitoring, and advocacy programs. With increasing levels of democratization and cross-sectoral collaboration, it becomes more likely that developing-country governments will at least parallel donors in ensuring some measure of NGO accountability, if not eventually replace them. Some NGOs are not comfortable with the notion of oversight of their activities and argue for unfettered autonomy, but increasingly the establishment of transparency and accountability is seen as important for NGO credibility and legitimacy, both as service providers and as policy advocates.[10]

Measurement and Implementation Issues

Concern for metrics that can be used for assessment of an enabling environment arises on a number of fronts. Since features of the enabling environment are being employed as criteria to decide which countries receive international donor grants and loans under initiatives such as the MCA, measurement of these criteria takes on fundamental importance. This is not the place to engage in a detailed discussion of the choice and utility of the MCA and other selectivity indicators, which others have dealt with extensively (see Radelet 2003, 2004; Jafari and Sud 2004). The point is to recognize that the intense focus on indicator selection and eligibility thresholds, which have preoccupied donors, countries seeking donor resources, and other interested parties, has limited attention to other aspects of measurement related to enabling environments.

In terms of making progress toward the MDGs with NGO participation, two other measurement considerations are important. Both of these concern the link between measurement and implementation. The first consideration is a focus on capacity assessment. As noted here, as well as by numerous other analyses, a critical issue for the enabling environment is whether societal actors, both in and outside of government, have the requisite capacity to establish and sustain appropriate enabling conditions to support NGO efforts that will advance the MDGs. This issue suggests that efforts to measure institutional capacity are a necessary complement to tracking enabling-environment indicators. It also raises two related questions. First, what measures might provide indications of progress toward a better enabling environment? Second, what strategies and interventions will build the needed institutional capacity?[11]

The second consideration is a focus on monitoring and measurement of the enabling environment for purposes of performance improvement and change management. The relevant managerial perspectives here are several: for example, public-sector managers in government service-delivery agencies, policymakers reviewing public agency performance and allocating resources, and managers of NGOs working on MDG-related programs. This measurement focus relates to a body of research and practice regarding strategic management, in which the items identified in tables 5.1 and 5.2 would be used to inform assessment and strategy formulation for managing change.[12] Given the dynamism of the enabling environment, this type of monitoring and measurement is called for on an ongoing basis, rather than as a one-shot undertaking. As poverty-focused NGOs participate in negotiating relative entitlements to public benefits and mobilizing political power in support of the MDGs, a strategic orientation to the enabling environment will be helpful.

Finally, related to implementation capacity, there is the issue of global and transnational impacts on an individual country's enabling environment. How much of creating an enabling environment is within the control of a particular government and its governance partners? Globalization—removal of trade barriers, liberalization of capital markets, rapid technological change—has, in the view of many observers, challenged the sovereignty of the nation-state as well as posed serious burdens on state capacity to cope with greater economic, political, and social interdependence (see Rondinelli and Cheema 2003). Coupled with these forces, as previously noted, donor-imposed conditionalities and transnational civil society add to the external pressures that developing-and transitioning-country governments face. However, to the extent that global forces push governments in the positive direction of improving their enabling environments, the issue shifts away from lack of control toward capacity constraints.

Conclusions

The MDGs contain ambitious targets whose achievement depends upon the concerted effort of national and international actors, supported by substantial investment of resources. The enabling environment in a particular country strongly influences the effectiveness of those actors' efforts —in the public, NGO, or private sectors—and the sustainability of MDG-promoting investments. The features of the enabling environment have been targets of investment and capacity building, as well as, more recently, criteria employed to assist donors in deciding *ex ante* which countries are "good bets" for development dollars and for specifying conditionalities associated with these dollars.

NGOs are important to the fight against poverty, and through their roles in service delivery, policy advocacy, and constituency empowerment they can contribute to making progress on the MDGs. Maximizing these contributions depends upon government actions to create an appropriate enabling environment, as elaborated in this chapter. Local NGOs themselves can take steps to push their government to implement these actions, but in many cases they cannot do it alone. International NGOs can provide support and fill gaps when necessary, using either their own or donor-provided resources. International donors, intervening directly, can also address the implementation issues raised here in various ways.

Through conditionalities, as already mentioned, they can induce governments to facilitate NGO participation in the MDGs. Through targeted investment in pilot activities they can demonstrate the constructive roles NGOs can play. Through the convening of neutral forums, they can bring government and NGOs together to engage in information sharing, dialogue, and negotiation. Government resistance to NGOs derives to some degree from political concerns, but it can also stem from ignorance and lack of capacity. Sometimes NGOs are the resistant parties, with a hostile or fearful orientation to government.

To the extent that countries move in the direction of the features of the enabling environment for socioeconomic development identified in table 5.1, the likelihood increases that government will take actions to support NGO involvement in the production of public goods (table 5.2). While restricting international donor assistance to countries where these features are already positive can ensure that resources will be well spent and progress made, the real challenge remains to develop strategies for NGOs and the MDGs where these features are weak or absent.

Notes

1. A few examples include: (a) Interactive symposium, Creating an Enabling Environment for Achievement of the Millennium Development Goals, Washington, D.C., October 2, 2002; (b) The Nonprofit Partnership Conference, An Enabling Environment: The Legal and Policy Framework Required for a Vibrant NPO Sector, Johannesburg, South Africa, March 25–27, 2003; (c) World Bank, Community Driven Development Learning Module, Enabling Environment for Civil Society in CDD Projects, Washington, D.C., April 19, 2001; (d) USAID/Nigeria, Request for Assistance (RFA) No. 620-04-003, Enabling Environment, (USAID/Nigeria, 2004); (e) Asian Development Bank, Grant No. PRC 36445-02, Strengthening the Enabling Environment and Building Institutional Capacity to Combat Land Degradation, September 2003.
2. There are many ways to define NGOs. The definition used in this chapter is intentionally broad, encompassing what has variously been identified as the third or nonprofit sector, civil-society organizations, nongovernmental development organizations, and grassroots organizations. Brinkerhoff and Brinkerhoff (2002) discuss definitional questions and cite the issue of "sector blurring," which recognizes that the lines distinguishing the public, private, and NGO sectors are not always bright.
3. Both the World Bank researchers' analyses and the modified lending policies are topics of intense debate, among Bank staff as well as outside observers. For recent critical discussion of the empirical research base for performance-based selectivity in lending, see Mosley et al. (2003) and also Radelet (2004). This debate fits within the ongoing arguments regarding the

utility, appropriateness, and effectiveness of conditionality (see, for example, Killick 1997; Santiso 2001; Koeberle 2003).

4. These are not the only clarifications that are in order. Other questions that arise include, in what ways are the conditions interrelated? Are some conditions more important than others?

5. The extant development literature widely addresses the topics in this table. For some useful treatments that aggregate and synthesize research findings, see World Bank (1997, 2002) and UNDP (2002).

6. To elaborate on the specifics of government-NGO relations is beyond the scope of this paper. For an overview see Brinkerhoff and Brinkerhoff (2002).

7. The International Center for Not-for-Profit Law has done extensive documentation of legal frameworks affecting NGOs and civil society in a wide range of countries. See the publications and online library available at www.icnl.org.

8. Many analysts of NGOs in developing countries have noted the existence of NGOs of dubious parentage, suspicious purposes, and outright phoniness; see Fowler's (1997, 31–32) discussion of NGO "pretenders." On NGO legitimacy and accountability, see Slim (2002).

9. The percentage of countries by region (excluding Western Europe) ranked by Freedom House in 2003 as "not free" or "partly free" are: Sub-Saharan Africa, 77 percent; Middle East/North Africa, 94 percent; Central/Eastern Europe and former Soviet Union, 56 percent; Americas, 34 percent, and Asia Pacific, 54 percent. Calculations are based on data from www.freedomhouse.org/research/survey2003.htm.

10. Issues of performance accountability relate most directly to NGOs in their role as service providers, where the focus is on downward accountability to beneficiaries and upward to funders, whether international donors or governments (see, for example, Ebrahim 2003; and Edwards and Hulme 1996). NGOs as self-proclaimed representatives of, and advocates for, various special groups (the poor and marginalized, ethnic/religious minorities, women, children, etc.) face pressures for democratic accountability in both national and international policy arenas. For a useful discussion of NGO legitimacy and accountability that addresses both performance and democratic dimensions, see Slim (2002).

11. Capacity assessment and capacity building are topics of perennial discussion, debate, and diatribe in the international development community. The UNDP has sought to play a leadership role in addressing issues of capacity development and technical cooperation; see, for example, Fukuda-Parr et al. (2002). For a recent highly critical perspective, see Dichter (2003).

12. A large literature provides analysis and guidance on change management and performance improvement. Brinkerhoff and Crosby (2002) offer a toolkit for public-sector reformers that is also relevant for NGOs. Lusthaus et al. (2002) provide a useful compendium of insights and advice on performance enhancement and enabling environments. J. Brinkerhoff's (2002) book on partnership is helpful for NGOs working with government or the private sector.

References

ADB (African Development Bank). 2002. Achieving the Millennium Development Goals in Africa: Progress, prospects, and policy implications. Abidjan: ADB, in collaboration with the World Bank, Global Poverty Report, June.

Bloom, G. 2000. Equity in health in unequal societies: Towards health equity during rapid social change. IDS Working Paper No. 112. Brighton, U.K.: University of Sussex, Institute of Development Studies.

Boris, E. T., and C. E. Steuerle. 1999. *Nonprofits and government: Collaboration and conflict.* Washington, D.C.: Urban Institute Press.

Brinkerhoff, D. W., and B. L. Crosby. 2002. *Managing policy reform: Concepts and tools for decision-makers in developing and transitioning countries.* Bloomfield, CT: Kumarian Press.

Brinkerhoff, D. W., and A. A. Goldsmith. 1992. Promoting the sustainability of development institutions: A framework for strategy. *World Development* 20(3): 369–385.

———. 2003. How citizens participate in macroeconomic policy: International experience and implications for poverty reduction. *World Development* 31(4): 685–701.

———. 2005. Institutional dualism and international development: A revisionist interpretation of good governance. *Administration and Society* 37(2): 199–224.

Brinkerhoff, J. M. 2002. *Partnership for international development: Rhetoric or results?* Boulder, CO: Lynne Rienner.

Brinkerhoff, J. M., and D. W. Brinkerhoff. 2002. Government-nonprofit relations in comparative perspective: Evolution, themes, and new directions. *Public Administration and Development* 22(1): 3–19.

Burnside, C., and D. Dollar. 2000. Aid, policies, and growth. *American Economic Review* 90(4): 847–868.

DFID (Department for International Development). 2003. Better government for poverty reduction: More effective partnerships for change. Consultation document. London: DFID.

Dichter, T. W. 2003. *Despite good intentions: Why development assistance to the third world has failed.* Amherst, MA: University of Massachusetts Press.

Dollar, D., and J. Svensson. 1998. What explains the success or failure of structural adjustment programs? Policy Research Working Paper No. 1938. Washington, D.C.: World Bank.

Ebrahim, A. 2003. Accountability in practice: Mechanisms for NGOs. *World Development* 31(5): 813–829.

Edwards, M., and D. Hulme, eds. 1996. *Beyond the magic bullet: NGO performance and accountability in the post-Cold War world.* West Hartford, CT: Kumarian Press.

Fisher, J. 1998. *Non governments: NGOs and the political development of the third world.* West Hartford, CT: Kumarian Press.

Florini, A. M., ed. 2000. *The third force: The rise of transnational civil society.* Tokyo and Washington, D.C.: Japan Center for International Exchange and Carnegie Endowment for International Peace.

Fowler, A. 1997. *Striking a balance: A guide to enhancing the effectiveness of non-governmental organizations in international development.* London: Earthscan.

Fox, T., H. Ward, and B. Howard. 2002. Public sector roles in strengthening corporate social responsibility: A baseline study. Washington, D.C.: World Bank, Private Sector Advisory Services Department.

Fukuda-Parr, S., C. Lopes, and K. Malik, eds. 2002. *Capacity for development: New solutions to old problems.* London: Earthscan and the United Nations Development Programme.

Independent Sector. 2001. The nonprofit almanac in brief. Washington, D.C.: Independent Sector. www.independentsector.org/PDFs/inbrief.pdf.

Jafari, S., and I. Sud. 2004. Performance-based foreign assistance through the Millennium Challenge Account: Sustained economic growth as the objective qualifying criterion. *International Public Management Journal* 7(2): 249–270.

Jenkins, R., and A. M. Goetz. 1999. Accounts and accountability: Theoretical implications of the right-to-information movement in India. *Third World Quarterly* 20(3): 602–622.

Karim, M. 2000. NGOs, democratization, and good governance: The case of Bangladesh. In *New roles and relevance: Development NGOs and the challenge of change,* ed. D. Lewis and T. Wallace. Bloomfield, CT: Kumarian Press, 99–109.

Killick, T. 1997. Principals, agents and the failings of conditionality. *Journal of International Development* 9(4): 483–495.

Koeberle, S. G. 2003. Should policy-based lending still involve conditionality? *World Bank Research Observer* 18(2): 249–273.

Lakshman, N. 2003. The political economy of good governance for poverty alleviation policies. ERD Working Paper No. 39. Manila: Asian Development Bank, Economics, and Research Department, May. http://www.adb.org/Documents/ERD/Working_Papers/wp039.pdf.

Lusthaus, C., M-H. Adrien, G. Anderson, F. Carden, and G. P. Montalvan. 2002. *Organizational assessment: A framework for improving performance.* Ottawa and Washington, D.C.: International Development Research Centre and Inter-American Development Bank.

Mosley, P., F. Noorbakhsh, and A. Paloni. 2003. Compliance with World Bank conditionality: Implications for the selectivity approach to policy-based lending and the design of conditionality. Research Paper No. 03/20. Nottingham, U.K.: University of Nottingham, Centre for Research in Economic Development and International Trade, November.

Najam. A. 2000. The four C's of third sector–government relations: confrontation, co-optation, complementarity, cooperation. *Nonprofit Management and Leadership* 10(4): 375–396.

Picciotto, R., and E. Weisner, eds. 1998. *Evaluation and development: The institutional dimension.* New Brunswick, NJ: Transaction Publishers, for the World Bank.

Radelet, S. 2003. *Challenging foreign aid: A policymaker's guide to the Millennium Challenge Account.* Washington, D.C.: Center for Global Development.

———. 2004. Aid effectiveness and the Millennium Development Goals. Working Paper No. 39. Washington, D.C.: Center for Global Development, April.

Rondinelli, D. A., and G. S. Cheema, eds. 2003. *Reinventing government for the twenty-first century: State capacity in a globalizing society.* Bloomfield, CT: Kumarian Press.

Santiso, C. 2001. Good governance and aid effectiveness: The World Bank and conditionality. *Georgetown Public Policy Review* 7(1): 1–22.

Slim, H. 2002. By what authority? The legitimacy and accountability of nongovernmental organizations. Geneva: International Council on Human Rights Policy, http://www.jha.ac/articles/a082.htm.

Thindwa, J. 2001. Enabling environment for civil society in CDD projects. Washington, D.C.: World Bank, Social Development Family, CDD Learning Module, April 19. www.worldbank.org/participation/enablingenvironment/EnablingenvironmentCECDD.

UNDP (United Nations Development Programme). 2002. *Deepening democracy in a fragmented world.* Human development report 2002. New York: Oxford University Press, for UNDP.

———. 2003. *Millennium Development Goals: A compact among nations to end human poverty.* Human development report 2003. New York: Oxford University Press, for UNDP.

USAID (U.S. Agency for International Development). 1988. Sustainability of development programs: A compendium of donor experience. AID Program Evaluation Discussion Paper No. 24. Washington, D.C.: USAID.

USAID/Nigeria. 2004. Country strategic plan 2004–2009. Washington, D.C.: USAID, www.dec.org/pdf_docs/PDABZ265.pdf.

World Bank. 1985. Sustainability of projects: First review of experience. Report No. 5718. Washington, D.C.: Operations Evaluation Division.

———. 1997. *The state in a changing world.* World development report 1997. New York: Oxford University Press, for the World Bank.

———. 2002. *Building institutions for markets.* World development report 2002. New York: Oxford University Press, for the World Bank.

6

The Politics of Global Partnership

Martha Finnemore

Much of the conversation surrounding implementation of the Millennium Development Goals (MDGs) is very technocratic in tone and content. People worry about program design and efficiency. They worry about effectiveness and what techniques or programs will work. They worry about evaluation and specifying concrete measures for success. These are all important concerns. Indeed, they are crucial, and one of the very important contributions of the MDGs has been to set concrete, measurable goals that focus attention on some of these technocratic problems of evaluation. But technocratic know-how is only half of what is needed to meet the MDGs. Political know-how is also required.

Implementing the MDGs is as much a political problem as a technical one. Very often, we know what will move us toward these goals but we cannot implement pro-poor policies because of political opposition. The drafters of the MDGs recognized this and Goal 8 highlights the need for political cooperation as well as some potential benefits from it. Goal 8 calls for "global partnerships" and cooperation between a wide variety of political actors (UNDP 2003). It calls for cooperation among governments, both in the wealthy global North and in the poor global South. It calls for cooperation between governments and the large intergovernmental organizations (IGOs) crucial to realizing the MDGs—the World Bank, the International Monetary Fund (IMF), the World Trade Organization (WTO), and others. It calls for cooperation of both governments and IGOs with private companies, such as technology and pharmaceutical firms that can provide the means to health and well-being for the world's poorest. It also requires cooperation with NGOs who are so often the advocates for and implementers of antipoverty programs around the world.

In standard UN-speak, the MDGs and the Millennium Declaration use high-minded language to call on all these political players to get along, cooperate, and do the right thing. However, anyone involved in poverty-alleviation work is well aware that political cooperation is not a naturally occurring phenomenon. Indeed, cooperation is problematic in most forms of social life. It is not effortless in families, in offices, and certainly not among governments. It has to be actively fostered, built, and nurtured by the partners in this implementation effort.[1]

In this chapter, I explore a few basic issues surrounding the politics of global partnership. As a political scientist, the first questions I would ask about implementing the MDGs are not technocratic ones about how to design efficient and effective programs. The first questions I would ask about the Goal 8 call for global partnerships are: why would these actors—these governments, firms, IGOs, and NGOs—want to cooperate at all? Why would any of these actors want to work toward implementing the MDGs? What's in it for them? Equally important, what motives might undercut their work toward implementation? Without understanding what motivates these political actors, we will not get far in implementing our programs, no matter how beautifully designed they are.

NGOs understand this. Working to achieve the MDGs, they must navigate often-complex political minefields, and the strategies they choose to do this vary across regions and sectors. Detailed consideration of these strategies would require far more than this chapter. My purpose here is simply to point out that beneath all the technocratic planning and program design lie some serious political challenges, opportunities, and issues. Here, I consider five of these.

1. Mixed Incentives of Partners

It is not at all clear that many of the "partners" named in Goal 8 really *do* care about implementing the MDGs beyond paying lip service. Of course, all of these various actors will sign onto the UN-sponsored platitudes and aspirations. However, one does not need a PhD in political science to know that commitments like this are made all the time but do not receive the sustained support needed for success. Why might this be? Many of these actors have very mixed motives when it comes to the nitty-gritty of MDG implementation. They may sincerely support the MDGs at some elevated level of rhetoric, but most face very powerful incentives that run counter to or distract from MDG support.

Governments, in both the North and the South, have many other demands on their time and resources. Like any other goal, alleviating poverty, especially among citizens in foreign countries, must compete with other policy priorities for the attention of decision makers and for government resources. To compete successfully, a policy usually has to offer some clear political payoff for governments, so it is worth asking: what is the political payoff to governments in implementing the MDGs? The answer is not obvious. The poor tend not to be politically powerful anywhere, not in poor countries or rich ones.[2] Pats on the back from the UN or other actors for implementing MDG-directed policies do not obviously translate into political benefits that will help governments stay in power or win elections.

Intergovernmental organizations, such as the IMF and the WTO, have mandates and missions that do not always or obviously put pro-poor policies at the forefront of concern. IMF staff are not convinced that poverty alleviation is their job; neither are WTO staff, and it is not at all clear that either institution is well set up to implement the MDGs. The IMF is staffed by macroeconomists who understand their job to be promoting macroeconomic stability. This is not some misapprehension by staff. Many powerful member governments provide clear direction that this is to be the fund's primary concern. Alleviating poverty is often understood to be the World Bank's job, and many staff at the Fund will say so in private if not in public (Barnett and Finnemore 2004; Evans and Finnemore 2001; Woods 2006). Similarly, the WTO is staffed by trade lawyers and economists who believe their primary job is to promote agreement among members on trade rules, not the alleviation of poverty. Member states decide whether trade rules will help the poor, not staff. Macroeconomic stability and expanded trade may help the poor, but the MDGs are add-on goals for these institutions, not core missions (Kruger 1998).

Business firms may see public-relations benefits to supporting the MDGs, and some business people may genuinely be willing to roll up their sleeves and get involved, but their overarching concern will always be about the bottom line. Businesses need to make money and shareholders need to be satisfied. Again, poverty alleviation needs compete with other, very pressing, concerns (Haufler 2001).

In sum, supporting the MDGs has a mom-and-apple-pie quality. How can you be against helping the poor? But there is a lot of symbolic politics going on in these negotiations that mask very powerful countervailing interests. Creating sustained support for the MDGs among these partners will require addressing these mixed incentives.

2. Turning Words into Deeds

Symbolic politics is not empty politics. Powerful governments, IGOs, and other actors often make symbolic and rhetorical commitments with little expectation that they will ever be forced to follow through. However an increasing body of research in political science is documenting ways in which these actors can become trapped by their commitments and forced to deliver. NGOs are crucial to this process. Generalizing, the research suggests that when states, IGOs, or businesses make public commitments, these commitments become focal points for political mobilization. NGOs and publics mobilized by these commitments monitor performance and follow-through by actors, exposing nonperformance and creating political costs for those who do not deliver. Such cases have been well documented in human rights and environmental activism.[3] Similarly, the UN's Global Compact is set up in part to take advantage of this dynamic since it explicitly relies on NGOs to monitor business compliance with Compact commitments (Hurd 2003).

3. Bring Advocacy Back In

Chapter 4 (Brinkerhoff, Smith, and Teegen) mentions the advocacy role of NGOs without exploring it in detail, but this role is essential to the politics of successful implementation. It is only through strong advocacy for the MDGs and constant pressure to implement them that the various global partners will be able and willing to follow through with the often-demanding measures needed for success.

NGOs have some important tools with which to shape behavior of more powerful actors. At first glance, this is not obvious. Most NGOs are very weak by traditional measures of political power. They are usually much smaller, with fewer people and resources than other "global partners" such as states, IGOs, or transnational companies (Keck and Sikkink 1998). However, NGOs can be essential to creating and maintaining the political climate that gives other actors political reasons to follow through and implement the MDGs. They can do this in a variety of ways, many of which involve either creating political costs for reneging on commitments to the MDGs or creating new political benefits from implementation.[4]

Collection and dissemination of information is one such tool. NGOs often provide watchdog functions, making sure that other actors deliver on promised behavior. They publicize failures and hypocrites; they also can and should praise those who meet their obligations. They issue reports critical of laggards; they may rate or rank the best/worst performers; they collect information on relative successes and failures; and they disseminate information about best practices. NGOs often make *publicity* of this information a central portion of their mission and their advocacy, in this case for the MDGs. They use techniques of *shaming* to impose costs on large institutional actors who care about their reputations both internationally and domestically. They can also engage in *emotional appeals* to create a climate of broad public awareness of and support for the MDGs. This climate, in turn, shapes incentives for larger actors who require public support or might be sensitive to public opinion.[5]

Many of the characteristics identified in chapter 4 as contributors to NGOs' effective performance also enhance their performance as advocates. NGOs are often skilled at working at many levels—at the apex of policy-making and on the ground during implementation. They can be skillful intermediaries both between partners and between different levels of government. They are often more flexible than other actors and face fewer bureaucratic constraints and formalized accounting procedures. This kind of flexibility also makes it possible for NGOs to be creative and entrepreneurial in ways that other partners may not be. Big, ossified bureaucracies have trouble generating new ideas and implementing them quickly. This is much easier for the smaller, more flexible NGOs; and new ideas about how to engage partners and publics often come from the NGO sector. Finally, in the advocacy realm NGOs often benefit from public assumptions about their altruism and principled commitment, assumptions not generally accorded to governments, business, or even many prominent IGOs. These assumptions often give NGOs a certain moral authority that buttresses their information claims and enhances the effectiveness of their publicity (Wapner 1995; Keck and Sikkink 1998.) Indeed, this often seems to work even when NGO leaders, publics, and politicians all understand that NGOs also have "private" agendas of their own that may have little connection to altruism or achieving the MDGs.

4. The Myth of Being Apolitical

Advocacy is inherently a political action, but the advocacy function of NGOs can create tensions when it collides with the often strongly held view that these organizations must be impartial and apolitical. Humanitarian organizations often perceive themselves, and promote themselves, as being above politics, outside of politics, or otherwise apolitical. They imply that their allegiance is to humanitarian ideals, which they want to portray as universally accepted. They explicitly or implicitly claim that, "We all want to relieve hunger, spread education, promote health, and alleviate poverty. How could anyone be opposed?" Mobilizing support for humanitarian programs often depends crucially on the ability of advocates to foster this view of humanitarianism and poverty alleviation as everyone's goal. Indeed, much of the legitimacy and moral authority of humanitarian NGOs flows from a perception that they do not take sides in partisan politics, or that if they do so, it is only because they are fighting for the weak and dispossessed, and that they will work with any party or group who shares these concerns.

NGOs are not alone in cultivating this nonpartisan, apolitical image. The World Bank, the IMF, the UN, and most other IGOs similarly cultivate the image that they are neutral and impartial. As for NGOs, this perception is central to the legitimacy and influence of these organizations.[6]

However, this apolitical image presents something of a paradox for many of the "global partners" involved with implementing the MDGs: they want to be apolitical but there is no apolitical ground on which to stand. Implementing the MDGs is fundamentally a political process. It calls for a change in "who gets what, when, and how," which is a classic definition of politics (Lasswell 1936). The best these partners can hope for is to make implementation of the MDGs so widely accepted as an important goal that it *appears* apolitical because it is impossible for actors to say publicly that they oppose it. This surface consensus eliminates none of the countervailing incentives described earlier. MDG implementation will continue to be a political process in which advocates for pro-poor policies must compete with advocates of other goals for the time, attention, and resources of policymakers and other key stakeholders in society. Further, they must do this while continuing to cultivate the image of being apolitical in order to maintain legitimacy and support. We cannot eliminate this paradox, but we can be aware of it and learn to use it strategically. Certainly advocates, especially NGOs, use the fact that it is difficult to oppose pro-poor policies as an opportunity to exert pressure for action.

5. The Missing Partner: Publics

Achievement of the MDGs will require participation, not just by large institutional actors such as governments, IGOs, and multinational firms. It will require broad support from mass publics, both in the South and in the North. The development community has understood for two decades now that broad participation and "ownership" of antipoverty programs in poor countries is essential to implementation and success. The mixed success of efforts to promote this kind of public involvement has been widely studied, and efforts to improve mechanisms for involvement will and must continue.

Publics in Northern countries also have an important role to play in generating the political support that will allow or require governments, IGOs, and firms to implement pro-poor policies. Indifference or outright opposition in these countries is often a major barrier to implementation. Reducing agricultural protection, increasing foreign-aid budgets, and altering drug patent protections have all become lightning rods for political opposition. Overcoming these forces will require well-organized campaigns to mobilize public support for pro-poor policies in the North and give politicians there reasons to make favorable decisions. Changes in trade rules that would help realize the MDGs, for example, will entail political battles within and among developed countries, and pro-poor policies will only prevail if publics in the North actively support them. Eliminating protection and subsidies in rich countries' agriculture sectors will be particularly contentious. Domestic agriculture has strong, well-organized lobbies in all these countries, and they will fight hard to protect protection. Without public support within member states of the Organisation of Economic Co-operation and Development for revised trade rules to eliminate these protections, it will be difficult, probably impossible, to change the rules. Politicians who championed such a change would be committing political suicide, and suicidal tendencies are not common in politicians. It will be the job of advocacy groups to make it possible for politicians to take the desired decisions at some reasonable political cost.

There is some reason to be hopeful on this score. Official and NGO aid are in some respects complements rather than substitutes. In particular, the domestic (political) constituency for adequately funded and rigorously evaluated foreign aid can be formed by citizens who become personally engaged in voluntary-sector activities as well as who donate to and learn from poverty-focused international NGOs (Smith 2005, 195).

Implementing the MDGs is not just a management problem. It is a political problem. It requires the creation of political reasons to support implementation and the creation of political will to take action where little may now exist. This means restructuring people's expectations about what is necessary and what is possible. More people in more places need to be persuaded that implementing the MDGs are both. Changing people's minds, raising their consciousness can only be done with constant advocacy and lobbying of not only the obvious "global partners" (governments, IGOs, firms) but also of the publics to which they answer.

Notes

1. For a thoughtful overview of organizational and political issues involved in partnerships such as those entailed in the MDGs and the Global Compact, see Ruggie (2003).
2. For an excellent analysis of the rise of foreign aid and global poverty as a concern of governments in the developed world, see Lumsdaine (1993). For a discussion of the institutionalization of poverty as a concern of the World Bank, see Finnemore (1996, chapter 3).
3. See Keck and Sikkink 1998; Thomas 2001; Risse et al. 1999; Khagram et al. 2002.
4. For an overview of recent studies of NGO activist efforts to shape the behavior of more powerful actors, see Price 2003; Finnemore and Sikkink 2001.

5. Analysis and examples of these techniques are discussed in Keck and Sikkink 1998; Thomas 2001; Risse et al. 1999; Khagram et al. 2002; Finnemore and Sikkink 2001.
6. For an extended analysis of this phenomenon with reference to intergovernmental organizations, see Barnett and Finnemore 2004.

References

Barnett, Michael, and Martha Finnemore. *Rules for the World: International Organizations in Global Politics.* Ithaca: Cornell University Press, 2004.

Evans, Peter, and Martha Finnemore. "Organizational Reform and the Expansion of the South's Voice at the Fund." United Nations Conference on Trade and Development, G-24 Discussion Paper Series no. 15, December 2001. http://www.unctad.org/en/docs//pogdsmdpdg24d15.en.pdf

Finnemore, Martha. *National Interests in International Society.* Ithaca: Cornell University Press, 1996.

Finnemore, Martha, and Kathryn Sikkink. "Taking Stock: The Constructivist Research Program in International Relations and Comparative Politics." *Annual Review of Political Science* 4 (2001): 391–416.

Haufler, Virginia. *A Public Role for the Private Sector: Industry Self-Regulation in a Global Economy.* Washington, D.C.: Carnegie Endowment for International Peace, 2001.

Hurd, Ian. "Labour Standards through International Organizations." *Journal of Corporate Citizenship* 11 (Autumn 2003): 99–111.

Keck, Margaret, and Kathryn Sikkink. *Activists beyond Borders.* Ithaca, NY: Cornell University Press, 1998.

Khagram, Sanjeev, James Riker, Kathryn Sikkink, eds. *Restructuring World Politics: Transnational Social Movements, Networks, and Norms.* Minneapolis: University of Minnesota Press, 2002.

Kruger, Anne O. ed., with the assistance of Chronia Aturupane. *The WTO as an Organization.* Chicago: University of Chicago Press, 1998.

Lasswell, Harold. *Politics: Who Gets What, When, and How.* New York: Smith, 1936.

Lumsdaine, David H. *Moral Vision in International Politics: The Foreign Aid Regime, 1949–1989.* Princeton: Princeton University Press, 1993.

Price, Richard. "Transnational Civil Society and Advocacy in World Politics." *World Politics* 55 (July 2003): 579–606.

Risse, Thomas, Stephen Ropp, and Kathryn Sikkink, eds. *The Power of Human Rights: International Norms and Domestic Change.* New York: Cambridge University Press, 1999.

Ruggie, John G. "The United Nations and Globalization: Patterns and Limitations of Institutional Adaptation." *Global Governance* 9, 3 (July–Sept 2003): 301–21.

Smith, Stephen C. *Ending Global Poverty: A Guide to What Works.* New York: Palgrave Macmillan, 2005.

Thomas, Daniel C. *The Helsinki Effect: International Norms, Human Rights, and the Demise of Communism.* Princeton, NJ: Princeton University Press, 2001.

United Nations Development Programme. *Human Development Report.* New York: Oxford University Press, 2003.

Wapner, Paul. "Politics Beyond the State: Environmental Activism and World Civic Politics." *World Politics* 47, 3 (April 1995): 311–40.

Woods, Ngaire. *The IMF, the World Bank, and International Relations.* Ithaca, NY: Cornell University Press, 2006.

7

The Need for Political Will: A Short Note on the Millennium Campaign

Carol Welch

The Millennium Development Goals, or MDGs, stem from the Millennium Declaration and UN conferences and summits of the 1990s. NGOs worked at these events to create concrete outcomes and targets for various issues, which are now articulated in the eight MDGs.

The Millennium Declaration was unanimously adopted by the heads of all UN member states at the Millennium Summit in September 2000. The Declaration is based on a human-rights framework and embodies freedom, equality, solidarity, tolerance, respect for nature, and shared responsibility. In adopting it, the governments of UN member states committed to freeing their fellow citizens from the "abject and dehumanizing conditions of extreme poverty, . . . to making the right to development a reality for everyone and to freeing the entire human race from want."

The eight MDGs that stemmed from the Millennium Declaration are more than commitments; they offer a "program of action" to combat many of the world's ills through global partnership. The MDGs are unique relative to other international agreements in several ways. The first is that they are a deal between the Global North and the Global South, prescribing roles for both developed and developing countries to fulfill toward the realization of the goals. Second, they are monitorable and measurable, with clear targets set for each MDG. Furthermore, the MDGs are timebound in that there is a clearly defined date by which they should be achieved: 2015. Finally, the MDGs can be adapted to various country contexts and the targets adjusted to appropriately reflect the development realities of different states.

The UN has been using the MDGs as a framework, integrating them into its programs as a way of measuring outcomes and successes. Interestingly, many NGOs, including CARE and the UN Foundation, are doing the same. Part of the commitment that UN member states made in adopting the MDGs was to provide "country reporting" on their activities to meet the goals. These country reports can serve as a useful tool by NGOs to challenge governments on the pace of progress toward the Goals and to compare with their own development findings at the local, regional, and national levels.

The UN also established the Millennium Project and the Millennium Campaign to assist in the effort to achieve the MDGs. The Millennium Project, led by Professor Jeffrey Sachs, spearheads analytical work on policies, institutions, and investments needed to achieve the MDGs. The Millennium Campaign, led by Eveline Herfkens, is charged with awareness raising, advocacy, and mobilization, both globally and in specific countries.

To ensure that the MDGs would not become just another set of UN commitments, the Campaign was established to build political will amongst all member states to meet their commitments. It also serves the purpose of empowering different constituencies with the information they need to conduct campaigns on the MDGs. This includes facilitating civil-society strategy meetings and linking civil-society organization (CSO) groups with the UN's resources.

Furthermore, the Campaign was designed to educate the public about the MDGs. In 2003 it joined in a partnership with the British Broadcasting Corporation (BBC) to raise awareness of the MDGs. The objective of the collaboration is to provide evidence through the voices of ordinary citizens across the world on the progress made in achieving the Goals via the BBC World Service programs. Africa and Asia were selected for the pilot initiative of the project because the MDGs face their most significant challenges in these regions. During 2003 the project began development of pilots that were a combination of radio programs and related broadcast events, and a television program. A second phase will expand the number of radio and TV series and broaden the coverage to other languages and regions. The Campaign has also tapped into the influence of the UN Goodwill Ambassadors, who record and air public-service announcements on the MDGs in the United States and Europe.

The Campaign played a large role in educating the public and drawing attention to the 2005 G8 summit in England, for which the MDGs had been set as the center of international discussions. Similar efforts were made for the Millennium +5 Summit in September 2005, where UN member states reviewed the progress made and challenges lying ahead in realizing the MDGs.

The activities of NGOs were integral in the creation and adoption of the MDGs and will prove critical in achieving these targets by 2015. NGOs will play a particularly vital role in realizing Goal 8: "developing a global partnership for development." Currently, political leaders can neglect these issues because they can afford to, from both an electoral and public-relations standpoint. However, if NGOs are able to create public awareness and attention around these issues, political leaders will be compelled to act on these commitments.

NGOs will also play a large role in transparency and making sure that resources are used appropriately. They will help ensure that the emphasis in achieving the goals is on both a national and a local scale. This oversight will see that progress toward the MDGs is not reduced to meaningless aggregates that filter out the most vulnerable, but actually achieves meaningful change for those who need it most. Finally, the MDGs provide an umbrella for groups working on a broad range of issues, including health, education, human rights, transparency, and environmental integrity, to become part of a bigger, more powerful effort in achieving their goals.

Developing countries will play a large role in determining the success of the MDGs. NGOs will assist governments in reaching the targets by holding them accountable on spending, fighting corruption, tracking spending, and making sure services are delivered at the local level. NGOs will also help governments measure the effectiveness of their programming, for instance, by ensuring that resources are geared toward universal primary education rather than subsidizing tertiary education for the elite and focusing resources on decentralized rural development schemes rather than on large-scale infrastructure projects such as construction of dams.

As an example, Social Watch Philippines (SWP), a national network of NGOs, has shifted its focus to the MDGs as they provided a good platform from which to address SWP's issues of concern. However, the organization's aims go beyond the MDG framework because certain issues, such as unemployment, are not addressed within the Goals and because certain timelines for achieving them are not appropriate in the Philippine country context. So, in this sense, in the Philippines, the MDGs serve more as a starting point—serving as "minimum" development goals.

SWP has an organized presence in the Philippine Islands and coordinates national and local consultation with various CSOs to help launch an MDG literacy campaign and to identify key development issues in both local and national contexts. These include special considerations for the war-torn island of Mindanao, where peace and post-conflict development are key. SWP engages the Philippine government on the MDGs and challenges the assumptions made in the country's official MDG Status Report. The government has acknowledged some points raised in an alternative country report by SWP and, as a result, made amendments to its original draft. Philippine government assessments show that many of the MDG targets will be met at the national level; however, the NGO community there has advocated the importance of going beyond national averages and looking at subregional and local situations. CSOs have been actively consulting with local governments to determine what the needs of the most vulnerable are.

CSOs in developed countries are also taking a country-specific approach to the MDGs. Campaigners in Ireland have worked toward Goal 8 by focusing on eliminating the country's trade subsidies, particularly in the dairy sector. The Campaign has focused its attention on "laggard" countries, such as Italy and Spain, where little in the way of meeting commitments on the MDGs had been accomplished, but where civil society pressure is now bearing fruit in terms of political discourse.

The Campaign has targeted existing organizations such as the influential and broadly based peace movement in Italy in order to create awareness and spark action around the MDGs. It used a large peace march to get hundreds of thousands of students, church groups, and other CSOs under the umbrella of the peace movement educated on the MDGs. By tapping into the existing peace movement, a great deal of media attention around the Goals was created. Stakeholders for each Goal made an individual gate representing the subject of this particular goal, and these gates have traveled around Italy, providing a visual symbol of the MDG movement. Italian celebrities have also been drawn into the campaign, with the AC Milan soccer team signing a petition in support of the MDGs and setting up the eight Millennium Gates for game attendants to pass through on their way into the San Siro stadium. The Gates also traveled to the capital city of Rome, where parliamentarians have formed a working group with the aim of rewriting the Italian development cooperation law. All of this attention and action around the MDGs was generated in less than six months, which offers an encouraging example of the influential role that CSOs play in bringing development issues into the national spotlight.

Spain is another country where the Campaign is focusing a great deal of its efforts. The Aznar Government had a very low aid as a percentage of Gross Domestic Product volume, at 0.25, with much of that aid tied to trade credits. The new Spanish government plans to increase official development aid from 0.25 percent to 0.5 percent of the GDP by 2008 and remove the strings attached to these funds—a large victory in terms of overseas development assistance (ODA).

More focus is being placed on international development issues in Spain, which is becoming a new aspect in the country's political landscape. One example of this new emphasis is the Public Education Forum 2004, held in Barcelona over the course of 141 days. The conference involved large- and small-scale exhibitions, workshops, markets, performances, round tables, and debates on three main themes: cultural diversity, sustainable development, and conditions for peace. Spanish CSOs also worked with the regional coalition government of Catalonia, which has long had a goal of increasing ODA to 0.7 percent of GDP, to put pressure on the national government to increase Spain's volume of international aid.

In the United Kingdom, as CSOs geared up for the 2005 G8 Summit, they put pressure on Tony Blair and Gordon Brown in particular to bring MDG issues to the table. Brown proposed the creation of the International Finance Facility (IFF) in which developing countries pursuing anticorruption policies for stability and economic development would receive an extra $50 billion a year in ODA—a sum projected necessary to meet the MDGs. Blair also established the Africa Commission, a high-level panel consisting of African and developed-country leaders, which will closely examine the development needs of the continent.

CSOs wanted the British G8 hosts to take the opportunity to put these issues on the agenda in order to pull other G8 leaders into firmer commitments to meet the MDGs and replicate the politics of the Jubilee Movement. These groups worked on catchy ads and visuals to promote the MDGs' importance and create a more personal message regarding why the Goals are important to the people of the UK.

Finally, action in the United States is crucial to success in achieving the MDGs. Despite the fact that it is the largest volume donor of ODA, the United States is actually the least-giving country in terms of its economic power and population. Therefore, if it does not act to meet its MDG commitments, there is little hope that real progress will be made. There are a growing number of NGOs in the country, from service delivery NGOs to longtime antipoverty/hunger groups such as Bread for the World and Results, which want to campaign under a common banner to advance broad efforts toward the MDGs. Student AIDS organizations are also engaged. Faith-based organizations such as the Episcopalians for Global Reconciliation, who propose giving 0.7 percent of their personal, parish, diocesan, and national budgets to help achieve the MDGs, are becoming increasingly involved in the effort. The city councils of Nashville, San Jose, and Los Angeles have also passed pro-MDG resolutions, and the Mayor of Denver has issued a proclamation in support of the Goals.

Polling has shown that Americans think that they give much more ODA than they actually do and that what they give is sufficient. The poll results have also found that Americans respond favorably to the MDGs and to the concept of aid being given in a different way than in the past—in ways that avoid corruption and empower people to help themselves. Reactions regarding the MDG targets raised some questions and concerns amongst those polled. However, my perspective on the matter is that you can argue about the timeframe set for the goals, but the bottom line is that it is helpful to set targets and timelines.

In closing, the goal of the Millennium Campaign is to help foster a loose uniting of groups, working toward the MDGs under a common slogan or logo. We want to multiply our efforts, create a buzz in the media and among policy makers, and educate constituents around the country on these issues.

Part III

Application of the Theoretical Framework

8

Organizational Comparative Advantages of NGOs in Eradicating Extreme Poverty and Hunger: Strategy for Escape from Poverty Traps

Stephen C. Smith

This chapter builds on the framework introduced in chapter 4 to examine in more detail the organizational comparative advantages of nongovernmental organizations (NGOs) with specific reference to eradicating extreme poverty and hunger, and looks in greater depth at some of the resulting strengths that NGOs may bring to bear on innovation and implementation of poverty programs. In doing so, it will examine the types of poverty traps faced by those in extreme poverty, and consider in this light NGO programmatic responses.

Analysis of poverty traps helps to clarify the distinctions between chronic (or structural) and transitory poverty. Evidence suggests that perhaps one-third of all families that are poor at any one time are chronically poor, which is proxied by evidence that an individual has been poor for at least five years. McKay and Baulch (2003) provide a well-regarded "guesstimate" that about 300–420 million people were chronically poor at the $1 per day level in the late 1990s. The other two-thirds are among a larger group who are vulnerable to poverty and are extremely poor from time to time. This larger group includes families usually poor but occasionally receiving enough income to cross the poverty line, and those that are usually nonpoor but occasionally experiencing a shock that knocks them temporarily below the poverty line (McKay and Lawson 2003; Hulme and Shepherd 2003).

While all poor, and indeed vulnerable people, are properly of concern to the UN, aid agencies, and poverty-focused NGOs, chronic poverty is of special economic as well as humanitarian concern. It is not clear that existing microfinance and other poverty programs, to the degree that they reach into extreme poverty at all, primarily benefit those who are chronically destitute rather than temporarily poor.

This divide between the sometimes-poor and the always-poor suggests the deeply disconcerting thought that we could halve poverty (the target for Goal 1) without improving the lives of any of the families that are chronically poor. Indeed, the very measurement of poverty as the fraction living below the $1 per day level gives the rather perverse incentive of meeting the target by helping those living just below rather than far below the poverty line. While this states the problem in particularly stark terms, the fear that something close to this could occur is reflected in the reorientation of poverty-program efforts by Building Resources Across the Countries (BRAC) and other NGOs in light of the finding that even their best programs often fail to reach the poorest of the poor (Emran 2003). But there is much reason to doubt whether government or the private sector has done much to improve the well-being of the poorest, so the question is how NGOs can play a special role in reaching the always-poor—those stuck in poverty traps—in helping them to join the economic mainstream.

In the remainder of this chapter, first, Goal 1is briefly reviewed. Then, the problem of poverty traps is introduced. Thirteen types of traps are identified that will need to be addressed if better progress is to be made in helping to bring those in chronic, or structural, poverty into the economic mainstream. To consider the specific role of NGOs in Goal 1, I then examine the organizational comparative advantages of NGOs in addressing poverty traps. Finally, links between the traps and NGO comparative advantages and programmatic responses are analyzed.

The First Millennium Development Goal: A Brief Review

Appropriately, the first goal is to eradicate extreme poverty and hunger. The targets are more modest, to get halfway to this goal by 2015, according to two measures: reduce by half the proportion of people living on less than a dollar a day; and, reduce by half the proportion of people who suffer from hunger. On current trends, we will not be able to achieve even the first half on schedule. In the 1990s, according to the UNDP (2003), income poverty increased in 37 countries and hunger in 21 countries. South Asia is on track to halve income poverty, but hunger would not be halved until the twenty-*second* century. In sub-Saharan Africa, the poorest region in the world, income poverty is actually increasing. Poverty is also increasing in the transition countries, while little progress is being made in Latin America. In contrast, East Asia has already nearly met these two targets, although some observers fear the region remains vulnerable to a bursting bubble in China. Although there are continued concerns about distribution of the gains of this growth, absolute poverty has been falling in China even as inequality has increased.

To ultimately achieve the first goal of eliminating, or even halving, extreme poverty and hunger, one cannot think about poverty only in terms of achieving a threshold level of income, or meeting minimum caloric requirements, without taking into account the other seven goals. One cannot ensure income without health, nor health without nutrition. Adequate income may not be attainable without gender equity, and gender equity is not likely without improved incomes for women. Agricultural incomes are precarious in the absence of environmental sustainability and of lowered tariff barriers and developed-country agricultural subsidies that are at the core of what we mean by global partnership for development. Thus, the significance of this topic and discussion can only be appreciated in context of all the chapters of this book.

In a sense, the halving-poverty target is even more modest than halfway, because the first half is likely to be a lot easier than the second half. This is not only because the poorest require more income to reach the $1 per day poverty line, but because they may be stuck in chronic poverty, caught in more binding poverty traps; this problem is taken up in the next section.

In considering the MDGs as a whole, we inescapably turn our attention to the problems of social exclusion from local society and global community. Social exclusion refers to the systematic, possibly unwritten, barriers that often prevent classes of poor people from having access to opportunities to develop and use their capabilities, including access to health, education, training, employment, and a voice in their wider communities. Social exclusion, whether through active marginalization or simply through benign neglect, causes poverty to become reinforced and then perpetuated. Temporary access to income or basic needs does not generally address the deeper problem of social exclusion; addressing exclusion provides better opportunities to ensure that poverty reduction is sustainable.

As soon as the language about poverty moves from lack of income, and even lack of health and education, to social exclusion, the central role of NGOs becomes inescapable. As outlined in chapter 4 (Brinkerhoff, Smith, and Teegen), the roles of NGOs center on advocacy (along with targeted service and local public good and common-property resource provision). This includes advocating for groups excluded from the political process, and indeed from economic opportunity, as well as overcoming effective discrimination that excludes the poor from the social mainstream.

Although treated together in the MDGs and many discussions about poverty, dollar-a-day income poverty and hunger are not the same thing, nor are those in income poverty always the same people who are malnourished. For example, extra income is more likely to lead to reduced hunger when women have more power within the family to allocate resources (Thomas 1990, 1993). And there are circumstances in which the natural resources to which the poor have access provide sufficient caloric energy and protein, but allow for very little income for health care, clothing, shelter, basic education, and other needs. Although the income poor and the hungry are clearly overlapping groups, progress toward the two goals need to be separately and carefully accounted for. But what both severely income-poor and malnourished people, as well as the socially excluded, often have in common is the dilemma of being stuck in poverty traps.

Poverty Traps

Poverty becomes a trap when a vicious cycle undermines the efforts of the poor, in which conditions of poverty feed on themselves and create further conditions of poverty. The literature offers an increasing number of examples of such possible poverty traps. Some operate at the national-economy level and concern problems such as coordination failure in industrialization and have been systematically reviewed in the literature (Hoff and Stiglitz 2001; Todaro and Smith 2003, chapter 5), and some operate at the family or community level. However, in this section, I survey the range of types of family and local traps through a review thirteen key poverty traps that the best NGO poverty programs are working to address. These traps reflect the characteristic problems associated with the most extreme forms of poverty and hunger, where NGO involvement is likely to be required to achieve the first MDG.

1. Child-Labor Traps

Child-labor traps work in two dimensions—over time and across space. In an important example of the intergenerational transmission of poverty, if parents are too unhealthy and unskilled to be productive enough to support their family, the children have to work. But if children work, they can't get the education they need; so when they grow up, they have to send their own children to work (see Galor and Zeira 1993; Basu 1999). In a regional child-labor trap, if most children work, unskilled-labor supply is large, so that wages are too low for parents to refrain from sending their children to work; but if few children work, even though total income is lower with children not working, family income is sufficiently high for parents to realize their preference that their children not work (see Basu and Pham 1998; Basu 1999). According to estimates by the International Labor Organization (ILO), approximately 180 million child laborers are exposed to "work that is hazardous to children," while "some 110 million children in hazardous work are under age 15"; moreover, "seventy-three million working children worldwide are less than ten years old" (ILO 2002).

2. Illiteracy Traps

Closely related to the problem of a child-labor trap is the illiteracy trap. Even if the family does not need the meager wages the children could earn, parents may not send their children to school because they cannot afford transportation, a school uniform, or a modest school fee. If a family could borrow this money, the higher incomes received a few years later by their now-literate children could pay back these loans manyfold. But if the poor lack access to credit, they may not be able to get loans to finance otherwise very productive schooling. One could borrow the money one's children would earn, and thus afford to send them to school, only there is no collateral one can put up, which denies one the chance of borrowing even the small amount of money required. Looked at the other way around, child labor can also be seen as a kind of alternative to credit. If parents need money for survival today, they may send their kids to work, even though this "loan" will be repaid with their children's far lower earnings later in life (see Baland and Robinson 2000; Jacoby 1994). According to UNESCO estimates, there are some 860 million completely illiterate adults in the world; well over 40 percent of all adults in South Asia are illiterate. It has been estimated by the World Bank that in 2003 more than 100 million children were unable to go to school due to their poverty. They are thus deprived of their chance to escape poverty when they grow up.

3. Low-Skill Traps

If there is no visible employer in a region that is seeking modern job skills—for work in basic manufacturing, for example—there is no incentive for individuals to invest in gaining these skills. But if there is no workforce available with these skills, outside investors are not likely to invest in the region, particularly when these skills are readily available in other developing regions. This type of trap could be described as a chicken-and-egg problem—which comes first, the investment or the skills? The failure to achieve a scale sufficient to benefit from agglomeration economies is related to this type of trap (Todaro and Smith 2003, chapter 8). Governments can help with training and incentives for firms if they have resources, but when they lack resources (resulting from such conditions as a very high debt burden) this may be difficult or impossible to resolve from within the trapped economy (see Acemoglu 1997; Kremer 1993). While there are no systematic estimates of the extent of low-skill traps per se, the striking concentration of high skills in a few countries and regions suggests the concentration of low-skilled people in other areas, which are unlikely to attract much investment.

4. Working-Capital Traps

Lack of credit also plays a role in other poverty traps. In a working-capital trap, a microentrepreneur has too little inventory to be very productive. This means she will also have too little net income to acquire the resources to hold a larger inventory in the future. For example, consider a woman trying to make ends meet by selling door to door, with a small inventory of costume jewelry, say, or the few used American jeans that are all she can afford to hold. This makes the chance of a sale—a matching style and size that the customers want—so low that her income will be so meager that she will be unable to go out with a larger inventory the next day (see, e.g., Banerjee, Besley, and Guinnane 1994; Banerjee and Newman 1993; Ghatak and Guinnane 1999). Despite the explosion of microfinance institutions (MFIs) in the last fifteen years, it has been estimated that MFIs are serving just 11 percent of the world's 240 million poorest families (Daley-Harris 2002). This estimate suggests that working-capital traps are still pervasive.

5. Debt-Bondage Traps

But the wrong kind of debt from the wrong kind of lenders can also lead to a trap. Colluding moneylenders may calibrate loan amounts and interest payments to ensure that a peasant can never get out of debt (Ray 1998). Sometimes the rate of pay for impoverished people working for their creditors is so low that it is insufficient even to pay back the interest they owe. Such is the plight of tens of thousands of low-caste salt workers in rural India. Although bonded workers are allowed to keep a subsistence income (as slaves used to be) so they can work, the moneylender may essentially extract the entire surplus in an endless cycle of debt. But terms may be designed so that the more you work or the more productive you become, the more you must pay to your masters, in what could be called a quicksand of poverty. All too often the children of the bonded laborers are then themselves born into bondage, never to escape. The result is effective slavery of these individuals. The NGO Free the Slaves estimates that there are some twenty-seven million people serving in debt bondage and related forms of effective slavery around the world today.

6. Uninsured-Risk Traps

Unanticipated events put the poor in developing countries at risk of losing their few assets such as land, livestock, home, and microenterprise assets, as well as their basic nutrition and health. For example, a majority of the poorest are farmers, and they are generally unable to get any weather insurance. As a result, they have to orient their whole approach to farming to minimize the risk of a catastrophic drought or other shock in which their families face ruin. But this approach to farming also makes it unlikely that they can take advantage of opportunities to do much better and begin to build assets that can lift them out of poverty in the long run. As a result, they are unable to change their circumstances in a way that would let them gain more security against high risks in the future. In addition, insecurity of land and other property tenure may induce risk-averse behavior such as not leaving the property (Field 2002; Jacoby and Mansuri 2006) or refraining from long-term investments in real estate, such as fertilizer, irrigation, and improvements to buildings. Analogous distortions are found in the behavior of microentrepreneurs. Although the poor show great ingenuity in developing informal risk-sharing arrangements in their communities, the result can be considerable distortions and inefficiencies that also retard the rate of economic progress (see, e.g., Townsend 1994; Udry 1995). Almost all farmers in developing countries can be regarded as underinsured relative to those in the developed world. One of the potential consequences of this lack of insurance is that farmers may become trapped in low income and low consumption.

7. Information Traps

Impoverished day laborers, housemaids, and others among the poorest of the poor work long hours every day just to put one or two meals on the table. Even though there are alternatives available that may pay a higher wage, such as rickshaw pulling, one has no time or energy to learn about what these occupations pay or how to take them up. Of course, employers have no incentive to help their laborers learn about better opportunities, and may work to prevent it. There is no systematic evidence on the degree and consequence of information traps, but it is likely to be a significant problem, as evidenced by the apparently high frequency with which participants in credit-plus programs, such as those offered by BRAC and Freedom from Hunger, switch income-earning activities after being exposed to alternatives as part of the training and solidarity components of the program. Those too poor to participate in microcredit programs are likely to be even more vulnerable to information traps.

8. *Undernutrition and Illness Traps*

In undernutrition traps, found during famines and in deeply impoverished areas, an undernourished person is too weak to work productively, so her resulting wage is too small to pay for sufficient food to improve her nourishment, and she continues to work with low productivity for low wages (see Dasgupta and Ray 1986, 1987). A similar vicious cycle can keep chronically ill (but treatable) people in poverty. Related problems include poor-shelter traps: inadequate shelter from the elements can also lead to low productivity, for example by reducing sleep and making recovery from illness difficult, and thus reducing earnings and making it difficult for the family to improve their shelter. The UN Food and Agriculture Organization (FAO 2003) has reported that the number of people suffering from chronic extreme hunger increased by 18 million during the last half of the 1990s. Thus, 842 million people are severely undernourished. It is unclear that more than a minority of these people are in classic undernutrition traps (Strauss and Thomas 1998). Nevertheless, it is plausible that such traps are operating in famine-affected areas such as Ethiopia, northern Kenya, and Niger, and chronically undernourished regions such as Bihar state in India and northwest Bangladesh.

9. *High-Fertility Traps*

If most families in your area have many children, and there are few decent jobs to go around, then you must have many children or face the likelihood that no child of yours will have the means and the willingness to take care of you when you are too old to work. If all could have lower fertility, all might be better off; but it is implausible that individuals could coordinate such a change (see Dasgupta 1993, 1995; Todaro and Smith 2003, chapter 7). Fertility remains extremely high in some regions in Africa.

But the sharp drops in fertility in many low-income countries suggest that fertility traps are being overcome. Still, given the relationships between population growth and income growth in the cross-section data (Barro 1997), it seems likely that in rural Africa, more broadly, fertility remains above what would be consistent with per capita income maximization from a social perspective, as well as above what surveys suggest are consistent with preferences of mothers.

10. Subsistence Traps

Specialization—and the proficiency in economic activities that take advantage of natural abilities and available local resources—is a key to increasing productivity. But one can only specialize if one can trade for the other goods and services one needs. In the extreme, if everyone in your region is practicing subsistence agriculture, there is no one to sell to and you have to remain producing for subsistence. (In practice, there will be a modest degree of local trading, but the fundamental point holds.) The alternative is to produce for more distant markets. But to do so, you have to first know about them, and you must somehow get your products to markets where people have money to buy them, and indeed to convince distant buyers of their quality. Middlemen can play a key role by effectively vouching for the quality of the products they sell; they can do this because they get to know the farmers they buy from as well as the product. It is difficult to be an expert in the quality of many products. So in order for a specialized agricultural market to emerge, there needs to be a sufficient number of concentrated producers with whom a middleman can effectively work. But without available middlemen that the farmers can sell to, specializing is not a viable strategy, so there is no incentive to specialize in the first place; farmers will thus have to continue producing their staple crop or goods, primarily for personal consumption and limited sales within the village. The result can be an underdevelopment trap in which a region remains stuck in subsistence agriculture (Emran and Shilpi 2004).

11. Farm-Erosion Traps

In environment degradation traps, the poor are so desperate for food for their children this year that they have to overuse their land even though they know the result will be lessened fertility next year, eventually even desertification. In poor countries, especially in times of famine, impoverished farmers have been known to eat the seeds they saved from the last harvest to plant in the next sowing season. They have to do this so they do not starve before the next season. This is not myopia but the need to survive today. This is a metaphor for the basic problem. Even though you know you are overusing your soil and that it will degrade if you do not rest it or plant less aggressively, the problems come at some point in the future. You have to grow more food today to keep your family from becoming badly undernourished. But in the end, of course, you are simply trapped in a cycle of poverty. Any or most gains in productivity, as new techniques are learned, can be negated by the poorer quality of soil. While fertilizers and other land improvements might be a good investment by conventional calculations, they are of no help if you cannot afford them or borrow to finance them (see, e.g., Perrings 1989; Todaro and Smith 2003, chapter 11). Worldwide, about two billion hectares of crop and grazing land is believed to be distressed due to moderate to severe soil degradation. The FAO (1995) has estimated that five to seven million hectares of land valuable to agriculture is lost worldwide every year through erosion and degradation.

12. Common-Property Mismanagement Traps

Similarly, lakes are overfished; forests are not managed sustainably; land is overgrazed (World Bank 2004a). Part of the problem is a breakdown of community management of common-pool resources, which in turn is the result of colonial practice followed by rapacious post-colonial regimes. But once broken, cooperative social agreements about responsible use of shared resources are difficult to restore—another kind of poverty trap akin to the famous prisoners' dilemma problem. Put in stark terms, if I do not fish today even at unsustainable levels, someone else will catch those fish instead of me; either way, I will catch fewer fish tomorrow (see, e.g., Larsen and Bromley 1990; Todaro and Smith 2003, chapter 11). Closely related are collective-action traps. Many times a community of the poor, or a village including many poor people, could improve its circumstances by working together on joint projects. But it would require a leader who could take time to organize, and generally the poor do not have the time and resources to do this. In a poor village or community of the poor, even if one could do so, few of the benefits go to any one person, such as the organizer; rather, they are diffused around the community. Moreover, any such actions can be risky, with the reward very uncertain. It can be difficult for individuals to initiate corrective action (see, e.g., Olsen 1965). For evidence on the seriousness of the common-property-resource mismanagement problem in developing countries, see Jodha (1995) and Seabright (1993).

13. Powerlessness Traps

Poverty leads to social and political powerlessness, but such powerlessness leads to an inability to command entitlements to public services that could help the poor to break out of the cycle of poverty (World Bank 2000a, 2000b, 2004b). Moreover, depression and anxiety appear to be pervasive among the poor in developing countries. Narayan et. al. (2000) and Patel (2000, 2001) argue that such outcomes are commonly the consequence of extreme poverty and its associated powerlessness. Worse, in a real sense, depression and anxiety are inflicted on the poor deliberately, for the rich all too often abuse and terrorize the poor to keep them from gaining any bargaining power. Compounding this, women face domestic violence and abuse along with a lack of personal identity—factors contributing to the much higher incidence of depression in women than men in countries such as India. But once depression takes hold, a poor person can become listless, exhausted, unable to take initiative—and so depression also becomes a cause of poverty. A vicious cycle ensues, making poor mental health a form of poverty trap. For a survey of evidence on these problems, see Patel (2000, 2001). Drug and alcohol abuse is also increasingly common in developing countries and becomes a related form of trap. Furthermore, a culture of criminality may emerge in disempowered communities of the poor, in which the poor are preyed upon, families lose their sons to gang violence, and resources are diverted to protect lives and property. In turn, such criminality traps may be included among a broader category of "neighborhood effects," such as those examined by Hoff and Sen (2005).

In sum, there is an extraordinary range and variety of poverty traps that is probably an important cause of structural poverty—in a large group of people who are always poor, and who are more difficult to assist with standard poverty programs. An improved knowledge base on the incidence and severity of poverty traps in different developing regions is an important priority for future research.

Organizational Comparative Advantages of NGOs in Addressing Extreme Poverty

When organizational characteristics, such as those that define the nature of NGOs, are exogenous or inflexible, that is, given in advance, organizations have a tendency to specialize in ways that reflect their resulting organizational comparative advantage. The concept of organizational comparative advantage is introduced in Smith (1994). In the private sector, firms have a tendency to specialize in the products or subproduct qualities in which their organizational structure puts them at an advantage relative to other firms. For example, cooperative enterprises specialize in goods for which small-scale innovations contributed by production workers are important to maintaining competitive advantage. Insights into the specialization and behavior of NGOs may similarly be gained by analyzing the types of activities that offer advantages to organizations with NGO characteristics relative to organizations with other characteristics, such as private or state ownership.

What are some of the advantages and limitations of NGOs in designing and implementing poverty programs capable of achieving Goal 1? As discussed in chapter 4, most activities in which NGOs have comparative advantage appear to lie between conventional private and public goods. That is, in the dimensions of rivalry and excludability, services provided by NGOs tend to be partially rival, partially excludable, rival but not excludable, or excludable but not rival. (Of course, the relevant dimensions in this analysis must go beyond rivalry and excludability.) It is proposed that NGOs have seven, partially overlapping, types of organizational comparative advantage in hunger and poverty activities. Some of the resulting comparative advantages and responsibilities appear to confer naturally to international NGOs, and others to local organizations such as federations of community-based organizations (CBOs). Each of these categories is itself quite diverse, and more specific applications of this framework would have to take further differentiation of organizational forms into account. In each case, the emphasis is placed on comparative advantage in addressing poverty traps or structural poverty.

1. Innovation

NGOs can play a central role in innovations in poverty-program design and implementation, particularly with respect to programs that reach the poorest of the poor, with which they may be more closely in touch. Unless there is a request for proposal (RFP), individual profit-making firms (although not necessarily the private sector as a whole) lack incentives for poverty innovation. Indeed, many of the needed innovations are so unexpected that no RFP could be written to draw them out. In many cases, government has an advantage in scaling up established programs. But as a working hypothesis, government is relatively unsuccessful at significant program innovation, compared with, or at least without a prod from, the NGO sector. Indeed, empirically, some of the most important innovations in programs designed to address poverty traps have been conceptualized and initially developed by domestic and international NGOs.

Consider the case of child-labor traps and illiteracy traps. Because of the at least partially public-good character of provision of basic education, government is usually viewed as having comparative advantages and hence as playing the central role (World Bank 2004a). But often, government programs have not reached the poorest families. By its nature, government tends to offer uniform services, whereas the poor may have special needs different from the mainstream populations. NGOs have played the pioneering role in such areas as nonformal primary education (NFPE), community literacy campaigns, educational use of village theatre, and use of technology, particularly computers. In this case, the role of NGOs as innovators is clear. The open question is whether, once they are established as working models, the government and private sector are then capable of scaling up these NGO innovations as well as or better than the innovating NGO. In any case, if governments or private-sector firms are unable or unwilling, the experience of BRAC shows that NGOs may do this scaling up to a substantial degree (BRAC NFPE enrollment currently exceeds one million), at least until the government is finally ready to step in. In addressing the development of ideas, innovations are nonrival but are potentially excludable, particularly if detailed information is not transmitted easily.

2. Program Flexibility

As organizations independent of government, NGOs in general are less constrained by the limits of public policy or other agendas such as those of donor-country foreign-assistance priorities, or by domestic, national, or local governmental programs, than are government agencies. Indeed, national NGOs, such as BRAC, are in principle relatively unconstrained by the preferences of the international NGOs (and vice versa), particularly to the degree that they can become majority self-financed as BRAC. Of course, independence from government can be compromised by budgetary dependence or other forms of government pressure—the actual degree of independence in any given case is an empirical question. And international NGOs can and do influence choices of local NGOs through their own budgetary power and suasion. But the broad point holds, at least as a matter of degree.

Moreover, once a potential solution to a poverty problem has been identified, NGOs may have far greater flexibility in altering their program structure accordingly than would be the case for a government program. NGOs may be better able to make use of informal (that is, nongovernmental) participation mechanisms, unconstrained by the formal strictures, and/or implicit prerogatives for elites, that prevail in the public sphere. There are also limits to this flexibility, as NGOs may have a tendency to tailor their programs to fit the available funding, and as a result come to resemble their funders, at least in their priorities and approaches. This phenomenon is sometimes called donor capture, or sector blurring (Brinkerhoff 2002), although the latter term also has broader uses. Flexibility enables NGOs to better identify traps, oppose vested interests that benefit from them, and devise locally adapted programs addressing the key traps afflicting the structural poor in a given region. Flexibility can be interpreted as localized innovations or minor adaptations of program innovations to suit particular needs.

3. Specialized Technical Knowledge

International NGOs in particular, but national NGOs in some cases (such as seen in Bangladesh), may be greater repositories of technical expertise and specialized knowledge than local government. In particular, international NGOs can draw upon the experiences of many countries that may offer possible models for problems of poverty faced by any one country, and of possible solutions. Of course, this forms part of the basis for credibility. These technical skills may be invaluable for developing effective responses to locally binding poverty traps. NGOs' knowledge of local economic conditions as well as international development experiences may also be helpful in addressing low-skill traps and information traps. Specialized knowledge is acquired in the process of doing specialized work with the poor. Consider the Grameen Phone Lady model, in which microcredit and training is provided to village women to purchase and operate a cell phone available to community members on a fee basis. This program reflects program innovation coupled with local NGO advantages in certain technical knowledge (or knowledge of how to effectively contract it) and in understanding the role of information traps. Knowledge, understood as an economic good, is also excludable but nonrival.

4. Targeted Local Public Goods

Quasi-public goods, which are rival but excludable, including those targeted to socially excluded populations, may be best designed and provided by the NGOs who know and work with these groups. Examples may include local public-health facilities, nonformal education, participatory road building and maintenance in remote areas, provision of village telecommunications and computing facilities, codification and integration of traditional legal and governance practices, creation of and specialization in local markets, community mapping and property registration, community negotiation with higher levels of official government, and development of locally suited innovations and other productive ideas (Smith 2005). Targeted local public goods such as toll goods are nonrival but excludable. There is nothing automatic about the relative effectiveness of NGO work in these areas; the extension of local public goods to meet the needs of the poorest is not easy, and NGOs such as BRAC have had to do substantial innovation and organizational development to make progress.

5. Common-Property Resource Management Design

NGOs, including federations of local CBOs, have an important role to play with respect to common-property management and targeted local public-goods provision. Throughout the developing world, there has been a poor track record in ensuring sustainability of forests, lakes, coastal fishing areas, pasturelands, and other commons (World Bank 2004a). But preserving these resources is very important for Goal 1 when the poorest rely on local natural resources for food security and basic survival. A large fraction of the world's population still relies upon local natural resources for most of their income and consumption. Targeted NGO programs—including training, assistance with organizational development, efforts to change noncooperative cultural characteristics, and initiating measures such as community- and common-property policing—can help to address common-property mismanagement traps and other forms of collective-action problems. In some of these cases, CBOs may be sufficiently developed to play these roles, but they will often need assistance of national, or in many cases international, NGOs to realize their potential. Common-property resources are rival but nonexcludable. This role may be understood in a broader framework of community mobilization for facilitating and maintaining collective action, with common-property resource management as only one application, if likely its most important one.

6. Trust and Credibility

In practice, NGOs may have other advantages over government when it comes to gaining the trust of, and providing effective services to, those in extreme poverty. Clearly, as reviewed in chapters 3 and 4, NGOs are a highly heterogeneous group of organizations. However, with the caveat that there are some significant exceptions to this generalization, those NGOs with a strong local-level presence and relationships, frequent communication, and greater avenues for participation are likely to develop greater trust among the poor. Although in a highly decentralized and socially inclusive participatory democratic setting there is no reason why government cannot be even more trusted than NGOs—since, after all, the government may be elected into office unlike an NGO—this idealized model of government does not fit the reality on the ground in many developing countries. Of course, many regions where the poor live are at best democratic in name only. But even majority rule can be of little benefit to the socially excluded, particularly when the majority population or its representatives actively marginalize the poor. When government resources are sharply limited, trade-offs between benefits for established or excluded groups can take on added significance. But democracy may also little benefit the socially excluded even when they experience benign neglect and a lack of established communication channels with the government. And once this history is established, it may be difficult for even a new and well-meaning government to overcome this legacy. Well-functioning NGOs are often more trusted in several of their component dimensions, particularly assumed competence, benevolence, reliability, established personal contacts, and perception of consistent behavior across different settings that may not be possible to monitor. In sum, in part because of their presence and ongoing interaction in the community where the poor live, NGOs may not suffer from as great a "credibility gap" as government agencies, being more trusted by the poor and their CBOs.

It is important to note that self-serving individuals can, and sometimes do, establish NGOs for largely private gain and without adequate controls for quality of service and costs. Donors may have difficulty separating effective from opportunistic NGOs. One de facto screening mechanism is that many NGO founders often work for years building up an organization before they receive more than a token salary for their work, in a civil-society version of sweat equity. But this screening mechanism is not always adequate, for example when political pressures lead to expectations that large-scale outside development funding (such as from the World Bank) to support NGOs should be very widely disseminated among organizations, or when funders lack the ability or the political will to demand, and then act upon the findings of, rigorous program evaluations.

To the degree that NGOs follow explicit bylaws requiring democratic practice, accountability, and responsiveness, credibility is enhanced over time. Partly as a result, NGOs may also be more trusted by local government than less responsive or accessible official actors such as United States Agency for International Development and the World Bank. Foundations and certain other donors may trust only NGOs to address poverty traps;

developing-country governments may be perceived as corrupt or incompetent. Thus, NGOs help mobilize resources that would otherwise not be available at all for those in structural poverty. Finally, private-sector firms may prefer to partner with NGOs over governments or other official actors to gain credibility in socially responsible investment activities (Doh and Teegen 2003). Thus, the efficient degree of responsibility given to NGOs for halving poverty depends in no small part on their responsiveness. Many NGOs may enjoy higher trust than other organizations among all the major parties concerned, including the poor, developing-country local and national governments, and donors. Trust is related to the capability to do effective advocacy.

7. *Representation and Advocacy*

NGOs have some advantages in understanding the needs of poor people and poor communities, who otherwise are often excluded from political processes and even local-community deliberations of all kinds. They may play an important role in the aggregation of preferences, and thus of representation of community needs. To the degree that NGOs have a better understanding of locally binding poverty traps, they should be in a position to more effectively represent the needs of the poor. This also reflects the advocacy role of NGOs, including CBO federations, in advocating for the needs of poor and socially excluded peoples. Minorities may need special protections in a majority-rule representative democracy, and such constitutional protections as exist are not always sufficient. It is not a comparative advantage of either the private or the public sector to advocate for the poor or the excluded. Individual donors, foundations, agencies, or other funders of advocacy will want to ensure that the advocates they sponsor are working diligently and incorruptibly. Working for an NGO at the expense of higher income and benefits and promotion opportunities is an imperfect but useful signal of commitment to do so. And if it is government that needs to be lobbied or influenced, it is unlikely to be the comparative advantage of government to fulfill this function—certainly to the degree that trust is at issue—although an office of ombudsman or of citizen protection can play some valuable part in this objective as well. Again, variability within the NGO sector must be taken into account; these observations rarely apply to "briefcase NGOs," but it is a characteristic that the NGO organizational form lends itself to. Advocacy is largely nonrival and nonexcludable, and might thus be considered more properly a public good; but it is generally done in the face of government inaction or detrimental action.

When considering the role of NGOs in achieving reductions in extreme poverty and hunger, it is useful to consider which of these seven comparative advantages is being utilized. If the NGO is playing a role different from any of these seven, this is worth considering carefully. It may be that a new form of comparative advantage has been identified; but perhaps the NGO is failing to play to its natural strengths.

Sometimes, exceptional failures of either government or the private sector create situations under which NGOs can temporarily step in to fill the void; in these circumstances efficiency may be enhanced. This vacuum-filling responsibility is a reasonable way to describe some activities of multiplex NGOs, and can represent another and more positive form of "sector blurring." For example, BRAC is involved with producing private goods such as chalk, sanitary napkins, and seeds, under conditions of a dysfunctional private sector, at least in rural areas. Africare is involved in what are normally thought of as efficiently government responsibilities, such as (at least financing) road building (which has public-good characteristics), in the face of government neglect. In such cases, it is worth considering how conditions may be established to turn these functions over to the private sector (such as through spin-offs or privatization) or to government, including traditional local government (such as through a transfer agreement), in accord with underlying comparative advantage, when conditions warrant, as indeed is an explicit part of Africare policy. The goal would be to enable NGOs to specialize in areas in which they can naturally contribute most, not merely in areas in which they can somehow manage to compete as a result of failures of other actors.

Mapping Poverty Traps into NGO Comparative Advantages and Program Activities

The comparative advantage characteristics identified in the previous section can make NGOs better-suited than public- or private-sector actors in responding to poverty traps. To see this more explicitly, consider first a mapping of the thirteen traps into areas of NGO comparative advantage. Table 8.1, column 1 lists the thirteen poverty traps examined above. In column 2, the comparative advantage that can be utilized by NGOs in addressing each of these traps is indicated. Most of these follow directly from the review in the preceding section. In columns 3 and 4 of table 8.1, the corresponding NGO programmatic activities and specific examples of such activities are indicated. More details on these programs are found in Smith (2005). For the purposes of this chapter, these often innovative examples are intended to be illustrative of types of programs fitting within each category; further evidence, and in many cases further research, is needed to gauge the impact and efficiency of many such NGO programs both in absolute terms and *relative to* comparable or related activities in the public (and private) sector.

First, in unlocking *child-labor traps,* NGOs have used their potential advantages in program innovation and flexibility to design alternative school programs that can reach child laborers in ways that government schools have not. Well-known examples include the BRAC nonformal primary education program in Bangladesh and Save the Children schooling programs for child laborers in countries including Mali and Uganda.

Second, *illiteracy traps* have been addressed by attacking the problems that keep children out of school even when they do not have to work. Donors have paid school fees and other costs often via NGOs through representatives of the local voluntary sector. NGOs have played key advocacy roles in pushing to eliminate school fees, required uniforms, and other expenditures in countries such as Kenya and Uganda. They have also provided key services such as tutoring and accelerated learning necessary for the children of the poor to catch up sufficiently to the level of the nonpoor children to make their continued schooling feasible, as illustrated by the programs of Pratham in India.

Third, in India, Self-Employed Women's Association (SEWA) has sponsored innovative programs to develop new markets and help its members to develop the skills they need, and also help communities in which members live to overcome *low-skill traps.* (Although SEWA is technically a trade union and therefore arguably part of the private sector, it has many of the characteristics of an NGO.) In Peru and Bolivia, Small Enterprise Assistance Fund (SEAF), through its investment funds, has helped companies to expand so as to take better advantage of existing regional-worker skills in fields such as traditional fabrics and stonework, and to help the companies and their employees further upgrade these skills. Endeavor has performed similar roles in working with gifted but early-stage entrepreneurs whose firms' expansion has significant potential to generate employment in South Africa and several countries in South America.

Fourth, NGOs have responded to *working-capital traps* by developing MFIs which frequently go beyond provision of credit to jointly address other problems the poor face, such as lack of a social network, need for business and other training, and even health and nutrition. Examples include Grameen and BRAC in Bangladesh, FINCA in Uganda and Freedom from Hunger in Ghana. This reflects NGOs' innovation skills and their role as repository of specialized knowledge relevant to escaping poverty traps.

Fifth, NGOs have played a central role in identifying *debt-bondage traps* as a widespread problem, raising public awareness of the problems, and

Table 8.1 Types of poverty traps and NGO responses

	Type of response		
Type of trap	Areas of NGO comparative advantage	Specific NGO programmatic activities	Illustrative program examples
Child labor traps	Innovation, flexibility, advocacy	Designing school programs to reach child laborers; advocating improved conditions	BRAC—nonformal primary education (BEP); Save the Children—nonformal schools in Africa, e.g., Mali; Uganda; Peru STC school for street children; legal advocacy
Illiteracy traps	Innovation, flexibility	Designing effective literacy programs for the very poor	Pratham—accelerated learning, India
Low skill traps	Local public goods (including club and toll goods), innovation, knowledge	Developing training programs targeted to low-skill marginalized groups; mentoring for local entrepreneurs with potential for employment expansion	SEWA—developing new markets and skills for members, India; Endeavor, South Africa, South America; SEAF—entrepreneurial skill development and access to capital, Peru, Bolivia
Working capital traps	Innovation, knowledge	Providing microfinance, alone or with complementary basic services, solidarity, etc.	Grameen, FINCA, BRAC, Freedom from Hunger, etc., Bangladesh
Debt bondage traps	Advocacy, innovation, flexibility	Raising awareness, lobbying; identifying bonded laborers; developing alternative work opportunities	Anti-Slavery International; Sankalp, India; Kamaiya FMMC, Nepal

Uninsured risk traps	Innovation, local public goods	Innovating targeted microinsurance for farmers	BASIX/KSB, India
Information traps	Knowledge, innovation	Providing information about alternative livelihoods and training	Grameen Phone Lady, BRAC—Targeting the Ultrapoor Program (TUP), Bangladesh
Undernutrition traps	Advocacy, knowledge	Providing targeted food supplements; advocating for affected areas	Programs operated by International Rescue Committee (IRC)
High fertility traps	Innovation, flexibility	Community mobilization and "cultural transformation"	CARE, Ethiopia
Subsistence traps	Knowledge, local public goods	Helping villages identify and market alternative crops	Africare, Africa Now; BRAC, Bangladesh
Farm erosion traps	Knowledge, flexibility	Providing targeted packages of credit, training, and inputs	TechnoServe and its partners, Tanzania
Common-property mismanagement	Common resource management	Mobilizing, training community organizations	Gram Vikas, India; Suledo, Tanzania
Powerlessness	Trust, flexibility	Building self-esteem, providing legal and comprehensive training	ADEW, Egypt; Child Helpline, India; World Vision, Peru

lobbying at both international and national levels for legislative reform. Examples include the work of Sankalp with bonded quarry workers in India and that of several NGOs united under the Kamaiya Freedom Movement Mobilization Committee (FMMC) in Nepal. NGOs have helped these workers achieve alternative sources of income that have ranged from buying the quarries in which they work to migrating and entering entirely new types of employment.

Sixth, *uninsured-risk traps* have recently been addressed with creative strategies. For example, crop insurance has been difficult because it is prone to moral hazard (in this case, working less hard because one knows one is insured, or even cheating), costly to provide to small farmers, and relatively easy for large farmers to monopolize ex post public distributions. Recently, some NGOs have worked with insurance companies to provide microinsurance to small farmers analogous to microcredit instruments. Rather than based on levels of output, which farmers can control, payments are based on the amount and calendar distribution of rainfall, which they cannot control. NGOs, working with CBOs, organize and distribute the insurance products, which entail transaction costs too great for conventional insurers. A good example is the recent Krishna Bhima Samruddhi Local Area Bank in Maboobnagar (BASIX/KSB) experience in India.

Seventh, NGOs have worked to help overcome *information traps* by providing the rural poor with improved knowledge about alternative livelihoods and training and otherwise preparing them to move into these activities. An interesting example is the Grameen Phone Lady program in Bangladesh, which both provides a viable alternative source of income and simultaneously increases the flow of information into and out of the village. The program reflects specialized technical knowledge and capacity for innovation.

Eighth, relief agencies such as the International Relief Committee , have worked to address *undernutrition traps*. They have combined provision of food nutrition supplements with job training, credit, and other necessary capacities to use improved health and energy productively.

Ninth, CARE in Ethiopia has responded with innovation and flexibility to *high-fertility traps*. It developed a program of community mobilization and cultural transformation to support family planning, focused on identifying and training natural leaders to play leading roles to facilitate program credibility and sustainability.

Tenth, Africare has undertaken projects in remote rural areas to help villagers overcome *subsistence traps,* working with them to identify, specialize in, and market alternative crops suitable to their local environments and capable of generating relatively high value-added, such as temperate fruits in mountainous areas. These activities reflect specialized technical knowledge and provision of club goods.

Eleventh, TechnoServe, in partnership both with international organizations such as the Consultative Group on International Agricultural Research (CGIAR) and with NGOs and CBOs working at the village level, have worked to reduce *farm-erosion traps,* both through land management education and provision of training and complementary inputs that can make a switch to more sustainable agricultural practices economically feasible for those locked into short-time horizons due to their extreme poverty.

Twelfth, groups such as Gram Vikas in India have sought to overcome *common-property mismanagement traps* through facilitating the creation of CBOs and providing them with organizational development and training, to upgrade and maintain commons, particularly wooded areas and water sources. The Greenbelt Movement has engaged grassroots participation in needed reforestation in Kenya and elsewhere in Africa.

Thirteenth, domestic NGOs, such as Association for the Development and Enhancement of Women (ADEW) in Egypt, and international NGOs, such as World Vision in Peru, have worked to identify very poor people, particularly women, who are caught in *powerlessness traps.* These programs work to improve self-esteem while providing legal education and comprehensive family and vocational training. ADEW also works to address powerlessness problems among adolescent children of their clients through its innovative Girls' Dreams Program. The program designs reflect the trust of participants and the flexibility of NGOs. In sum, these examples demonstrate that local and international NGOs have utilized the identified NGO comparative advantages in addressing key poverty traps.

Concluding Remarks

A broad conclusion of this chapter is that an overarching organizational comparative advantage of NGOs in Goal 1 centers on identifying significant local poverty traps and then in creating and improving the keys to unlock these traps, particularly through the design and implementation of targeted poverty programs. This conclusion rests particularly on the argued advantages of NGOs in innovation in poverty program design, flexibility in program implementation, provision of public goods targeted to the poor, design of management strategies for common-property resources, establishment of trust and credibility among the chronically poor as well as donors, and capacity for representation and advocacy of and with the poor. Of course, there is no claim that most NGOs working in this field exhibit high levels of even a minority of these characteristics.

Considerable additional empirical work will be needed to confirm whether systematically superior performance is found by NGOs on average over government and private-sector contractors in these spheres, and to better identify the specific conditions and organizational features of NGOs in which efficiency in these activities is largest.

Certainly, there are other roles for NGOs in relation to the other MDGs. And while other NGO roles in Goal 1 are not precluded, the analysis points to a central NGO role in helping the poor to escape from poverty traps. In fact, most international and national NGOs working in the poverty field generally say their focus is on the poorest of the poor. Yet they often voice frustration at the slow rate of progress. This may be due to the failure to identify and design policies specifically to address poverty traps. Yet as the examples in this chapter demonstrate, it is possible for NGOs to do so.

The examples offered here are sufficient to demonstrate that each of the comparative advantages identified as useful in addressing poverty traps has been utilized by at least some NGOs. There is much else that we do not know, or do not know well enough. Which of these (and other) poverty traps are empirically most significant, and in which regions and contexts? Under what conditions have NGOs made the greatest difference in addressing these traps, and which of their types of interventions have been most effective? Under what circumstances is it efficient for NGOs to step out of their natural comparative advantages and assume responsibilities vacated by the private and public sectors (i.e., provide private and public goods)? How can NGOs most plausibly serve their role in advocacy for hunger and poverty problems facing the very poor, when they are generally not elected? What is the process by which programs are designed and implemented in different types of NGOs as well as in public and private sectors? There are also unresolved but important questions regarding the internal organization of NGOs. In particular, under what conditions are multisectoral NGOs and poverty programs more effective than specialized programs in seeking to achieve Goal 1, or indeed the MDGs as a whole (see Smith 2004)?

Finally, the fact that NGOs have a key role in poverty traps does not mean that governments and the private sector do not also have important roles to play in Goal 1. In fact, their participation is crucial. Designing and implementing poverty programs require long-term commitment of resources. Government can enable innovative and effective programs to reach greater scale, and for-profit firms can form effective partnerships with NGOs while contributing strategies that have the effect of lowering the effective prices paid by the poor. As a general conclusion, to achieve the first MDG, highly effective NGO programs to help the poor escape from poverty traps need to be identified and then actively supported by all sectors.

References

Acemoglu, Daron. "Training and Innovation in an Imperfect Labour Market." *Review of Economic Studies* 64, no. 3 (July 1997): 445–64.

Baland, Jean-Marie, and James A. Robinson. "Is Child Labor Inefficient?" *Journal of Political Economy* 108, no. 4 (August 2000): 663–79.

Banerjee, Abhijit V., and Andrew Newman. "Occupational Choice and the Process of Development." *Journal of Political Economy* 101, no. 2 (April 1993): 274–98.

Banerjee, Abhijit V., Timothy Besley, and Timothy W. Guinnane. "Thy Neighbor's Keeper: The Design of a Credit Cooperative with Theory and a Test." *Quarterly Journal of Economics* 109, no. 2 (May 1994): 491–515.

Barro, Robert J. *Determinants of Economic Growth: A Cross-country Empirical Study.* Cambridge, MA: MIT Press, 1997.

Basu, Kaushik. "Child Labor: Cause, Consequence, and Cure, with Remarks on International Labor Standards," *Journal of Economic Literature* 37, no. 3 (September 1999): 1083–120.

Basu, Kaushik and Van Hoang Pham. "The Economics of Child Labor: Reply." *American Economic Review,* 89, no. 5 (1998): 1386–1388.

Brinkerhoff, Jennifer M. *Partnership for Development: Rhetoric or Results?* Boulder, CO: Lynne Rienner Publishers, Inc., 2002.

Daley-Harris, Sam. State of the Microcredit Summit Campaign Report, http://www.microcreditsummit.org/pubs/reports/socr/2002/socr02_en.pdf, 2002.

Dasgupta, Partha. "The Population Problem: Theory and Evidence," *Journal of Economic Literature* 33, no. 4 (December 1995): 1879–902.

———. *An Inquiry into Well-being and Destitution,* Oxford: Oxford University Press, 1993.

Dasgupta, Partha, and Debraj Ray. "Inequality as a Determinant of Malnutrition and Unemployment: Theory," *Economic Journal* 96, no. 384 (December 1986): 1011–34.

———. "Inequality as a Determinant of Malnutrition and Unemployment: Policy," *Economic Journal* 97, no. 385 (March 1987): 177–88.

Doh, Jonathan P., and Hildy Teegen. *Globalization and NGOs: Transforming Business, Government, and Society,* Westport, CT: Praeger, 2003.

Emran, Matin. "Stories of Targeting: The BRAC Targeting the Ultrapoor Program," BRAC Research and Evaluation Division, 2003.

Emran, Shahe, and Forhad Shilpi. "Marketing Externalities, Multiple Equilibria, and Market Development," paper presented at the Northeast Universities Development Conference, Boston University, September 2001 (revised 2004).

Field, Erica. "Entitled to Work: Urban Property Rights and Labor Supply in Peru." Unpublished working paper, Department of Economics, Princeton University, New Jersey, 2002.

Food and Agriculture Organization (FAO). *Dimensions of Need, An Atlas of Food and Agriculture, on the 50th Anniversary of the FAO*, 1995, Rome: FAO.

———. *The State of Food Insecurity in the World*, November 2003, Rome: FAO.

Galor, Oded, and Zeira, Joseph. "Income Distribution and Macroeconomics," *Review of Economic Studies* 60 (January 1993): 35–52.

Ghatak, Maitreesh, and Timothy W. Guinnane. "The Economics of Lending with Joint Liability: A Review of Theory and Practice," *Journal of Development Economics* 60, no. 1 (October 1999): 195–228.

Hoff, Karla and Arijit Sen. "Homeownership, Community Interactions, and Segregation," *American Economic Review* 95, no. 4 (September 2005).

Hoff, Karla, and Joseph Stiglitz. "Modern Economic Theory and Development," in *Frontiers in Development Economics*, ed. Gerald Meier and Joseph Stiglitz, New York: Oxford University Press, 2001.

Hulme, David, and Andrew Shepherd. "Conceptualizing Chronic Poverty," *World Development* 31, no. 3 (March 2003): 403–23.

International Labor Organization (ILO). "Where, Why, Who, How: The Facts about Child Labor," 2002, http://www.ilo.org/public/english/bureau/inf/childlabour/factssheet.htm.

Jacoby, Hanan G. "Borrowing Constraints and Progress through School: Evidence from Peru," *Review of Economics and Statistics,*" 151–60 (1994).

Jacoby, Hanan G., and Mansuri, Ghazala. "Incomplete Contracts and Investment: A Study of Land Tenancy in Pakistan," World Bank, Policy Research Working Paper Series No. 3826, 2006.

Jodha, N. S. "Common Property Resources: A Missing Dimension of Development Strategies," World Bank Discussion Paper, WDPI69, Washington, World Bank, February 1995.

Kremer, Michael. "The O-Ring Theory of Economic Development," *Quarterly Journal of Economics* 108, no. 3 (August 1993): 551–75.

Larson, Bruce, and David Bromley. "Property Rights, Externalities, and Resource Depravation: Locating the Tragedy." *Journal of Development Economics* 33, no. 2, 1990: 235–262.

McKay, Andrew, and Bob Baulch. "How Many Chronically Poor People Are There in the World? Some Preliminary Estimates," CPRC Working Paper No. 45, Chronic Poverty Research Centre, 2003.

McKay, Andrew, and David Lawson. "Assessing the Extent and Nature of Chronic Poverty in Low Income Countries: Issues and Evidence," *World Development* 31, no. 3 (March 2003): 425–39.

Narayan, Deepa, Robert Chambers, Meera K. Shah, and Patti Petesch. *Voices of the Poor: Crying out for Change.* New York: Published for the World Bank, Oxford University Press, 2000.

Patel, Vikram. "Poverty, Inequality and Mental Health in Developing Countries," in *Poverty, Inequality and Health: An International Perspective*, ed. David Leon and Gill Walt, New York: Oxford University Press, 2000.

———. et al. "Depression in Developing Countries: Lessons from Zimbabwe." *British Medical Journal* 322 (2001): 482–4.

Perrings, Charles. "An Optimal Path to Extinction? Poverty and Resource Degradation in the Open Agrarian Economy," *Journal of Development Economics* 30 (1989): 1–24.

Ray, Debraj. *Development Economics.* Princeton, NJ: Princeton University Press, 1998.

Seabright, Paul. "Managing Local Commons: Theoretical Issues in Incentive Design," *Journal of Economic Perspectives* 7 (Fall, 1993): 113–134.

Smith, Stephen C. "Innovation and Market Strategy in Italian Industrial Cooperatives: Econometric Evidence on Organizational Comparative Advantage," *Journal of Economic Behavior and Organization* 23, no. 3 (1994): 303–321.

———. "Multiplex vs. Specialized Nongovernmental Organizations: Which Are More Effective and Under What Conditions?" draft, 2004.

———. *Ending Global Poverty: A Guide to What Works,* New York: Palgrave Macmillan, 2005.

Strauss, John, and Duncan Thomas. "Health, Nutrition, and Economic Development," *Journal of Economic Literature* 36, no. 2 (1998): 766–817.

Thomas, Duncan. "Intra-household Resource Allocation: An Inferential Approach," *Journal of Human Resources* 25, no. 4 (1990): 635–64.

———. "The Distribution of Income and Expenditure within the Household," *Annales de Economie et de Statistique* 29 (1993): 109–36.

Todaro, Michael P., and Stephen C. Smith. *Economic Development,* Boston: Addison-Wesley, 8th ed., 2003.

Townsend, Robert M. "Risk and Insurance in Village India," *Econometrica* 62, 3 (May 1994): 539–91.

Udry, Christopher. "Risk and Saving in Northern Nigeria," *American Economic Review* 85, 5 (December 1995): 1287–300.

United Nations Development Programme (UNDP). *Human Development Report,* 2003.

World Bank. *Voices of the Poor: Crying out for Change.* New York: Oxford University Press, 2000a.

———. *Voices of the Poor: From Many Lands,* New York: Oxford University Press, 2000b.

———. *World Development Report 2003: Sustainable Development in a Dynamic World: Transforming Institutions, Growth, and Quality of Life,* Washington: World Bank and Oxford University Press, 2004a.

———. *World Development Report 2004: Making Services Work for Poor People,* Washington: World Bank and Oxford University Press, 2004b.

9

The Role of NGOs in Health, Education, Environment, and Gender: Application of the Theoretical Framework

Jennifer M. Brinkerhoff, Stephen C. Smith,
and Hildy Teegen

This chapter examines the real and potential roles of nongovernmental organizations (NGOs) with respect to the Millennium Development Goals (MDGs) and targets related to health, education, environment, and gender. It builds on the commissioned practitioner and researcher sectoral contributions from the George Washington University conference and synthesizes the findings, applying the framework developed in chapter 4 to each of these sectors. The chapter concludes with implications regarding NGO roles, especially in responding to sector failures, comparative advantages, and effectiveness contingencies. Table 9.1 summarizes these findings.

Health

Health[1] is critically important in achieving poverty reduction and development, as well as vital to human well-being in its own right. Accordingly, health is given a prominent role in the MDGs, with three of the eight goals health related, and three others encompassing important health dimensions. The health targets themselves address a wide range of issues:

- **Goal 1, target**. Halve the proportion of people who suffer from hunger. Nutrition is a fundamental feature of health, and a majority of child deaths are related to nutrition, including weakened immune systems.

- **Goal 4, target.** Reduce by two-thirds the mortality rate among children under five.
- **Goal 5, target.** Reduce by three-quarters the ratio of women dying in childbirth.
- **Goal 6, target.** Halt and begin to reverse the spread of HIV/AIDS and the incidence of malaria and other major diseases.
- **Goal 7, target 1:** Reduce by half the proportion of people without access to safe drinking water (this is discussed later in this chapter in the environment application).
- **Goal 8, target:** In cooperation with pharmaceutical companies, provide access to affordable essential drugs in developing countries.

Clearly, there are very important overlaps between health and other goals. Indeed, it may seem as if health completely dominates MDG efforts. On the one hand, there are always opportunity costs, and clearly, resources devoted to health are no longer available for primary education or the environment. On the other hand, there is considerable complementarity between health goals and the other goals. Nevertheless, if the MDGs come to dominate all development resources, the fact that they are health focused may mean less attention to other critical areas for poverty reduction, such as expanded access for credit and insurance, bottom-up market development, access to technologies and markets, human rights for the poor, and community empowerment and development (S. Smith 2005).

Prospects for meeting the health MDGs are questionable. Many of the MDGs were selected to be consistent with progress in previous decades, such as the world rate of poverty reduction. However, with respect to the health targets, much accelerated progress, including broader infrastructural improvements, will be necessary to meet the goals, especially in sub-Saharan Africa. Levine (2004) points out:

> Short of major technological breakthroughs that are effective at a population level, progress depends on steady (and fast) improvements in the living conditions that affect health, including education and water and sanitation infrastructure; and improving access to, quality of, and effectiveness of health services.[2]

Thus, it is essential to bring all available resources and capacities to bear.

The health sector is striking in that all three actors—private firms, government, and the citizen sector—play large roles. Certainly, the health goals may be met in various ways, utilizing the three sectors in different proportions and combinations. The recent report of the UN Millennium Project (2005) and the Commission for Africa (2005) emphasized enhancement of capabilities and resources of the public sector. Neither the UN and aid agencies, nor developing-country governments need provide services themselves. For example, the Global Fund to Fight AIDS, TB, and Malaria buys services from other actors in any of the three sectors, including NGOs. This service-buying approach is a useful model. Among other things it can help to stimulate a more active market in which NGOs as well as for-profit firms can have opportunities to demonstrate their potential efficiencies.

Key among NGO roles in the health sector is the capacity to directly deliver local health services. In many instances, such delivery can be seen as sector extension. Religious-affiliated hospitals have a particularly large share of the market in Africa. NGOs may also have a comparative advantage when the activity represents specialized public goods, using specialized knowledge, and reaching hard-to-reach groups. Somewhat relatedly, NGOs play roles in social mobilization around health issues. They can help to coordinate communities to identify and respond to health needs. In the process, NGOs may use their comparative advantage in innovation in strategies for health-service delivery. NGOs also play key roles in capacity building of government. Finally, NGOs have played key roles in advocacy, such as pushing for better services in the HIV/AIDS sector (as in the case of The AIDS Support Organization, also known as TASO, in Uganda), and demanding attention to special health needs of minorities, among others.

With respect to local service delivery, these are often activities complementary to the private sector, although they sometimes serve as substitutes. According to Levine (2004), NGOs are often "engaging in activities that permit the public sector to better fulfill its mission." This includes, for example, disseminating public-health messages and acting as public-service contractors for the delivery of particular types of health services or service delivery to particular populations. Levine illustrates these points by way of the example of Profamilia in Colombia. Profamilia employs more than 1,500 staff and maintains 35 family- planning service centers throughout the country. It is partially funded, through contracts with the Colombian social insurance system, to deliver those services deemed best by the government to be offered through private sources, though publicly funded.

Some of these services can be offered directly in competition with (as substitutes for) the private sector as well as the public sector. This can occur, for example, for services that are generally considered to be in the purview of government, but for which government provision is inadequate due, for example, to financial, managerial, and political constraints. This is common in countries with failing public health systems, where citizens and donors alike seek alternative delivery mechanisms. The proliferation of health-related NGOs in Haiti, supported by the United States Agency for International Development (USAID) and other donors, is a case in point (ibid.).

The health-related MDGs "are unachievable without getting services to populations that currently have very little effective access—and particularly the poorest, who are at the greatest health risk and yet have the most limited physical, economic, and cultural access to health services" (ibid.). In the health sector, NGOs are considered—and often are—better at reaching particular population groups, most especially those at the margins of society, who may be underserved by public- and private-sector providers or not served at all. These groups include indigenous populations, women in restrictive societies, commercial sex workers, and slum dwellers. Examples of NGOs effectively responding to the needs of these populations include Prosalud in Bolivia, Building Resources Across the Countries (BRAC) in Bangladesh, Mexfam in Mexico, and Partners for Health in Haiti and Peru (ibid.). Other notable examples are provision of health insurance and key health care services by the Self-Employed Women's Association (SEWA) in India for its members, and Africare's nutrition program targeted to the most isolated people in Uganda and Burundi (S. Smith 2005).

NGOs are also active in health advocacy, whether targeting a specific population or health outcome. Examples include the numerous reproductive health, HIV/AIDS, antitobacco and other advocacy groups working in developing countries. Some of these have strong connections and support from developed-country organizations; others operate independently under the leadership of a committed individual or group (Levine 2004).

In what might be considered a cross between delivering services to hard-to-reach populations and advocacy, Levine highlighted NGOs' comparative advantage in focusing on vital, but socially controversial, health services, which the public sector may shy away from. These include family-planning service delivery, particularly to unmarried women and youth, and programs to combat HIV/AIDS, for example, candid public-information campaigns, promoting behavior change, and condom distribution. This comparative advantage makes NGOs particularly well positioned to make contributions to the maternal health and HIV/AIDS MDGs. While the rich may have ready access to health products and services regarded as controversial, such as condoms and AIDS information, the poor often lack the resources to obtain for themselves what the public sector cannot or will not provide.

Different types of NGOs contribute in different ways. Small NGOs can address local problems, and national NGOs, problems of a national nature, such as BRAC in Bangladesh. While they are not conventional NGOs, as discussed here, nonprofit medical foundations also play a role. Foundations may be able to work well with NGOs, including funding important NGO programs, such as the financial support of the Bill and Melinda Gates Foundation for community activities related to HIV/AIDS in Africa. Some poverty- and development-oriented NGOs are focused exclusively or almost exclusively on health activities, traditionally defined. However, many multisectoral NGOs are involved both in health and in several other fields, including those encompassed within the MDGs, such as education and environment, and those beyond the range of the MDGs, such as community empowerment. BRAC is one of the clearest examples of an NGO that has made major contributions to health, yet is also engaged in other important sectors such as microfinance, education, and legal rights.

NGOs have been key players in international health-policy agendas. The Center for Global Development conducted a review of major global public-health successes, with national, regional, or global scope, and a big health impact (i.e., sustainable for at least five years) that could be attributable to a specific program or set of interventions. The review included evidence to make that attribution using cost-effective methods. Of these, Levine cited five major successes in health programs in developing countries in which NGOs played a central role. These were:

- *Case 1.* Oral rehydration to treat dehydration due to diarrheal disease in Bangladesh, where BRAC played a central role (discussed later in this chapter).
- *Case 2.* Control of onchocerciasis (river blindness), where the first efforts to distribute antibiotics to 19 Central and East African countries (not already covered by the Oncho Control Program) were made by a group of international NGOs (INGOs). Though the Africa Program for Onchocerciasis Control was launched in 1995 and assumed major responsibility for the ivermectin distribution, INGOs have continued to play a large role—through substantial fund-raising, technical capacity, assisting distribution of ivermectin on the ground, and advising the WHO. An NGO coordinating group in Geneva advises the overall program.
- *Case 3.* Trachoma control in Morocco, where Helen Keller International was instrumental in providing services.
- *Case 4.* Guinea worm eradication in Africa, led by the Carter Center.
- *Case 5.* Polio elimination. Rotary International has played a large role in the global polio eradication campaign, having committed over $500 million and contributed hundreds of thousands of volunteers.

Big INGOs played a key role in the last four cases, which were targeted efforts that mobilized large resources for intensive campaigns against major diseases. INGOs were "absolutely essential in mobilizing the leadership, the funding, and actually assisting with the implementation" (Levine 2004).

In the other case (Case 1), a national NGO, BRAC, played the critical role. BRAC's top health official, Mushtaque Chowdhury, confirmed that it has played a central role for the case of oral rehydration therapy (ORT) in Bangladesh (Chowdhury 2004):

> until the 1990s the ORT for diarrhea was just another medical advance, a medical discovery which was kept within the four walls of hospitals. But, BRAC decided to take it to the homes of everybody in the country. Over the decade of the 1980s BRAC took ORT to all families, all mothers in Bangladesh, to their households. BRAC visited 14 million households in the country. So this makes this program the largest culture-based ORT program ever undertaken anywhere in the world.

Beyond teaching, BRAC worked to improve the overall system, focusing on effective monitoring for quality improvement. As a result, there is almost universal knowledge of ORT among the population in Bangladesh. Chowdhury highlighted BRAC's successful sustainability of the ORT program: "The knowledge that has been given in the '80s in Bangladesh is still there, and it has become a part of the culture, in the sense that mothers are transmitting the knowledge to their children."

BRAC also plays a key role in the control of TB in Bangladesh. It has achieved over 90 percent treatment completion through an innovative incentive program. Those seeking treatment are required to deposit roughly $5, which is returned on completion of the treatment. Those who default forfeit the money. BRAC works in close cooperation with the government and has reached about two-thirds of the country (ibid.). This example illustrates how an innovation can be developed and tested by an NGO. Although NGOs generally (outside of nonprofit medical organizations) do not innovate new medicines, they often innovate in service delivery.

With respect to contingencies, Levine (2004) cited four difficulties (paraphrased here) in carrying out the tasks that NGOs might otherwise be well suited for:

1. Weak management capacity and governance. Typically, she claimed, NGOs in a poorly governed country are equally (or almost equally) poorly governed.
2. Small scale, and loss of core comparative advantage when activities "scale up." Efforts to scale up may jeopardize the relationship between NGOs and the communities.

3. Political marginality. NGOs are often viewed "with extreme skepticism by the party in power, as they are often 'parking places' for opposition politicians," potentially restricting their scope of influence.
4. Financial and institutional vulnerability. NGOs typically operate with little reserves and are often dependent on external donors, making them financially vulnerable. They may also be institutionally unsustainable when they are closely tied to a charismatic leader.

Several of these contingencies limit NGO effectiveness in the other categories of comparative advantage as well.

On the other hand, governance of highly effective NGOs in the field of poverty reduction is often reasonably good, especially that of INGOs (for details with case studies from East Africa, see Smith 2004). When the NGO activity overlaps with those traditionally associated with the other two sectors, at their best, NGOs work to build the capacity of those sectors. An example is Africare's efforts to train local governments to take over AIDS education and outreach programs from the very inception of the program in a target district.

NGOs are important actors in the health systems of developing countries, working both with and sometimes at odds with governments. The most successful NGOs are likely to be those with a strong track record, diverse sources of support, and a strong relationship with the public sector (Levine 2004). On the other hand, skepticism is warranted, owing to some NGOs' small scale, financial insecurity, and antagonistic relations with government (ibid.). NGOs have a particular role to play in advocacy and as a watchdog to influence public-sector priority-setting and implementation. The extraordinary success of BRAC in Bangladesh demonstrates that these factors need not be fundamental constraints.

Education

Education[3] is addressed in MDG 2 and as an important target of MDG 3:

- **Goal 2, target:** Ensure that all boys and girls complete primary school.
- **Goal 3, target:** Eliminate gender disparities in primary and secondary education (preferred).

Debates about NGOs' role in the education sector no longer concern whether it is necessary and desirable to include them; rather, particularly after the 1990 Education for All (EFA) conference and the 1994 Delhi Declaration, policy debate focuses primarily on how best to work with NGOs and the private sector. EFA marked the first time NGOs acted as fully credentialed participants in a major international conference. One of the outcomes of deliberations is Article 7, which embraces a role for these and other actors: "National, regional, and local educational authorities have a unique obligation to provide basic education for all, but they cannot be expected to supply every human, financial or organizational requirement for this task" (quoted by Method 2004). Similarly, in 1994, the Delhi Declaration confirmed that the state is no longer considered the primary or solely responsible actor for these goals: "Education is, and must be, a societal responsibility, encompassing governments, families, communities and non-governmental organizations alike; it requires the commitment and participation of all, in a grand alliance that transcends diverse opinions and political positions" (ibid.). More recently, when launching USAID's (2005) new education strategy, James Smith, Acting Assistant Administrator, Bureau for Economic Growth, Agriculture and Trade, cited examples of this multisector embrace: in Burkina Faso, the Minister of Education stated, "If communities build my schools, it costs half the cost and then the communities maintain them." The Education Minister from Honduras told USAID, "I want to build a runway on which private investors can land" (ibid.).

In the last twenty years, expansion of partnerships, inclusive of NGOs, have proven key in terms of broadening civic participation in national-action planning and implementation, innovating and developing alternative approaches, and advocating internationally to maintain EFA as an international development priority. Multisector approaches are particularly needed to address complex needs, such as those of communities affected by HIV/AIDS; child labor; trafficking of children and other exploitative practices; and local infrastructure and community initiatives.

Method (2004) identifies roles for NGOs in the following areas:

- Diversification of education approaches and broad partnerships;
- Decentralization of education administration (not necessarily financing) with substantial roles for parent and community participation;
- Continued advocacy and action planning to increase education opportunities for girls and women, accompanied by administrative and policy reforms to increase school capacities for all;
- Diversification of education models, particularly toward small, multigrade, integrated community schools;
- Early childhood care and development;
- Education of adolescents and young adults, including second-chance options for schooling or schooling equivalent education;

- Special needs of the physically handicapped and those with learning impairments; and
- Education in emergencies, in failed/failing states and in postconflict contexts.

Reported highlights of INGOs' achievements with respect to related advocacy efforts include:

- Forging a coherent and independent network of national and INGOs with a common EFA agenda;
- Raising the visibility and status of basic education;
- Sustaining an international focus on financing EFA and how this relates to debt relief;
- Pressuring international organizations and the Group of 7 industrialized countries to make concrete resource commitments; and
- Securing a place for civil society in policy planning and monitoring at the national and international levels (Murphy and Mundy 2002).

More specifically, Gibbons (2004), drawing from Hartwell (2004), depicts the EFA/MDG problem as a local one, where there is exclusion of particular people in particular situations, and where, for tens of millions, local schools do not work. For example, in the northern regions of Ghana, community settlements tend to be small, sparsely populated, and widely scattered. Delivering EFA there is further complicated by the local belief that formal education alienates children from their original culture. Children in Balochistan, Pakistan, face similar challenges to accessing education, in addition to the complexity of the region's highly diverse population, with many ethnic groups and four major language groups. In urban areas, EFA does not reach the poorest, many of whom live in shantytowns. Countries facing civil conflict and resulting institutional breakdown are even more at risk. According to Gibbons, "Of those countries now unlikely to achieve EFA goals, almost half have areas where there is a history of civil conflict."

Where schools are operating, they do not necessarily contribute meaningfully to EFA. Many school systems are run by inflexible bureaucracies that do not account for or respond to the many constraints to attendance children may face. Furthermore, attendance does not ensure learning. For example, Gibbons reports that in Ghana, fewer than 10 percent of pupils in grade six are able to meet minimum mastery standards for reading comprehension on the national criterion Referenced Test. Additional barriers to attendance and learning include family reliance on child labor, distrust of the government education system, and difficulty in recruiting and retaining teachers who know the local language and culture and are willing to serve in remote areas. Government education systems typically do not conduct outreach and are not relevant for rural girls and women and pastoral communities more generally. For all these reasons, increased financing for the EFA/MDGs alone will not be sufficient to achieve them.

Gibbons summarizes NGOs' contributions as informing and demanding critical policy changes, and supporting and enabling critical policy implementation approaches. In the first instance, NGOs demonstrate outreach/inclusion models, negotiate accreditation and financing of alternative models and absorption of paraprofessional teachers, reorient planning on inclusion, and advocate for a stream of financing for NGOs and community-based action as part of the EFA system. In terms of supporting and enabling policy implementation, NGOs are key in processes of decentralization/localization for ownership, quality, and relevance; action learning/adaptive management for quality, inclusion, and responsiveness; and social mobilization/social action for inclusion and accountability.

A few examples serve to highlight NGOs' comparative advantages in making these contributions. In what Gibbons calls the first generation of NGO contributions, NGOs develop and implement alternative primary education—with multiactor approaches to ensure equity and effectiveness—that are scalable and operate at a systems level, i.e., negotiating sustainable inputs such as training and supporting teachers, governance and finance mechanisms, and appropriate policy frameworks. For example, the Balochistan Community Girls School Project provides full primary school for girls in poor, rural villages. The Project reviewed, revised, and expanded on the government curriculum. Enrollment of girls more than doubled in less than ten years. In the Schools for Life program in northern Ghana, teachers are locally recruited volunteers, with some secondary education. They are supported by the community, paid "soap money" of about $5 per month, and given short induction training and weekly in-service supervisions. BRAC's nonformal primary education in Bangladesh, reviewed earlier, is probably the most known example. Other, smaller-scale voluntary efforts also ensure girls stay in school and succeed. For example, in Egypt, the Coptic Orphans' Valuable Girl Project uses a girls-to-girls mentoring program. Success of these alternative models is attributed, in part, to leadership and commitment, assurance of quality standards, and development of a locally relevant, child-centered curriculum and pedagogy.

In the second generation of EFA contributions, NGOs have embraced a widening variety of approaches. With respect to action learning/adaptive management, Save the Children UK has developed a long-term collaboration in Ethiopia to build regional education-bureau capacity and push it to address underserved needs, and facilitated these bureaus' outreach to pastoral communities to develop alternative primary education. Also in Ethiopia, a range of local NGOs have facilitated decentralization and localization of services (e.g., Relief Society of Tigray, or REST, in the Tigray Region; Afar Pastoralists' Development Association, or APDA, in Afar; and the Forum on Street Children in Dire Dawa). And BRAC's Institute for Education in Development is now engaged in a major program to improve the capabilities of the public-school system.

In the area of social mobilization/social action, Vidayak Sansad in Maharashtra, India, has mobilized to organize a national federation of parent-teacher associations for migrant workers' children and pressured and negotiated with state and local government to finance and accredit alternative models as government services. In Zimbabwe and Ghana, the Campaign for Female Education, or CAMFED, has conducted multisector social mobilization to support girls' education in rural areas. They have negotiated with and enlisted traditional, business, and government leaders; organized a girls'/women's social support association; and facilitated a "girl-friendly" curriculum, materials, and infrastructure enhancements. Finally, national NGOs and networks have been created for advocacy purposes, for example, Haki Elimu in Tanzania, a national citizens' membership organization to support quality, equity, and diversity of education; and the Forum for Education NGOs in Uganda (FENU), a national network for Poverty Reduction Strategies Paper (PRSP) and EFA participants, with district chapters for experience sharing and training.

Environment

The environment[4] is addressed in MDG 7: "Ensure environmental sustainability":

- **General target**: Integrate the principles of sustainable development into country policies and programs and reverse the loss of environmental resources.
- **Target for 2015**: Reduce by half the proportion of people without access to safe drinking water.
- **Target for 2020**: Achieve significant improvements in the lives of at least 100 million slum dwellers.

Of all the MDGs, the goal pertaining to the environment and sustainability (Goal 7) stands out as one where serious concerns not only of achievement, but indeed of Goal conceptualization and specification, are at the fore; NGOs' role for achieving this Goal is therefore hampered. The MDG process is seen as a global public-policy innovation, whereby actors from many nations and from many sectors work toward common development goals. The process itself is progressive, potentially (and, in some cases, actually) effective, and certainly promising, owing largely to the measurability of the specific goals and targets (Levy 2004). However, Levy notes, "The environment hasn't found a very comfortable home in the Millennium Development Goal Process."

For most of the MDGs, there exists a sufficiently robust and legitimate body of knowledge to support the creation and assessment of the specific goals and targets. The environment Goal is definitionally ambiguous, and some argue that the knowledge base is insufficiently developed to warrant more definitional precision; without such precision, evaluation of success and capacity to scale up are frustrated (Levy 2004).

The target related to drinking water is the exception within this Goal: a strong knowledge base exists concerning what works for providing safe drinking water, and programmatic results are directly and clearly measurable. Yet safe drinking water tends not to be the domain of environmentalists—it is the work of development specialists who attend to the problem in ways that are largely unconnected with the rest of the natural environment such as watershed depletion issues (Levy 2004).

Although politically viable coalitions exist for some MDGs to work collaboratively for success, environmental problems are difficult to describe in ways that resonate with global decision-making bodies or conventions. The environmental community has largely been marginalized or out of the mainstream with regard to global processes for development (ibid.). Past environmental successes in the decades prior to the signing of the Millennium Declaration were won through "stealth" approaches that traded on opportunistic acts for environmentalists to record small wins that en masse appeared ad hoc (ibid.).

The first major global opportunity to move environmentalism into a more programmatic posture at the global level came with the 1992 Rio Earth Summit, where very ambitious conventions on biodiversity, conservation, and climate change were proposed without sufficient attention paid to implementation capacity by actors on the ground nor to generation of sufficient (global) political will to effect such grand change (ibid.). The Johannesburg World Summit Type II Partnerships, geared toward promoting cross-sectoral partnerships for environmental sustainability, produced little in the way of uniting the sectors, tended to reinforce existing practices and policies instead of promoting the MDGs, and were largely uncorrelated with the prevalence or severity of environmental problems (Teegen 2003a; Levy 2004). Similar effects of "rubber stamping" of existing initiatives are corroborated in the environmental program mapping initiative of the World Bank and Conservation International in 120 eco-regions in Latin America that showed hot spots such as the Amazon receiving relatively little environmental attention compared with urban areas such as Mexico City (Price 2004).

The genesis of Goal 7 itself speaks to the political challenges associated with global policy initiatives. UN Secretary General staff were instructed to identify the goals related to environmental sustainability that the member governments have already endorsed so as not to be controversial. An examination of the history of global declarations (and signatories) found little by way of consensus around the environment, in contrast to findings to support specific goals with prior backing on poverty, education, hunger, and the like. And no intergovernmental process was convened to develop such specific environmental goals—this important work is left on the table (Levy 2004).

These disappointing outcomes of international efforts to date occur despite the active and broad involvement of a wide range of international and local, Northern and Southern NGOs in fora such as the Johannesburg Summit (Odhiambo 2004). The inability of civil society to effectively coalesce across focus areas and geographic and political boundaries may be to blame (Starik 2004; Odhiambo 2004). Nonetheless, many bilateral agencies (e.g., Germany), multilateral lenders, and developing countries have incorporated the MDGs into their own conceptualizations of, and commitment to, sustainable development (Levy 2004). For example, the World Bank's environmental impact statements have two decades of accumulated institutionalization (Price 2004), which allows for a more ready acceptance of the MDGs into their decision-making architecture.

A significant challenge for Goal 7 concerns the perceptions of, and realities concerning tradeoffs between environmental protection and human development. Climate change and biodiversity initiatives are prominent examples where common perceptions impose an at-odds relationship between environmentalism and human development, yet on-the-ground efforts undertaken by NGOs working in the developing world actively address the inherent connections and possible synergies between the natural environment and human development (Levy 2004).

One approach for resolving this perceived tension between Goal 7 and the other MDGs would involve embedding Goal 7 within the other MDGs—specifying individual targets that relate to environmental sustainability for each other Goal (Anonymous 2004). Yet this approach might orphan nonhuman issues such as biodiversity that are principal components of environmental sustainability (Levy 2004). Another approach would be to utilize specific targets for the environmental sustainability goal that map more closely to the spirit of human development, such as access to acreage of arable land (Price 2004). Ultimately, the MDG process will consider ways to recognize some natural linkages among the other Goals and environmental sustainability, while being honest about the very real trade-offs that may exist in the short and/or long run (Levy 2004).

Current practice increasingly exacerbates the conflict between environmental sustainability and achievement of the other goals (viz. the general absence of considerations on environmental sustainability in the PRSPs), which threatens the ability for the environment to "have a place at the table" in future development discussions (ibid.). This may stem from an "elitist" association with environmental sustainability that privileges natural protection over human development. Differences in citizen perceptions and conceptualizations of environmental challenges between the North (species preservation, wild lands preservation) and the South (safe water, breathable air, trash collection), as seen in opinion polling, bear this out (Price 2004). Redefining environmentalism in terms of human productivity maximization may provide a path for promoting human and environmental development in tandem (ibid.).

Other challenges regarding the conceptualization of the Goal and its implementation remain. The current environmental targets are urban-centric, yet much environmental degradation and problems of poverty are found in rural areas, where roughly half of the world's population—and up to three-quarters of those in extreme poverty—lives (ibid.). Environmental improvement inherently promotes the well-being of largely agrarian rural poor communities (ibid.). The targets are also silent on the environmental pressures stemming from concentrated population growth in many developing areas. Population growth may well present the single biggest challenge to environmental sustainability and overall human development in the future (ibid.).

NGOs cannot act alone in addressing these issues; the scale of environmental problems are often too vast for NGOs' capabilities and resources (Schmidt-Traub 2004). The pressing problems may require regulatory reform and enforcement at the national level (Odhiambo 2004), but such approaches are complicated in matters that span national borders, such as climate change (Teegen 2003a). In these cases, INGOs can fill important roles as brokers between the sectors to bridge differences in incentives and perspectives between otherwise local players in effecting positive environmental impact (Teegen 2003b).

Private-sector involvement, whereby market-based incentives are leveraged, is also key. Examples of successful initiatives include Care Kenya's introduction of reasonably priced packaged chlorine for at-home treatment of piped water from (polluted) Lake Victoria (Odhiambo 2004), and Starbuck's association with the Smithsonian Migratory Bird Center's efforts to promote and market shade-grown coffee from Central America (Price 2004).

Scaling up these programs requires the involvement of many actors working in coordinated fashion. Where local NGOs are small and compete fiercely for donor funding and local legitimacy, such coordination is difficult to achieve (Odhiambo 2004). The inherently long-term nature of environmental solutions makes these efforts less politically attractive and less pressing in terms of citizen engagement (ibid.). National or international programs to promote awareness of, and transparency in, environmental programming might be a first step in enabling greater collaboration and/or avoiding duplication of efforts in the future, but the costs involved in such reporting activities are great for participants and coordinators alike (Price 2004; Odhiambo 2004).

Schmidt-Traub (2004) provides a summary of key issues for the targets associated with Goal 7, overall targets 9, 10, and 11, as well as associated contingencies that relate to the role of NGOs in achieving this Goal. Target 9 (the first listed under Goal 7 in table 1.1) seeks the integration of principles of sustainable development into country policies and programs and the reversal of environmental resource loss. The target is problematic for a number of reasons. First, it is nonquantitative and poorly defined. Second, it poses challenges to both developed and developing countries, though the particular environmental challenges and associated environmental results differ greatly. Third, meeting the target is highly dependent on progress in other sectors (e.g., environmentally sustainable agricultural practices). With respect to NGO roles, a large number of INGOs are active in this area and provide funding to initiatives in developing countries. NGOs have played a particularly strong role—both at the international and local levels—in conservation and biotechnology. In this area, more than any other, international processes are highly developed and have been very supportive of a strong role for civil society (e.g., the Rio and Johannesburg summits, Agenda 21, and the UN Commission on Sustainable Development). More locally, some NGOs are well positioned to facilitate negotiations among local stakeholders as well as to deliver training and behavior-change programs.

Target 10 (the second listed under Goal 7, table 1.1) seeks to halve, by 2015, the proportion of people without sustainable access to safe drinking water and sanitation. Progress to meeting this target has slowed dramatically in many developing countries (especially in sub-Saharan Africa and South Asia) since the decline of resources after the Water Decade of the 1980s. No intergovernmental process focuses specifically on this target. Financing is critical, as the poor cannot afford to pay the full operating costs, let alone the capital costs. It is critical to distinguish, and attend to, financing, delivery, and operation and maintenance of the systems.

In most developing countries, financing remains the responsibility of government. Aside from resources, the target is also complicated by the differentiated needs and associated strategies for urban and rural areas. Many NGOs, mostly local, are active in water and sanitation. They mobilize communities and build awareness for developing sustainable clean water and sanitation systems. This includes negotiating among community stakeholders and across sectors, as well as delivering hygiene education. Through advocacy and community-sensitization campaigns, NGOs can contribute to larger-scale change, often drawing on low-cost technology. Sometimes these efforts begin with NGOs' demonstration of innovations. Sometimes these NGOs represent women and address the gender dimension and inequities associated with water and sanitation. Some INGOs, such as WaterAid, also play an important role, especially in advocacy and innovation dissemination. On the other hand, integrated water-resources management requires government intervention, and NGOs are not capable of providing the scale necessary to meet all of the needs.

Target 11 (the third listed under Goal 7, in table 1.1) more generally addresses the need for significant improvements in the lives of slum dwellers—at least 100 million by 2020. As with water and sanitation, there is no intergovernmental or international process to support target 11. In most MDG reports and PRSPs, target 11 is not mentioned. On the other hand, target 11 is not unreasonably ambitious. Current trajectories indicate that within one generation roughly 1.8 billion people are expected to live in slums. This means the target would be met by improving the lives of less than 10 percent of projected slum dwellers. Proportionally, sub-Saharan Africa has the largest population of slum dwellers, while the largest numbers live in South Asia.

Schmidt-Traub (2004) notes the high activity of local NGOs and community-based organizations (CBOs) in slum upgrading. They have formed national federations (e.g., in India, Thailand, and South Africa), and some of these have recently formed international partnerships to facilitate knowledge and experience exchange. Local NGOs are well placed to negotiate among stakeholders within slum communities, as well as represent these communities to other actors and coordinate joint construction of water and sanitation or other service delivery. They can mobilize communities for construction, operations, and maintenance as they introduce low-cost technologies, demonstrating innovative approaches to meet slum dwellers' needs (e.g., in solid-waste disposal). NGOs may also provide savings and credit services that enable slum dwellers to pay for some services. On the other hand, policy reform is still required to meet target 11; for example, slum dwellers often need reform in land-tenure rights as well as zoning laws, and NGOs typically lack the capacity for large-scale infrastructure (e.g., energy and transport).

Gender

The gender component of the MDGs is most explicit in Goal 3, "Promote gender equality and empower women." As of this writing, the first MDG target has been missed: to eliminate gender disparity in primary and secondary education "preferably" by 2005. While this target, alone, would not ensure Goal 3, it is a significant contributing factor.

It is difficult to consider NGOs' role in implementing Goal 3 without first acknowledging the controversy surrounding gender and the MDGs.[5] According to Grown (2004), on the one hand, the presence of Goal 3 signifies an important success on the part of women's organizations and the women's movement to put gender squarely on such a mainstream agenda. On the other hand, Goal 3 is a very incomplete extension of other international agreements to date, most notably the Cairo Program of Action (International Conference on Population and Development, 1994) and the Beijing Platform for Action (Fourth World Conference on Women, 1995). And Goal 3 raises the perennial question of whether or not the effectiveness of addressing gender issues is compromised by creating set-aside programs and goals. Indeed, gender issues are implicated in all eight of the MDGs, though this is not made explicit in their targets.

In response to these weaknesses, the UN Millennium Project Taskforce 3 (for Goal 3)[6] has developed a Framework of Gender Equality and Empowerment, which encompasses three domains: capabilities (as measured through education, health, and nutrition), opportunities (includes access to economic assets, resources such as income and employment, and political opportunities), and security (reduced vulnerability to violence and conflict). This framework emphasizes that gender is multidimensional and that progress in one domain to the exclusion of the others will not lead to gender equality and women's empowerment. Accordingly, the framework outlines six priorities for action, reincorporating many of the aims set forth and agreed to in the earlier international gender conferences. These priorities encompass girls' and women's access to secondary education; sexual and reproductive health services and education; gender-supportive infrastructure; property, inheritance rights, and job opportunities; and representation in national politics. The sixth priority is to combat violence against girls and women.

Grown (2004) also outlines some implications of the MDG controversy for NGOs. Most importantly, and following from the controversy outlined above, gender needs to be mainstreamed into all of the MDGs in order to achieve gender equity and women's empowerment. This will require participation in, and ownership of, the process on the part of women's organizations and NGOs to champion these issues, advocate strongly for this mainstreaming, and demonstrate effective approaches for meeting the targets. While NGOs may have comparative advantages in these activities, it is not clear that women's organizations will feel compelled to use the MDGs as a platform for advocacy and action. As noted earlier in this chapter, already, the MDGs represent backpedaling on earlier agreements that these organizations championed. And the experience of local NGOs and women's organizations in the national PRSP processes confirms that when these organizations are invited to participate, their contributions are not often reflected in the final PRSP. On a much more operational level, these organizations do not have sufficient funding to effectively press for accountability with respect to gender and the MDGs. Such efforts will require sustained participation, data collection, and analysis. Funding for such activities is limited for government mechanisms as well.

Richardson (2004) presents additional implications for NGOs' role in achieving Goal 3, based on five trends. First is the proliferation of business models, which NGOs are expected to adopt for social development. Specifically, NGOs are pressured to scale up and to be results focused. These approaches tend to drive out attention to process and promote top-down approaches based on efficiency—characteristics that tend to further marginalize women and contradict the way women have traditionally organized. Second is an emphasis on funding projects as opposed to integrated, holistic approaches. Third, 9/11 shifted the focus of human security to a more macro-level global and state security, potentially overriding women's presence in the debate and response to human security at the microlevel. Fourth is the mobilization against reproductive health and related education, which limits women's organizations' ability to empower women and meet their holistic needs. Finally, the very success of women's emphasis on mainstreaming has yielded further limits on women's organizations' ability to track progress on gender equity and women's empowerment. Many organizations claim they are working toward these goals but they do not produce data to confirm these efforts.

Local NGOs are impeded by these trends (Richardson 2004). Taking, for example, the target of girls' access to secondary education, local NGOs understand that girls' access (and attendance) is dependent on a complex set of interrelated socioeconomic factors, not just the existence of the services themselves. Hence, without community mobilization, this and other gender targets are not likely to be achieved. Yet, the trends outlined above do not support such community mobilization for integrated, holistic approaches. Furthermore, once girls acquire secondary education, in order to be empowered, they will need to have access to other strategic resources and opportunities. This relates to local NGOs' desire for intergenerational approaches that would address both girls and women.

Richardson (2004) provided examples from the Centre for Development and Population Activities (CEDPA) to illustrate the kind of integrative approaches that are possible and desired by target communities. The Better Life Pro-Actions for Girls Model seeks to link the health and education sectors by providing a holistic, nonformal education curriculum of life-skills training. The curriculum includes gender issues, civic participation, engaging with partners, and reproductive health. Outcomes have included delayed marriage, links to formal education systems, and community support. Based on community demand, the model was extended to boys. CEDPA also responds to the intergenerational concern noted earlier in this chapter by focusing on parenting, which includes women's literacy.

Kek Galabru (2004) provides a more in-depth case discussion of gender issues in Cambodia. She specifies four main obstacles to achieving gender and women's empowerment in that country. First is political will. As with the human-rights treaties that have gone before, the Government of Cambodia has endorsed the MDGs but shows no signs of political will to actually implement them. Second is the legal system, which is known to be partisan, incompetent, and corrupt. Third, corruption is more generally widespread and is both the product of, and a contributor to, the lack of political will and ineffective judicial system. Finally, women face discrimination in a range of spheres. Related priorities of women's organizations in Cambodia are access to health care, education, legal aid, employment, participation in local government, and combating violence against women.

NGOs in Cambodia play essential roles in each of these priority areas. In the health sector, they provide training of local providers, nurses, and midwives, and deliver reproductive health services. NGOs are also making antiretroviral drugs available to those infected with HIV/AIDS who would otherwise not be able to afford them. NGO-trained doctors still provide service for a fee, though significantly less than what the market might prescribe, given the low supply. These doctors are thus in high demand and cannot reach all those in need. Approximately 51 percent of women in Cambodia are illiterate, and a recent Oxfam report (2003) found that only 22 percent of women can read the newspaper. In the education sector, NGOs provide informal education to children for free (with support from UNICEF) and skills and vocational training to women.

In the legal sector, NGOs provide legal assistance to women in prison and to victims of violence and of trafficking for prostitution and forced labor. NGOs also raise awareness of these crimes against women and provide shelters to women who are rescued from them. NGOs provide support to women factory workers, again, raising awareness regarding working conditions, wages, and the violation of labor standards. NGOs also provide training on labor rights to women seeking employment in factories in other countries. Finally, women's organizations are working to promote women's participation in local government, focusing particularly on commune elections, as well as promoting women as judges, prosecutors, and police.

In the area of violence against women, NGOs have lobbied the Government to pass laws to enable the prosecution of domestic-violence offenders, but to date a drafted law has not been approved by the Cambodian National Assembly. NGOs also provide counseling, shelter, and humanitarian assistance to victims of violence. As President and Chair of the Cambodian League for the Promotion and Defense of Human Rights (LICADHO), Galabru documented her organization's experience providing legal aid to victims of violence (e.g., rape, trafficking, acid attacks), recounting the many challenges to prosecution, from the absence of a legal framework, to lack of political will, corruption, and the society itself. For example, government and party officials, who ideally would take a lead in combating these crimes against women, are instead implicated in cross-national trafficking webs and patronage of child brothels. LICADHO engages in advocacy, training, and raising awareness to combat these obstacles. NGOs also work to rehabilitate and reintegrate victims into their family and society.

Galabru also identified challenges within the NGO sector in Cambodia. In short, this sector is not immune to the corruption endemic in society. There have been cases where staff members of an NGO shelter for women rescued from prostitution "resold" the women into another brothel. Government–NGO relations are also tense, leading government officials to set up their own NGO and "infiltrate among the workers." Thus, the NGO sector itself cannot know who to trust and cannot rely on the judicial system to hold NGOs and their representatives to account.

Cambodia's experience reveals how in some countries the burden for service delivery and particularly for achieving Goal 3 is falling to under-resourced NGOs. Should NGOs be doing the work of governments? This perspective supports the agenda of mainstreaming gender issues. However, the women's movement may have moved too fast in its mainstreaming efforts, losing autonomy and space in the process. And mainstreaming remains a daunting challenge.

Wolchik (2004) stresses the importance of context when considering the prospects for achieving the MDGs and NGOs' role in a particular country. Focusing on Central and Eastern Europe, she emphasizes the importance of history with respect to women's and NGOs' roles and opportunities. She also highlights the challenges of trying to achieve these MDGs in political situations that are in flux, with unstable party systems. As many countries in the region are joining the European Union (EU) or seeking EU membership, they are required to harmonize their legal frameworks, including those related to gender equity and women's empowerment. However, it remains to be seen if individual countries will assert the political will to implement these laws once they join the EU. Some of the experience in Poland is relatively more promising. Here, women's groups have had an impact on policy through providing expertise and information to lawmakers, for example, regarding laws on violence against women. Generally, the greatest challenges to achieving gender equity and women's empowerment in the region concern political will, and the dispersed and under-resourced nature of national women's movements. Wolchik concludes by stressing the importance of international organizations, such as the UN and the EU, to hold national governments accountable in following through on their commitment to the MDGs and related legal frameworks.

Findings

While each of the sectors has unique characteristics and challenges, several themes emerge from this application. First, as table 9.1 illustrates, NGO roles frequently emerge in response to limitations in the other sectors. Second, the general potential comparative advantages of NGOs are consistent across the sectors. Similarly, many of the effectiveness contingencies are common across the sectors. Overall, the findings confirm NGOs' potential roles in the delivery of specialized public goods and services, common-pool resources, and advocacy. Examples in each of the sectors support the effectiveness contingencies identified in chapter 4.

On the other hand, the sectors vary in the potential for NGOs to fulfill these roles, and potentially in the desire for NGOs to do so. In the health and gender sectors, several of the targets remain politically controversial or socially stigmatic, presenting additional challenges to acquiring financial, regulatory, and institutional support. In the education sector, NGOs risk creating additional dependencies as they fill gaps in what would ideally be government roles and responsibilities. And in the environmental sector, the lack of clarity in the general target for Goal 7 potentially exacerbates NGOs' challenge to acquire legitimacy and resources as they address needs that are sometimes (perceived or otherwise) contradictory to other MDG targets. Chapter 10 further explores these findings and the contributions of the other chapters to explore policy implications for identifying appropriate roles and contingency factors for NGO contributions to achieving the MDGs.

Table 9.1 NGO roles, sector response, comparative advantages, and effectiveness contingencies

Roles	Sector response	Comparative advantages	Effectiveness contingencies	Examples
Health				
Deliver local health services (Specialized public goods, using specialized knowledge, filling gaps) Addresses targets in Goal 1 (nutrition programs), Goal 4, (preventive and curative services to reduce the child mortality rate), Goal 5 (preventive and curative services to reduce deaths in childbirth), Goal 6, (preventive and curative services to combat HIV/AIDS, TB, malaria, and other major diseases), and Goal 7 (train and support communities in building and maintaining safe-water supplies)	• Extend activities when government is unable to reach remote areas, meet specialized needs, or has expertise and resource constraints or when government is unwilling to target/specialize to particular populations or regions • In some countries in Africa, civil society organizations with religious roots, including NGOs, operate on the order of half of the hospital beds, and are often the sole providers of health services in some rural areas	• Innovation • Demonstration • Flexibility • Knowing clients and local communities • Reaching the hard to reach, particularly the poorest of the poor as well as marginalized communities • Potential legitimacy as a broker among various stakeholders • Community/social mobilization • Cross-national sharing of lessons learned • Community understanding and trust, enabling community commitment and buy-in	• NGOs may exhibit financial and institutional vulnerability, which may be reduced through sustainable financing through mainstreaming into government policy and implementation frameworks • Weak management capacity and governance • Small scale, and inability to effectively "scale up" • Political marginality, viewed as base for opposition • NGO credibility and access to decision-making bodies • Commitment to understanding and meeting specialized needs	• Immunization and nutrition boosters: Save the Children, Indonesia • Maternal- and child-health services delivery programs: BRAC in Bangladesh, Project Hope in Malawi • Family-planning services: Profamilia in Colombia (delivered through 35 centers throughout the country) • Safe-water provision: Roundabout Playpumps (associated with a for-profit firm) in South Africa, Mozambique, and Zambia • AIDS Services: The AIDS Support Organization, Uganda • Health services for the poor: Partners for Health in Haiti

Developing and adapting strategies for health-service delivery	• Working with program participants and clients to develop new strategies for health-service delivery	• Credibility with communities targeted for mobilization	• Deworming: International Christian Support Fund, Kenya
	• Innovation	• Local knowledge of/experience with community	• Identifying health needs of members, responding by creating women's cooperatives to address them, such as midwifery: Self-Employed Women's Association in India
		• Repository of expertise	• Starting with addressing a need that is widely recognized and prioritized by clients, such as day care, and expanding programs to address health care needs that emerge in service provision: Mother Child Day Care Center Services, Uganda

(Continued)

Table 9.1 (*Continued*)

Roles	Sector response	Comparative advantages	Effectiveness contingencies	Examples
				• Integrating health with needs of community development: Gram Vikas Rural Health and Environment Program, India
				• Integration of health and nutrition programs with microfinance: Freedom Fom Hunger Credit with Education program, Ghana; Project Hope health banks, Ecuador, Honduras
				• Prosalud in Bolivia
				• Health shebika program, oral rehydration therapy education program: BRAC
				• Mexfam in Mexico
				• Health insurance programs for the poor: NGOs such as SEWA, BRAC, Grameen

Function				
Capacity-building of other service providers	• International NGOs build government capacity, especially at local levels as well as build capacity of CBOs • Building capacity of private-sector actors in health, including cooperatives	• Expertise • Innovation in training and technology-transfer strategies	• Supportive policy framework • Recognized expertise and legitimacy of NGO by targeted providers	• NGOs training doctors in Cambodia. • Training volunteer-community family-planning workers: CARE in Ethiopia
Coordinate communities to identify and respond to needs	• Government capacity failure • Coordination failure	• Knowing clients and local communities; culturally and socially "close" to the communities that they serve, and trusted by patients and clients • Managing local conflicts and fostering joint learning • Reaching the poorest of the poor and marginalized communities	• Credibility with targeted communities • Limited personal risk to those who would participate • Local diversity does not prevent community problem solving	• Identifying, educating, and helping communities sustainably address nutrition issues such as *kworshiokor*: Africare Food Security Initiative, Uganda and Burundi
Social mobilization	• Government political will • Coordination failure	• Knowledge, experience, and potential credibility and trust with range of actors	• Credibility with diverse actors • As above	
Advocacy • Network mobilization	• Political will • Additive expertise/innovation	• Knowledge, experience, and potential credibility with range of actors	• Enabling legal frameworks	• TB program advocacy by Partners for Health notably in Haiti, Russia, and Peru

(*Continued*)

Table 9.1 (*Continued*)

Roles	Sector response	Comparative advantages	Effectiveness contingencies	Examples
• Media/public attention (both domestic and international) • Monitoring/accountability of commitments • Creating space for civil society in policy dialogues • Lobbying governments		• Potential legitimacy • Demonstration/innovation	• Credibility and access to decision-making bodies • Ethos of democratic practice, accountability, and responsiveness • Access to information, and information and dissemination networks (national and international) • Potential repercussions for inconsistent action • Mechanisms (formal and informal) for communicating with governments and donors • Local-level presence and relationships	• Organizing to ensure that women's health priorities were addressed in UN meetings and declarations, such as the 1994 Conference on Population Cairo Program of Action and the 1995 Beijing Fourth World Conference for Women Platform for Action • Playing lead both as donor and as advocate on major health issues, such as guinea worm eradication in Africa (the Carter Center), polio (Rotary)
Education				
Deliver alternative primary education (specialized public goods, filling gaps)	• Capacity limitations: government unable to reach remote areas, meet specialized needs, expertise and resource constraints	• Innovation • Demonstration • Flexibility	• Sustainable financing through mainstreaming into government policy and implementation frameworks	• Balochistan Community Girls School Project • Schools for Life, Northern Ghana

| | Political will: government unwilling to target/ specialize to particular populations or regions | • Knowing clients and local communities
• Reaching the hard to reach
• Potential legitimacy as a broker among various stakeholders
• Community/social mobilization
• Cross-national sharing of lessons learned
• Community understanding and trust enabling community commitment and buy-in
• Reaching the poorest of the poor
• Managing local conflicts and fostering joint learning | • Absence of regulatory constraints to experimentation and delivery
• NGO credibility and access to decision-making bodies
• Commitment to understanding and meeting specialized needs
• Credibility with communities targeted for mobilization
• Local diversity does not prevent community problem solving
• Local knowledge of/ experience with community
• Requisite capacity, expertise | • BRAC, Bangladesh
• Coptic Orphans Valuable Girl Project, Egypt
• UNICEF-funded informal education in Cambodia
• Vocational education for women in Cambodia
• Save the Children USA, nonformal primary schools, e.g., Mali, Uganda |
| Public-service delivery extension (decentralization/ localization) | • As above | • As above | | • Save the Children UK, Ethiopia
• Local NGOs in Ethiopia (REST, APDA, Forum on Street Children) |

(Continued)

Table 9.1 (*Continued*)

Roles	Sector response	Comparative advantages	Effectiveness contingencies	Examples
Capacity-building of other service providers	• Government capacity/expertise constraints	• Expertise • Supportive mission/will • Facilitation	• Supportive policy framework • Recognized expertise and legitimacy of NGO by targeted providers	• Balochistan Community Girls School Project • Schools for Life program, northern Ghana
Coordinate communities to identify and respond to needs	• Government capacity failure • Coordination failure	• Knowing clients and local communities • Potential legitimacy • Facilitation/ empowerment • Managing local conflicts and fostering joint learning • Reaching the poorest of the poor	• Credibility with targeted communities • Limited personal risk to those who would participate • Local diversity does not prevent community problem solving	• Balochistan Community Girls School Project • Schools for Life program, northern Ghana
Build community capacity to interface with other actors	• Government political will; government capacity to understand local needs, opportunities, and constraints	• Knowledge, experience, and potential credibility with range of actors • As above	• Credibility with diverse actors • As above	• Schools for Life, northern Ghana
Social mobilization	• Government political will • Coordination failure	• Knowledge, experience, and potential credibility with range of actors • As above	• Credibility with diverse actors • As above	• Vidayak Sansad, Maharashtra, India • CAMFED, Zimbabwe and Ghana

EFA MDG supportive advocacy • Network mobilization • Media/public attention • Monitoring/accountability of commitments • Creating space for civil society in policy dialogues • Infusion of expertise	• Political will • Additive expertise/innovation • Knowledge, experience, and potential credibility with range of actors • Potential legitimacy • Demonstration/innovation	• Enabling legal frameworks • Credibility and access to decision-making bodies • Ethos of democratic practice, accountability, and responsiveness • Access to information and information and dissemination networks (national and international) • Potential repercussions for inconsistent action • Mechanisms (formal and informal) for communicating with governments and donors • Local-level presence and relationships	• Haki Elimu, Tanzania • FENU, Uganda
Environment Advocacy for regulatory and policy changes	• Government political will • Knowledge, experience, and potential legitimacy as a broker among various stakeholders	• Operational capacity to operate at national and international levels	• Phasing out environmentally harmful subsidies • Logging concessions

(*Continued*)

Table 9.1 (*Continued*)

Roles	Sector response	Comparative advantages	Effectiveness contingencies	Examples
			• Political mandate to negotiate internationally	• Community rights, including those of slum dwellers
Negotiating among stakeholders/community problem solving	• Narrow view of challenge and potential solutions	• Knowing clients and local communities	• Credibility with targeted communities	• Communal access to grazing lands or forests
	• Common-pool resources/ free-rider problem	• Potential legitimacy	• Limited personal risk to those who would participate	• Water and sanitation access, operations, and maintenance
		• Facilitation/ empowerment		
		• Managing local conflicts and fostering joint learning	• Local diversity does not prevent community problem solving	• Slum upgrading and resettlement
		• Reaching the poorest of the poor		
Capacity building, community mobilization, and training and behavior change programs	• As above	• Knowledge, experience, and potential credibility with range of actors	• Credibility with diverse actors	• Agricultural extension
			• Limited scale	• Forest and water management
		• Ability (though not universal) to represent women's concerns	• As above	• Water and sanitation, e.g., Orangi in Pakistan
		• As above		• Hygiene education in support of clean water and sanitation

| Providing sector expertise | Limited incentives to develop particular expertise to support public goods and address externalities | • Commitment to public good, values, vision
• Flexibility
• Innovation and demonstration
• Disseminating low-cost technologies | • Capacity, credibility, and funding issues (including policy framework to enable NGOs to receive large amounts of external funding)
• Limited scale | • IUCN's (the World Conservation Union) work on biodiversity (e.g. Red List)
• World Resources Institute work on sustainable forestry and agriculture
• Local NGOs in water and sanitation, e.g., large-scale rural latrine programs (e.g., India)
• Sulabh double-pit latrine
• Solid-waste disposal in slums |
| Water and sanitation service delivery | • Capacity limitations: government unable to reach remote areas, meet specialized needs, expertise and resource constraints
• Political will: government unwilling to target/ specialize to particular populations or regions | • Innovation
• Demonstration
• Flexibility
• Cost efficiency
• Knowing clients and local communities
• Reaching the hard to reach | • Sustainable financing through mainstreaming into government policy and implementation frameworks
• Absence of regulatory constraints to experimentation and delivery | • Orangi, Pakistan |

(Continued)

Table 9.1 (*Continued*)

Roles	Sector response	Comparative advantages	Effectiveness contingencies	Examples
		• Potential legitimacy as a broker among various stakeholders	• NGO credibility and access to decision-making bodies	
		• Community/social mobilization	• Commitment to understanding and meeting specialized needs	
		• Community understanding and trust enabling community commitment and buy-in	• Credibility with communities targeted for mobilization	
		• Reaching the poorest of the poor	• Local diversity does not prevent community problem solving	
		• Managing local conflicts and fostering joint learning	• Local knowledge of/ experience with community	
			• Requisite capacity, expertise	
Gender				
Policy influence, political will	• Lack of political will	• Knowledge, experience, and potential credibility with range of actors	• Faith in the MDGs as an appropriate mechanism for pressing for gender	• ICRW
		• Potential legitimacy		• CEDPA

			equity and women's empowerment • Resources to support monitoring and advocacy	• LICADHO, Cambodia (domestic violence laws, labor laws, trafficking laws; includes advocacy and services for prosecution)
Policy influence, setting agendas; mainstreaming gender into all of the MDGs (e.g., Taskforce 3, Framework of Gender Equality and Empowerment)	• Narrow view of challenge and potential solutions	• Demonstration/ innovation • Community/social mobilization • Cross-national sharing of lessons learned • Expertise • Potential legitimacy as a broker among various stakeholders • As above	• As above • Credibility and access to decision-making bodies • Ethos of democratic practice, accountability, and responsiveness • Access to information, and information and dissemination networks (national and international) • Potential repercussions for inconsistent action • Mechanisms (formal and informal) for communicating with governments and donors	• ICRW • Gender Action

(Continued)

Table 9.1 (Continued)

Roles	Sector response	Comparative advantages	Effectiveness contingencies	Examples
			• Local-level presence and relationships	
			• Resources	
			• IGO and government political will	
Awareness raising	• Lack of political will	• Knowing clients and local communities	• Activist repercussions are not severe	• ICRW
		• Reaching the hard to reach	• Media and other information-dissemination outlets exist and are supportive	• LICADHO, Cambodia
		• Reaching the poorest of the poor	• Access to information, and information and dissemination networks (national and international)	
		• Community understanding and trust	• Potential repercussions for inconsistent action	
		• Potential legitimacy as a representative of clients and local communities	• Mechanisms (formal and informal) for communicating with governments and donors	
		• Community/social mobilization		
		• Cross-national sharing of lessons learned		

Service delivery

- Education: formal, nonformal, vocational, literacy
- Training: life skills, health-service providers, labor laws/rights
- Health: reproductive health services, HIV/AIDS treatment, maternal and child health
- Legal assistance: imprisoned women, victims of violence (e.g., domestic, rape, trafficking for prostitution, and labor, acid attacks)
- Humanitarian assistance: counseling, shelter, reintegration/rehabilitation

- Innovation
- Demonstration
- Flexibility
- Knowing clients and local communities
- Reaching the hard to reach
- Potential legitimacy as a broker among various stakeholders
- Cross-national sharing of lessons learned
- Community understanding and trust-enabling community commitment and buy-in
- Reaching the poorest of the poor

- Local-level presence and relationships
- Resources
- Legal frameworks supportive of service area (e.g., reproductive health, subsidized anti-retorviral drugs, education legal frameworks as above)
- Incentive structures and resource support for integrative, holistic approaches
- NGO transparency and reporting on gender programming, and gender-disaggregated program results
- Availability of effective legal recourse; functioning judiciary and government transparency

- CEDPA
- Better Life Pro-Actions for Girls Model
- LICADHO, Cambodia (vocational education for women, legal services, labor law training, health services, etc.)

(Continued)

Table 9.1 (*Continued*)

Roles	Sector response	Comparative advantages	Effectiveness contingencies	Examples
		• Managing local conflicts and fostering joint learning • Community mobilization for integrative, holistic approaches	• NGO sector has accountability ethos and recourse for prosecuting corrupt members	
Promoting participation of women in politics	• Political failure (non-representative)	• Community/social mobilization • Knowledge, experience, and potential credibility with range of actors	• Some degree of cohesiveness in women's movement • Mechanisms for representation exist	• LICADHO and other women's organizations in Cambodia • Asian Women in Politics (AWIP)

Notes

1. This section draws heavily from Levine (2004), with contributions from Chowdhury (2004).
2. Several previous UN conferences and agreements have addressed health and development. For example, as discussed in the gender section below, the Cairo Program of Action that emerged from the 1994 UN conference on population and development addressed reproductive health rights and goals, and the1995 Beijing Fourth World Conference for Women approved a Platform for Action setting out actions that governments are expected to take to promote women's empowerment, with women's health a central concern.
3. The overview of NGO roles at the macro level is based on Method (2004); micro level practice and examples are taken from Gibbons (2004).
4. The overview of NGO roles is based on Schmidt-Traub (2004); the limits to MDGs vis-à-vis the environment is based on Levy (2004) and Price (2004); micro level practices and examples are taken from Odhiambo (2004).
5. The discussion of the problematic nature of Goal 3 and the UN Millennium Taskforce 3 response draws from Grown (2004).
6. The UN Taskforces are charged with helping the UN system and member governments to develop operational strategies to support achievement of the MDGs. Taskforce 3 includes representatives of the women's movement, academia, and UN agencies.

References

Anonymous. Question posed of environment MDG panelists at "The Role of NGOs in Achieving the Millennium Development Goals" Conference, George Washington University International NGO Team, George Washington University, Washington, D.C., May 13, 2004.

Chowdhury, Mushtaque. Founding Director of BRAC's Research and Evaluation Division, Deputy Executive Director, BRAC, and Dean, BRAC University James P. Grant School of Public Health. "Achieving Health MDGs: NGOs can Play a Significant Role." Presentation at "The Role of NGOs in Achieving the Millennium Development Goals" Conference, George Washington University International NGO Team, George Washington University, Washington, D.C., May 13–14, 2004.

Galabru, Kek. Founder and President, LICADHO; Founder and Chair, Committee for Free and Fair Elections in Cambodia; Founder and Chair, Cambodian Committee for Women. Presentation at "The Role of NGOs in Achieving the Millennium Development Goals" Conference, session on Women's Empowerment and Gender Equity, George Washington University International NGO Team, George Washington University, Washington, D.C., June 7, 2004.

Gibbons, Michael. "How NGOs Can Contribute to EFA MDGs." Presentation at "The Role of NGOs in Achieving the Millennium Development Goals" Conference,

George Washington University International NGO Team, George Washington University, Washington, D.C., May 13–14, 2004.

Grown, Caren. Director, Poverty Reduction and Economic Governance, International Center for Research on Women. Presentation at "The Role of NGOs in Achieving the Millennium Development Goals" Conference, session on Women's Empowerment and Gender Equity, George Washington University International NGO Team, George Washington University, Washington, D.C., June 7, 2004.

Hartwell, Ash. Presentation to the Comparative International Education Society Annual Meeting, Brigham Young University, March 9–12, 2004.

Levine, Ruth. Senior Fellow and Director of Programs, Center for Global Development. "Achieving Health Millennium Development Goals: Roles of Non-Governmental Organizations." Presentation at "The Role of NGOs in Achieving the Millennium Development Goals" Conference, George Washington University International NGO Team, George Washington University, Washington, D.C., May 13–14, 2004.

Levy, Marc. CIESIN and Adjunct Professor at Columbia University. "NGOs and the MDGs." Presentation at "The Role of NGOs in Achieving the Millennium Development Goals" Conference, George Washington University International NGO Team, George Washington University, Washington, D.C., May 13, 2004.

Method, Frank. "Achieving Universal Primary Education: The Role(s) of NGOs in Achieving the Millennium Development Goals for Education." Presentation at "The Role of NGOs in Achieving the Millennium Development Goals" Conference, George Washington University International NGO Team, George Washington University, Washington, D.C., May 13–14, 2004.

Murphy, Lynn, and Karen Mundy. "A Review of International Nongovernmental EFA Campaigns, 1998–2002." Background paper prepared for *EFA Global Monitoring Report 2002.*

Odhiambo, Carolyne. NGO Practitioner from Kenya (Kenyan Public Benefit Environment). Presentation at "The Role of NGOs in Achieving the Millennium Development Goals" Conference, George Washington University International NGO Team, George Washington University, Washington, D.C., May 13, 2004.

Price, Marie. Professor of Geography and International Affairs and Department Chair, the George Washington University. Discussant remarks at "The Role of NGOs in Achieving the Millennium Development Goals" Conference, George Washington University International NGO Team, George Washington University, Washington, D.C., May 13, 2004.

Richardson, Yolanda. CEO, CEDPA. Presentation at "The Role of NGOs in Achieving the Millennium Development Goals" Conference, session on Women's Empowerment and Gender Equity, George Washington University International NGO Team, George Washington University, Washington, D.C., June 7, 2004.

Schmdit-Traub, Guido. United National Millennium Development Project Special Advisor on the Environment. Notes prepared as talking points for "The Role of NGOs in Achieving the Millennium Development Goals" Conference, George Washington University International NGO Team, George Washington University, Washington, D.C., May 13, 2004 (subsequent presentation not made).

Smith, James. Acting Assistant Administrator, Bureau for Economic Growth, Agriculture and Trade, United States Agency for International Development. Presentation to the Advisory Committee on Voluntary Foreign Aid, Washington, D.C., May 25, 2005.

Smith, Stephen C. "Governance of Nongovernmental Organizations: A Framework and Application to Poverty Programs in East Africa," Working Paper in GWU Law School Public Law Journal of the Social Science Research Network (SSRN), 2004, http://papers.ssrn.com/sol3/papers.cfm?abstract_id=628684.

————. *Ending Global Poverty: A Guide to What Works,* New York: Palgrave/ Macmillan (St. Martin's Press), May 2005.

Starik, Mark. Professor of Strategic Management and Public Policy and Director, Center for Environmental Sustainability, George Washington University. Commentary at "The Role of NGOs in Achieving the Millennium Development Goals" Conference, George Washington University International NGO Team, George Washington University, Washington, D.C., May 13, 2004.

Teegen, Hildy. "Business–Government–NGO Bargaining in International, Multilateral Clean Development Mechanism Projects in the Wake of Kyoto" (2003). In *Globalization and NGOs: Transforming Business, Governments and Society,* ed. J.P. Doh and H. Teegen, Westport, CT: Praeger, (2003a).

————. "International NGOs as Global Institutions: Using Social Capital to Impact Multinational Enterprises and Governments." *Journal of International Management* 9 (September): 271–285, (2003b).

United States Agency for International Development. *Education Strategy: Improving Lives Through Learning.* Washington, D.C.: Author, April 2005.

Wolchik, Sharon. Director of the Russian and East European Studies Program, George Washington University. Presentation at "The Role of NGOs in Achieving the Millennium Development Goals" Conference, session on Women's Empowerment and Gender Equity, George Washington University International NGO Team, George Washington University, Washington, D.C., June 7, 2004.

10

Conclusions and Policy Implications

*Jennifer M. Brinkerhoff, Stephen C. Smith,
and Hildy Teegen*

This volume and the conference that set it in motion were conceived as a means to more fully account for, and to understand the role of, nongovernmental organizations (NGOs) in achieving the UN Millennium Development Goals (MDGs), a global policy initiative of historic scope and scale. We anchor our collective interest in NGOs and poverty alleviation and development in general within the MDG framework, and integrate the perspectives of scholars, practitioners, and policy makers working in the MDG areas. As such, our efforts are intended to provide guidance to policy makers and practitioners struggling to achieve tangible progress in confronting the most critical issues facing global society. In pursuing this task we confront the problematic nature of the MDGs themselves, the complexity of defining NGOs, and the blurred roles of the various sectors in practice. The findings are applicable not only to the MDGs but to problems of poverty and development more broadly. Before presenting our findings, we first explore this context.

The Role of NGOs in Achieving the MDGs: Inherent Challenges

The choice of the MDGs as our policy anchor stems from many factors: most countries in the world have agreed to them; they have guided the framing and analysis of important and related global initiatives such as the World Economic Forum's Global Governance Initiative project and the Millennium Challenge Account in the United States; the targets are quantifiable and have "due dates" that allow for measurement and comparison of progress; all major bilateral and multilateral donors have incorporated the MDGs into their humanitarian assistance, development, and lending programs; the MDGs were developed in consultation with the poor themselves; there is implied recognition of the connections between and among causes of poverty and human suffering as captured in the eight goals; and a specific role is noted for all countries, including the rich countries that are called on to participate proactively in MDG achievement.

But as many contributors to the conference noted, this very anchoring of our work on NGOs and poverty alleviation to the MDG framework runs certain risks. The MDGs have been faulted as incomplete—matters of *global* governance and *supranational* issues such as climate change have not been included. Individual and community empowerment—garnering increasing attention by international donors such as the World Bank—are similarly excluded; yet as Smith (2005) details, powerlessness and social exclusion generate poverty traps that can effectively preclude the world's poor from enjoying gains in other areas such as health and education. Failure on certain MDGs (e.g., HIV) reduces the potential for success in others (e.g., education, incomes), yet this interconnectedness is not made explicit in the targets and indicators (Vandemoortele, chapter 2). Although most countries have signed off on the MDGs, they are often not aligned with national-policy frameworks, resulting in national initiatives that may work at cross-purposes to the MDGs (see D. Brinkerhoff, chapter 5). This misalignment may result from the MDGs' one-size-fits-all nature that calls into question the degree to which consultation with the poor on the MDGs is really more accurately construed as "choiceless participation"; without local and national ownership of the goals, their achievement may be illusory (Vandemoortele, chapter 2).

Furthermore, the quantitative indicators applied to the MDG targets are inherently linear, and social and human development deprivation increases nonlinearly; the "squared poverty gap" (P2) alternative more closely maps to the reality of poverty and deprivation. These targets also create perverse incentives for policy makers whereby the extremely poor—those arguably most in need of policy attention, and the most difficult and costly to reach— are neglected at the expense of those living at levels nearer the target. It is easier to demonstrate progress in moving citizens from 90 cents per day to $1 per day income levels than it is to move them from 50 cents per day to the $1/day MDG target. Extra income to someone with 50 cents per day may be worth five times as much in welfare as an equivalent income gain for someone with 90 cents per day (as implied by the squared poverty gap measure). Moreover, analogous incentives may apply to some of the other targets, for example in reducing hunger among those less calorie or protein deprived, or improving conditions of easier-to-reach and generally better-off slum dwellers. Like the oft-heard critique of the Millennium Challenge Account in the United States that favors countries with "good" track records in governance for overseas development assistance (ODA), leaving little room for those with governance challenges to "catch up" (with a moving target) (D. Brinkerhoff, chapter 5), the quantitative indicators for the MDGs may create vicious cycles for the extremely poor as policy makers consistently undertake development initiatives that prefer those relatively less badly off in society.

The targets are applied nationally, and are intended to form part of the national policy framework, yet indicator aggregation at this level invariably masks important differences in poverty within countries. Impressive gains made by countries such as India and China in recent years ignore serious, and in certain cases worsening, problems of poverty for certain sectors of those populations (Vandemoortele, chapter 2).

Although pressure to act may be prompted by the MDG timeframes, many development initiatives require investments with very long-term payoffs; some of these payoffs are only fully realized across multiple generations such as investments in family incomes that allow children to attend school instead of working. Drayton (Afterword) notes that many of the most-promising social-entrepreneurship endeavors do not expect returns for some fifteen years. Thus, the relatively short due dates for many of the MDG targets retard investments in critical projects with longer payback periods. The choice of time horizon conditions interpretations of success—resulting in further risk of manipulation and misinterpretation of the true status of poverty in a country. There is also the danger that the failure to achieve some of the specific indicators will lead to disillusionment and an excuse to decrease, rather than increase, efforts to end poverty. Clearly the Janus face of the MDG indicators' approach to development is one that requires further assessment.

Our explicit focus for the conference and for this volume is on the role of NGOs in achieving the MDGs. We note in chapter 4 that NGOs are but one set of relevant actors in the development arena—joined by their counterparts in the public and private sectors. There we outline ideal roles and comparative advantages for actors from each sector, based on the underlying concepts of rivalry and exclusivity conditions for the provision of a particular good or service. D. Brinkerhoff (chapter 5) extends the analysis and provides important grounding in the enabling environment that governments can and should provide for development per se, and for the citizen sector of NGOs in particular to effectively engage in the development process.

As Edwards (chapter 3) and Drayton (Afterword) convincingly argue, we must take great care in defining our terms and our focal organizations. The difficult work of the MDGs ultimately requires new ideas and inspiration for individuals to engage in activities that promote human development (Vandermoortele, chapter 2; Finnemore, chapter 6; Drayton, Afterword). In the conference and in this volume, we focus on NGOs as any and all groups of individuals from civil society that partake in activities geared toward the achievement of the poverty-related goals captured within the MDGs. This broad definition allows for the "surprises" (Edwards, chapter 3)—organizations that have appeared from unlikely quarters to work on behalf of the poor, and for the less formal network-type organizations harnessing and cross-fertilizing the actions of otherwise dispersed individuals working toward common goals (Florini 2003; Drayton, Afterword). NGOs defined thus are engaged in a range of activities, from direct service delivery, to advocacy, to capacity building and mobilization related to the MDGs. We note in chapter 4 that the "ideal" roles for NGOs in development are often not seen in practice, and that NGOs, through necessity and/or through opportunistic action, may find their niche in market-based activities (where we would otherwise expect private-sector firms to engage) and/or in the provision of basic public goods (where we would otherwise expect governments to take center stage).

These organizations make choices not only about their primary activity types (service, advocacy, capacity building, mobilization), but also about their reach or activity scope. We see examples of highly effective NGOs operating within very narrow geographic (e.g., a single village) and activity areas (e.g., polio vaccinations). But extreme-focus strategies such as these are not required or even always desirable for achieving great progress in poverty alleviation. NGOs such as the Building Resources Across the Countries, or BRAC, succeed by offering a multitude of services for the poor, including microcredit, nonformal education and basic healthcare; NGOs such as CARE are able to transfer learning across diverse geographical settings. Although somewhat tangential to our purpose here, we recognize the need for further work in understanding the specific contingencies associated with this scope question regarding NGO effectiveness.

Like many others, NGOs are often compelled through opportunity and/or through necessity to evolve over time. We see NGOs growing in size, often to achieve benefits of scale in production and delivery of services and reach for their advocacy activities. Some NGOs begin as informal associations of committed individuals—or in the extreme case as a single "social entrepreneur" with an innovative idea, passion, and energy to promote the cause and to enlist others in the effort (Drayton, Afterword). The AIDS Support Organization (TASO) in Uganda exemplifies this early stage of informality—a more formalized organization evolved over time in order to more effectively spread the benefits of its early innovations to a larger client base.

NGOs are associations of individuals, and their associational capacity and nature promotes further association between and among NGOs themselves—locally, across service areas, to provide holistic service packages to common clients, and internationally, to spur global awareness and to bring global resources to bear on problems in otherwise isolated or ignored areas of the world (Florini 2003). In this way NGOs may evolve into broad constellations of NGOs in far-flung (geographically or activity-wise) networks.

Some NGOs change their fundamental form—becoming for-profit ventures in the areas where they work. The participation of the Citigroup Foundation in Latin America, microlending in association with other NGOs, demonstrated attractive possibilities for Citigroup's commercial business to enter this market—either servicing "graduates" of the earlier nonprofit operations with larger, or longer term loans, perhaps secured with tangible collateral made possible through earlier nonprofit lending activities, or through market segmentation, whereby more commercially viable loan-candidate groups were identified through the earlier microlending activities (Hattel 2005).

This volume presents many important policy conclusions regarding the role and impact of NGOs in achieving the MDGs, which will be more fully recounted in the remainder of this chapter. Briefly, our main conclusions are summarized as follows:

- the MDGs represent a political "game" where NGOs can act, react, and impact others' actions;
- the MDGs are best understood within a *global* governance context where NGOs of various types play often evolving roles;
- NGO effectiveness for achieving the MDGs is informed by addressing:
  - ideal types for NGOs
  - scale considerations
  - scope considerations
  - conditioning contingencies
- accountability and responsiveness of NGOs and of the other organizations with which they interact are crucial in understanding MDG achievement and development sustainability; and
- careful and rigorous evaluation of NGO-initiated and/or NGO–related development programs and activities is called for.

The MDGs Represent a Political "Game"

There are several ways in which the MDGs can be described as a political "game." As Finnemore (chapter 6) argues, the needs of the poor are often ignored by politicians as they lack the political clout needed to incentivize national leaders to fully attend to their needs. NGOs can advocate for the poor in local venues and through activities elsewhere to pressure other actors, including the governments in advanced economies, to implement pro-poor policies, including demands for sufficient resources and the establishment of enabling environments to allow NGOs and the poor clients they serve to overcome serious development challenges (D. Brinkerhoff, chapter 5). The ODA policies of rich countries relate to another political aspect of the MDGs and NGOs' role. Through actions geared toward these government agencies and the international organizations where they wield significant clout as club members, NGOs can ensure that adequate funding and support— including capacity building for local communities and NGOs that provide local services—are provided, and promises made to this effect are carried out through diligent monitoring and publicity campaigns.

Politics are driven by incentives, and NGOs can and should work to promote the MDGs by reaching the relevant publics (Finnemore, chapter 6) and the "kitchen table" (Vandemoortele, chapter 2) so that this pro-poor policy initiative receives the widespread popular support that political actors ignore at their peril. Where the MDGs become mainstream, goes the argument, NGOs will have broader support for their important development work. The case experience of the MDGs related to gender issues, however, provides an important caveat—by mainstreaming gender issues in previous development initiatives, it has proven difficult for NGOs to garner sufficient development attention specific to gender (Brinkerhoff, Smith, and Teegen, chapter 9).

The MDGs and Global Governance

The eighth MDG—partnership—explicitly calls for participation of rich countries in global development initiatives. Similarly, the policy of 20/20 for social services, adopted at the 1995 Social Summit in Copenhagen, specifically links ODA funding with specific development programs (Vandermoortele, chapter 2). As indicated above, NGOs that advocate with rich-country governments and international organizations abroad can provide important benefits for policy in the developing world. However, the fact that all countries are deemed responsible for development within the MDG framework is but one element of the global governance dimension of development.

Many problems of development in a given poor country are caused or exacerbated by actions taken in other countries. Global coordination in trade that leads to reductions in harm to poor producers or consumers is not "naturally occurring" (Finnemore, chapter 6), but can be promoted by NGO activism and technical expertise in areas such as environmental sustainability (Brinkerhoff, Smith, and Teegen, chapter 9). Supranational development problems are often best addressed by international NGOs whose influence and operational capacity extend across national borders. By designing and promoting global standards and regimes, NGOs can galvanize development-oriented action at the level of nation states and local communities.

NGO Effectiveness Dimensions

In our framework chapter (Brinkerhoff, Smith, and Teegen, chapter 4), we note that NGOs are ideally suited to promote the achievement of the MDGs in areas where innovation, flexible programming, specialized knowledge related to the poor, targeted local public goods, common-property-resources management, and representation and advocacy are called for. By focusing their actions on these areas of natural comparative advantage, NGOs in the citizen sector can most effectively and efficiently further development throughout the world. In cases of market failure, NGOs may also fruitfully enter the "space" of private firms that will be insufficiently incentivized to engage in goods or services provision for the benefit of the poor. Similarly, where governments are weak, under-resourced, or corrupt, NGOs also play important roles in providing public goods and in establishing the institutions that enable subsequent activities to be successfully carried out. Each of these roles is demonstrated in the various sectors implicated by the MDGs, as described in chapters 8 (Smith) and 9 (Brinkerhoff, Smith, and Teegen).

A contemporary mantra in development privileges programs and activities that can be scaled to reach large numbers of the poor. The focus on scale finds its roots in the parlance of both economics and business management; by achieving scale, certain production economies, as well as learning-curve benefits that arise from repeatedly performing similar activities across time, can be enjoyed. Relatively small, local, NGOs may lack the resources and/or expertise to effectively scale up their activities. Yet these locally designed development approaches may be precisely what are called for to mitigate localized poverty traps (Smith, chapter 8). And scaling up, per se, does not guarantee poverty reduction or other development gains.

Some scaling up may involve the evolution of NGOs that pioneer the development initiatives in question; TASO in Uganda evolved from very informal beginnings to a more formalized organization to implement programs with broader reach. In other cases, NGO-pioneered actions are subsumed by governments (when sufficient public-sector capacity is present) or by private-sector entrants (when sufficient profit-opportunities exist) as the development innovations are applied in increasingly larger venues. Drayton (Afterword) notes that little incubations of ideas at the level of social entrepreneurs and NGOs can accumulate and provide scaled up advantages throughout the world where *ideas* (versus organizations or programs) are scaled up and applied broadly, and innovations are not "balkanized" within individual-country settings. NGOs play important roles in providing initial demonstration of initiatives' viability in development and in provoking further dissemination of these ideas through a range of conduits including advanced economies' development agencies, international organizations such as the World Bank, and development consultancies. International NGOs span territories and program areas and are thus well suited to identify high-potential extensions and efficiencies.

Although identification of the specific mechanisms underlying organizational scope is left for future work, we note here that the scope of NGO activities will also relate to these organizations' effectiveness. Given the connections inherent in the areas addressed by the MDGs, NGOs that can identify and leverage complementarities in the production of goods and services for development can more efficiently provide relevant solutions (Smith, chapter 8). This occurs when the costs associated with enlarged activity scope may be offset by important advantages that could not be enjoyed through more narrowly constrained activity scope. In making such calculations it is important to not discount the significant management challenges associated with broad development initiatives (Drayton, Afterword).

Through examination of the MDG application areas —health, gender, the natural environment, and education—we indicate in chapter 9 the series of contingent conditions that promote NGO effectiveness in achieving the MDGs. The delineation of these contingencies responds to the concern voiced by Edwards (chapter 3) that "we lack systematic evidence regarding transmission mechanisms for development across a sufficient number of different settings." Related research would be useful to sort out the enduring conundrums in development, including the case of modern China where, Vandemoortele (chapter 2) notes, impressive gains in economic growth have failed to reduce poverty more broadly. By recognizing these contingencies (detailed in tabular form at the conclusion of chapter 9 (Brinkerhoff, Smith, and Teegen), development actors from all sectors can be more confident that the actions undertaken by NGOs are well suited to a given situation and thus can be more readily expected to be effective.

Accountability, Responsiveness, and NGOs

The underlying premise for this volume is that NGOs might play an important role in achieving the MDGs. NGOs are agent organizations that must be responsive to dual principals—the clients they serve and the donors who provide them with the resources needed to conduct their work (see Brinkerhoff, Smith, and Teegen, chapter 4). Regarding accountability to the clients they purport to serve, NGOs must work to ensure that the poor are given a voice to shape and sustain the programs geared toward their development needs. Imposed from outside, standardized service offerings may fail by not addressing local needs or issues. Presumably, local NGOs will be more adept at finding appropriate solutions to development challenges.

Smith (chapter 8) notes that social exclusion can entrench poverty; where NGOs draw on the expertise of otherwise excluded members of the population in designing and implementing development programs, more sustainable gains can be made. Getting local ownership for development initiatives is important, although it may be insufficient for enduring development. Critical challenges such as ineffective national taxation systems (Vandermoortele, chapter 2) and weak local institutions (D. Brinkerhoff, chapter 5) may obviate the potential for local governments to take ownership of development programs. Some argue that (modest) user fees are important for getting the poor to take ownership for their own welfare promotion. Yet Vandemoortele (chapter 2) has argued that high transactions costs and negative externalities that serve to discriminate against certain groups in society are often the consequences of user fees and ultimately limit their net effectiveness. Indeed, even very small user fees can discourage participation in vital programs for poverty reduction such as deworming and agricultural improvements (Kremer and Miguel 2007). Where NGOs can work to redress some of these limitations, more permanent development solutions can be put into place.

NGOs are also ultimately accountable to the donor community. There is some risk that the poverty-reduction mission will be compromised by the need to follow the short time horizon as well as some of the other conditions for funding imposed by donors, such as USAID. Contrary to the simple, unidimensional, profit-performance metric common in the private sector, NGOs not only engage in activities with relatively long payback periods (Drayton, Afterword) but also in those that address development challenges that can legitimately be gauged along various dimensions, making performance assessment more difficult.

Current practice in the development community serves to protect donors from hostile environments (i.e., those that pose greater challenges to development effectiveness) (D. Brinkerhoff, chapter 5), yet NGOs should work to demand enabling environments to foster their development work and to hold other actors accountable for ensuring that development gains reach the poor (Finnemore, chapter 6). Power imbalances between the poor, the NGOs that represent their interests, and the donor community prompt Vandemoortele (chapter 2) to call for a peer-and-partner review process, whereby more suitable benchmarks and evaluators are employed to appropriately determine development effectiveness. NGOs can play important partner roles in such a process. Where NGOs adopt the MDG framework to guide and assess their own activities as does Social Watch Philippines (Welch, chapter 7), some minimum standards of accountability for governments and societies might be promoted. In sum, NGOs must give the poor an effective voice and role in achieving sustainable development and must carefully balance the needs of these clients with those of the donors who make the development work of many NGOs possible.

Looking Ahead: A Call for Rigorous and Careful Evaluation of NGOs and Their Programs

The nature of the MDGs and the role of NGOs in achieving them are sorely in need of careful evaluation. Such evaluation is occurring only in a very limited way, on a case-by-case basis, by the parties most affected by the evaluation. There is much important research to be done in terms of the NGO role in achieving the MDGs. Rigorous evaluation of poverty, hunger, and other development programs is crucial, given the suffering of the poor and the very limited resources available. Many of the issues in poverty strategy and the role of NGOs and other actors, as well as very specific program-design questions, including, but not limited to, those raised in this volume, can be addressed with rigorous evaluation methods.

The use of randomized trials is generally the most methodologically sound approach (because it addresses the key statistical problem of selection bias involving unobservable information).[1] In practice, it can also be the most ethical way to implement programs: given NGOs' very limited budgets, "drawing straws" is generally the fairest way to allocate program benefits among equally deserving participants. In addition to better evaluate programs, we can also benefit in practice—and in further development of theory—from studies that critically and carefully examine the process by which programs are designed and implemented in different types of NGOs as well as in public and private sectors. These are all areas where cooperation between development researchers in universities and development practitioners in NGOs could be very valuable. Insights gained through the conference that spawned this volume were similarly made possible by integrating the viewpoints of academic researchers and active development practitioners.

We conclude with a call to scholars and practitioners to participate in furthering this effort. Reports of actual (realized) NGO roles in development can be provided to correspond to each of the stated MDGs. These reports can be organized along the lines of the overview framework, paying specific attention to identifying relevant contingencies, assessment mechanisms, and outcomes from these previous NGO efforts. Drawing on these cases and the extant literature, we can further develop grounded theory and normative prescriptions for practitioners concerning the appropriate roles for NGOs in achieving the MDGs. The framework for appreciating the key roles for NGOs outlined in chapter 4, and the detailed examination of the main contingencies in applying this framework stressed in chapter 9, are intended to provide useful guidance for future work by academics and practitioners alike. A wide-ranging effort to refine our understanding of the critical roles of NGOs in development globally will help achieve the Millennium Development Goals and the broader objectives of ending poverty and realizing shared and sustainable development.

Notes

1. There are some difficulties and limits to randomization. Some, particularly internal validity problems such as "selective compliance," can be more readily addressed than others. More challenging are technical, budgetary, or political limitations. It can be difficult to isolate which features of successful but complex or multisectoral programs are most effective. For other contextual reasons, scaled-up programs can work quite differently than pilots; and programs can have different impacts in seemingly similar villages. This can lead to doubts about how well pilot-program impact study results apply to individuals not included in the study (external validity). Randomization is not always possible; using it in all places and contexts would be prohibitively expensive. In such cases when alternative strategies of evaluation are necessary, they need a higher level of care and rigor than has been common to date.

References

Florini, Ann M. *The Coming Democracy: New Rules for Running a New World.* Washington, D.C.: Island Press, 2003.

Hattel, Kelly. Director, MicroFinance Network. "MicroFinance Network Approaches to Service Delivery." Presentation at "The Effectiveness of Multiplex vs. Specialized Approaches to Microenterprise Development," GW International NGO Team Roundtable, George Washington University, Washington, D.C., April 8, 2005.

Kremer, Michael and Edward Miguel. "The Illusion of Sustainability." *Quarterly Journal of Economics,* forthcoming, 2007.

11

Afterword. The Power of Social Entrepreneurship

William Drayton

I want to contribute a historical perspective. There is a set of changes going on that just does not capture the shutter speed of the political process through the press. These changes are much more important, and I think much more hopeful, than what we read about. And what are these changes? They are in the citizen half of the world. The citizen half of the world has, over the last two-and-a-half decades, gone through the same structural transformation that business went through over the course of the preceding three centuries. This is a historically unprecedented event, and it has reached a scale now of momentum, size, and energy that it no longer can be ignored in terms of people's careers, or by business or government. If you are a scholar or journalist, and your job is to interpret the world and you do not understand this change, you are at risk of not doing a very good job, simply because we have now reached this scale of momentum.

Terminology

What is a *leading* social entrepreneur? Let me turn that around and ask you, who do you think is actually historically more important: Florence Nightingale or Andrew Carnegie? At the very least the question poses an arguable and important issue. Florence Nightingale was a great early pioneer social entrepreneur. We need entrepreneurs in education and human rights just as much as we do in energy and steel.

The heart of what it is to be an *entrepreneur*—to be creative—is, as we have come to understand, people who cannot stop—cannot be personally happy and satisfied—until they have changed the whole society. This characteristic makes them different from other people. Many people—scholars, artists—are satisfied when they can see and express an idea and share it: professionals when they make their client happy; managers when their organization works. None of that satisfies the entrepreneur. Entrepreneurs are only happy when they have changed the whole society.

I have one more point on terminology. At Ashoka, we have the rule that we never use the phrase *NGO,* and we also do not use *nonprofit.* Where do these words come from? Was it that the Europeans saw something new wandering around and they said, "Oh, what could this be? It's a nongovernment!"? Or that the Americans saw something new wandering around and they said, "Well, this is strange. These people are not looking for profit . . ."? Well, okay, one understands the etymology of where these terms came from, but you cannot define something this important by what it is not. You would not name a corporation the Non-Buggy Corporation. That says what you are not, but leaves utterly vague what it is that you actually do.

So we prefer the phrase *citizen sector,* or *citizen organization*, because that is the active ingredient. Someone or a group of people gets together and decides they are going to provide a service. They are working in the cause of change. They are going to take the initiative. So you will not hear from me the terms NGO or nonprofit—and hopefully no one from the social-entrepreneurship movement would ever use these dreadful phrases.

The Evolution of Social Entrepreneurship

As I mentioned, entrepreneurs are only satisfied when they have changed the whole society. That goal carries with it a whole set of requirements. It is a long-term process – they are in it for 10 to 20 years. You have to be very realistic. You have to be out there picking up the finest ideas available in the environment, and then, over 10 years, you change the idea. The notion that a social entrepreneur would have an idea and simply go implement it is just a complete fantasy. It does not work that way. As a social entrepreneur, every day, every month, you are changing the idea as the surrounding environment changes, as the idea evolves and goes through different stages, as you just learn the ropes. There is a constant iteration between vision and practical how-tos—so much so that these people tend to be psychologically testable as "double dominant" in the right and the left brain.

Now, ask yourself, what is the most powerful force in the world? I think it is at least strongly arguable that it is a person who is a good entrepreneur with a vision that represents a real pattern change in ideas. The combination of these two, plus an institution that's there to support it, is extraordinarily powerful. What drives all change ultimately? Someone has to have seen a potential change, and then he or she has to entrepreneur it.

I am going to try to do three things: one, expand on what this historical transformation is; two, articulate where we are in the transformation process; and, three, come back to the relevance—for us, personally, for the institutions we are associated with, and more broadly.

The Historical Perspective

First consider the perspective of history. William J. Baumol published a book (*The Free-Market Innovation Machine: Analyzing the Growth Miracle of Capitalism*, 2002) in which he asked the question, what caused the West to take off? It starts with some very interesting statistics. Prior to around the 1700s there was no growth in per capita income in the West at all. It's quite startling. Then in the 1700s it's 20 percent; in the 1800s it's 200 percent; in the last century, 740 percent. When you have a curve that does something like that you have to ask, what happened here? I think it's reasonably clear that business became entrepreneurial; starting in northern Europe, then crossing the Atlantic, and gradually moving out across the world. This development set in motion a compounding productivity—two to three percent a year—which by an ever-broadening base has driven history over these last three centuries. Now, how many newspaper historians over these last three centuries even talked about this underlying change in the structure of society? We heard about this tornado and that war and all these dreadful things that happened yesterday, but not this extraordinarily powerful force, and I think that is where we are in terms of the citizen half of this transformation.

Now, why did this takeoff occur in business and not in the citizen half? Because that is clearly what happened. The citizen half in every society did not go through this compounding in productivity. We focus on differences in economic growth across different countries, but within each country there has been a very productive compounding and productive business sector—and a social sector that has fallen way behind. Let's think about our reputation, our self-esteem, our competitive salaries as workers in the citizen sector. Two decades ago it was really pathetic. The fact that this has changed dramatically is one indication of the historical transformation of the last decade or so.

Why did the citizen sector fall behind? Because it was so easy to tax the new wealth that business generated. The money flowed through government: we built the canals, school systems, and the welfare systems. There was no pressure to change, in fact, because the money flowed through a monopoly; and no monopoly of any sector wants competition because it can't survive it. It was a negative incentive. Hence the smaller gap in productivity of the citizen sector across countries.

The Florence Nightingales, the Maria Montessoris, the William Lloyd Garrisons—they were extraordinary outliers. The system did not change yet, but they began the process. The history of the last two-and-a-half decades has been the flipping of the architecture of the field as a whole. As a result, the citizen sector has been going through a period of 9 or 10 percent productivity growth because this is a period of catch-up with the potential level as seen by looking at the private sector. As a result, we have experienced explosive growth in the citizen sector over these last two decades.

Other sources of the expansion of social entrepreneurship and the citizen sector included the accumulation of problems that have built up and are accelerating. And the failure to solve problems for three centuries has consequences. On the other side, we have succeeded in having a better-educated population, a more confident population. And so, supply and demand were coming together.

There are also some specific local factors. In Asia, the postindependence generation was coming of professional age, hitting their 30s. In Indonesia, Venezuela and other places, the new generation was moving—not everyone, a small percentage of people perhaps, but a significant absolute number. This is a generation that did not go through the colonial trauma. Their parents thought getting rid of the British or the Dutch or the French was the key, and then they would get control of the government, which they did. They used it very aggressively, but their children thought, "Oh, this is frustrating and inefficient," and so on. Conditions were ripe for a new approach. So the generals in Latin America fled around then, the Wall came down, and the Soviet empire collapsed in 1989. This all reflected the deep underlying pattern of everyone becoming a changemaker. The democratic revolution—all these pieces fit together.

At that point there was not even a word to describe social entrepreneurs. If you said that word, people would look at you blankly. The smart ones would say, "That's an oxymoron." But it was hard to describe how impossible things were when you did not even have a word that described the field.

Where Are We Now?

Here is a set of figures about the rate of growth of the citizen sector. The first, figure 11.1, is of countries from four different continents.

When Ashoka first went into Indonesia we could find only one environmental group; 15 years later we counted over 2,000. In Slovakia, when the Wall came down, there were 10 or 11 citizen groups; a decade later over 10,200 were registered. Brazil went from under 5,000 to over a million citizen groups from 1980 to 2000. You cannot even begin to understand the impact of this statistic. The United States went from

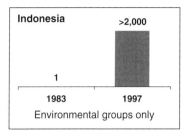
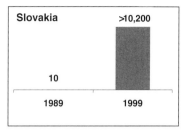
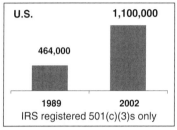
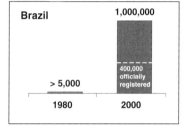

Source: Urban Institute, Ministry of Economics (Brazil), Walhi (Indonesia)

Figure 11.1   Number of citizen groups

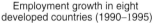

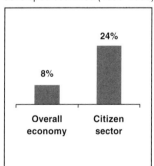
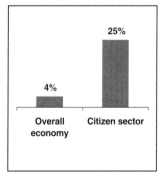

Source: Johns Hopkins

Source: John E. Seley, City University of New York; Julian Wolpert, Princeton University (2002)

Figure 11.2   Employment growth rates

464,000 registered IRS tax-deductible organizations in 1990 to over 1.1 million in 2002.

Figure 11.2 presents a different cut at the same issue. It illustrates the growth in full-time–equivalent employment in our sector versus elsewhere—three to six times that of the overall economy.

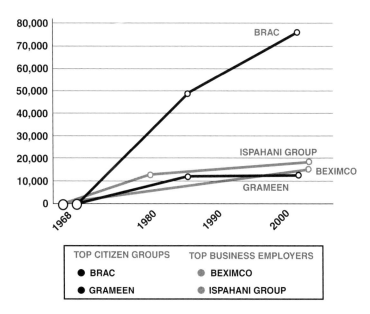

Figure 11.3   Number of workers—Bangladesh

In member countries of the Organisation of Economic Co-operation and Development (OECD), it is roughly 2.5 times the rate. New York City is obviously much more than that. And it is not just the number of organizations and the number of employees; now we have second- and third-generation modern, competitive, entrepreneurial, highly confident citizen organizations. Figure 11.3, on Bangladesh, illustrates the four biggest organizations other than the government.

As you can see, BRAC is four times bigger in terms of full-time equivalent than the biggest business. Grameen is roughly tied for third place, and this does not include their international staff.

Confirming the Relevance

When we got started in this transformation two to two-and-a-half decades ago, I cannot tell you how many people said, "Oh, they're just a drop in the ocean. It doesn't amount to anything." People don't say that anymore because when you have a million citizen groups in Brazil and they impeach the president, and the next president comes from our sector and so on and so forth, you *can't* say that anymore. It is obvious. We are finding more and more evidence of this power as the field is moving out on the global level, as reflected in figure 11.4.

We now have an International Criminal Court—and citizen groups blasted it out of the attic for those nation-states that kept it locked up for 50 years. This is extraordinarily radical, which is why the nation-states hate it so much. Now, under very limited circumstances, every human being has a right to go to an institution of law, a sovereign institution, without the permission of their national governments. So, suddenly in a small way— it's like the beginning of courts in common law—we now have citizenship as something bigger. It is only the beginning.

When we started working in Europe, people said, "Oh, this doesn't apply to us, especially in Europe where the government does everything." Well, here's your historical force at work, unheralded, unappreciated, and it is true in Germany and France too. As illustrated in figure 11.5, if you

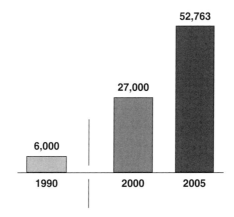

Figure 11.4   Number of international citizen groups

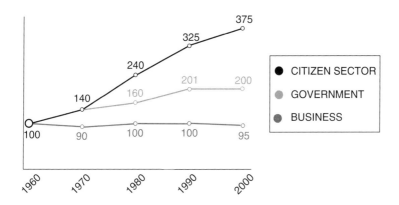

Figure 11.5   German employment indexed to 1960

take 1960 as your base year and look at business, government, and our sector, you'll see that over that period businesses actually lost full-time employees. In Germany, which represents the pattern for Europe, the employment index has dropped from 100 to 98. Government has roughly doubled, but employment in that sector is no greater than it was a decade or so ago. And the only sector that is growing in terms of employment in Germany is us, the citizen sector.

This has to be a really powerful, historical force. I could show you a whole series of different measures of something that you do not see recorded in the newspapers. The reality is way ahead of the perception, and that is one of the reasons this volume and the conference that informed it are so important, and I think that everyone here has got a major set of opportunities.

How Does It All Work?

Given that this is the history, let me try to delve for a minute or two into how this is going on. What are the mechanisms at work? Consider applying Thomas Kuhn's work on scientific revolutions to looking at how scientific change works through a society. You have a major change, and then it bumps down and changes one industry, and then it gives this industry a competitive advantage over the next industry, and so this second industry has to respond. And over several decades the change works its way through. I think it is exactly the same process for primary social change. And that, of course, is what leading social entrepreneurs do. They are in business to cause a change in the pattern of society all across society.

Consider what that means at the local level. Look at the fellow in this picture, just to give you a sense. This is a picture of Rodrigo Baggio (figure 11.6)—he was in his early 20s.

Rodrigo was after the digital divide. He had been working on it since he was a teenager. He had a very simple idea: people want to get to the other side of this divide. They have plenty of motivation: they'll do the organizing; they'll pay for it; they'll get the space; and they'll provide the people. Rodrigo knew that all he had to do was provide some technical assistance, software, and the building. He is now operating in some 15 countries. There are millions of graduates of his programs; 95 percent are either self-employed profitably or become employed within a couple of months of graduation. These are kids that do not have imposing resumes.

Now, let's contemplate what this means. Baggio comes in to this concept and presents his idea. People get organized; things change. Well, this upsets a lot of the existing patterns. It challenges the schools and all the things they failed to do. It challenges the idea that things must stay the way they are.

Figure 11.6   Rodrigo Baggio

In my mind, this is sort of like plowing a field before you seed it. Of course the entrepreneur makes the seeds as well. If you are an entrepreneur, you want lots of people in communities all over to say, "Oh, that's a good idea. I'm going to do that." Your seeds have to be user-friendly. If you are plowing and seeding, you get change. And specifically you support local changemakers because you do not get change unless you go through local changemakers.

Rodrigo's impact in many, many, barrios and villages across the world is that he has plowed and seeded. And local changemakers have come out of this process. The more local changemakers there are, of course, the more there will be, because it gets easier and easier. They are role models, not only Rodrigo, but all the other social entrepreneurs.

All right, so that is one changemaker. What happens when you go from one to two to ten, or a hundred in a country? What happens when you wire this field together so that ideas flow from Bangladesh to Nigeria to the United States and back? The rate of plowing and seeding just keeps multiplying. The network becomes a distribution channel. This is enormously liberating. It's telling people they can. It's showing them how through examples, not through theories or pamphlets. That is how people learn. They get to see this is something they can do.

As more local changemakers and more institutions begin to accept this, it gets easier with the next generation of primary entrepreneurs, and you have more and more of them. That is the core mechanism. That is part of the way you understand specific processes that have been so historically extraordinary these last two-and-a-half decades. Our work at Ashoka has been to nurture these primary entrepreneurs.

Changemaking in Community: The Continuing Agenda

But this leads to something that we in Ashoka could only come to understand and articulate in the past year. It is intuitive, but it took Pierre Omidyar, the founder of eBay, to push us. He said, "What you are describing is an intermediate goal. What are you really after?" In his own experience, he had understood online auctions, but he had missed all this universal economic democracy that started to emerge out of eBay. Well, we worked on articulating our ultimate goal, and we decided that it is an invitation for people to step up and do things differently. That first change touches a series of people who were not doing this before. They are not passive anymore; they are full citizens; they are changemakers. As a result of this new understanding, Ashoka embraced the goal of "everyone a changemaker." If everyone could be a changemaker, the implications for society would be startling. The numbers of angry, frustrated, and unhappy people would be dramatically reduced. And the probability of problems outrunning the capacity of problem solvers would go away.

Let us go back to history again. When the agricultural revolution came, it produced a surplus big enough for 2 or 3 percent of the world's population. Ever since then, for thousands of years, 2 or 3 percent have run things. And that is the way families are set up. Except that does not work anymore. We really need everyone to be changemakers. So it is a little bit like changing from a mechanical-engineering model to a biological model where everyone is a cell and can take actions as long as they are well connected with the others—upside down, right, left, and various combinations. Here is another analogy: everyone would become like a white blood cell coursing through society, seeking and solving problems. If you see something that could be better and you find a way to fix it, that is very satisfying and empowering for you. If you see something that is stuck, you can change it. And you know how to do that: you know how to work together with other people. This is a fundamental change in the architecture of society as a whole. The leading social entrepreneurs have played a very key role in initiating the change that this is about.

I mentioned the fact that these cells have to fit together, and it is not just the individuals. People constantly misunderstand the United States as a bunch of individualists. Well, it does not work unless we know how to work together, unless we really master the ability to see ourselves in people's shoes so we can be empathetic and guide ourselves—unless we know teamwork.

The same thing is going on at bigger levels. So what we are doing now is building the field, building the social infrastructure for society, getting the wiring right, setting up patterns of how we work together, and developing institutions to support that. And this is an absolutely critical part of the challenge that everyone here has. We are so privileged. We live at the moment where this process has built up a level of maturity. In the main areas of the world, we have several million citizen groups. We have advanced groups, high-level citizen organizations. We have to develop how we are going to work together, and how we are going to work or not work in business and in government. What are the patterns going to be? We have to think about a five-year window of opportunity. We have the maturity. We can push things in directions so the field will be much smarter, but we have got to think this through.

Additional Features of the Changemaking Agenda

Now, I am just giving you a couple of examples of this agenda. Everyone I am sure can add more.

Global Integration

First, I think it is absolutely essential that our field is globally integrated. All the national laws make this very difficult, but this is something we can do. If we can work together as an integrated field, we will be much more effective. The world's problems are increasingly unsolvable (at least in part) unless we deal with them at the global level; or at least they can be solved better at the global level. And even where that is not true, if we work together, think together and collaborate, we can do a much better job. So, our field has to be integrated from the local level right up to the global. The economies of scale are enormous. In no one country are there enough social entrepreneurs to have a conversation where you can see the goal, because there are pieces all over the world. And if you work together it is dramatically more powerful.

The jury is out. The social entrepreneurs in the network do not know if they are going to be able to do that. But if we set that as a goal and we all work on it, then of course the institutions we build together are going to work better for the world. Jean Monnet, one of the great social entrepreneurs of the last century, consciously set out to overcome this balkanization and come together. We need to do at the global level what Jean Monnet did for Europe. For years I wondered who would be this new Jean Monnet that I was looking for, but then it suddenly dawned on me: it is not one person in an organization; it is the whole dynamic of our sector at the global level.

Now that these 2,000 groups got the International Criminal Court, many, many other human-rights groups are saying, "How can I get my issue on the agenda of the Court?" And in fields such as the environment that are still in denial about globalization, maybe someone is going to eventually say, "Well, we can do for the environment what the women's groups and the human-rights groups have done in those sectors." We cannot solve our problems unless we do it through institutions that work. With experience the idea gets stronger: we are citizens of the world; we can create the needed institutions. That is exactly what Monnet did for Europe.

Partnering with Business

Second, for three centuries, business and society diverged. They did not like one another; they spoke different languages, and there were completely different levels of activity. This is incredibly dysfunctional, a nonsensical historical accident. Partnerships between social entrepreneurs and business are profoundly important for the health of both. They can create hybrid value chains and help end the divergence between the consumer and citizen sectors. Business can use social networks to reach new markets. And the citizen sector can use the marketplace to gain financial sustainability. If we can get the strengths of the two delivery systems, business and society, working together to serve the same clients, we can get them better served at substantially lower cost. And we are actually working on a series of examples that do this for slum dwellers, forest dwellers, small farmers, and health care. Everyone wins when we overcome the habits of division and start working together.

Methodologies for Measuring Success

Turning to methodology, the third feature of this agenda, I cannot stand all this business about how we should have more performance measures and be like business. I think this is one of the things that could really derail us. It has hurt business terribly. We got into this mode because we have this available hammer of financial statistics, and every bureaucrat in the world wants to use it because you can avoid judgment. And all those 20-year-olds with their computers on Wall Street, they can push the numbers. They do not have to ask harder questions about whether the management of this company is vital or not. Or, is this company ready to take the next steps in terms of having the scientific experts?

We do not want to make that mistake. Of course we want to do analysis and have statistics. You can do it for some things. You can compare the relative efficiency of digging water wells, because a lot of wells are dug, and the statistics are not perfect but they are useful. But you cannot do that when you are trying to find the best social entrepreneurs before they have a track record. Their impact will not come for 15 years. Their idea will change 70 percent in the intervening decade. Some Ashoka Fellows' impacts are illustrated in figure 11.7.

These are major impacts but difficult to quantify in a standardized way. You have to have a process that recognizes judgment, and that uses disciplined judgment. We need to design our field to be able to do that. But at the end of five years we can begin to get some quantified measures.

One of the most difficult judgments is identifying and selecting social entrepreneurs to support. We have a process and a clear way of doing it. Figure 11.8 presents the outline of this process.

We train people, and now have individuals in over 50 countries applying this process. We have some results, illustrated in figure 11.9.

Ninety-seven percent of the Ashoka Fellows are working full time on the same idea at the end of about five years. Eighty-eight percent have had other

- Persuaded country to enact comprehensive victim's rights laws
- Throws open historically Kafka-like justice system
- Now spreading reform to FSU, other countries

Petra Vitousova
Czech Republic, 1995

- Created National Network Against Trafficking in Wild Animals
- 580 organizations, 30,000 individuals
- Achieved policy changes
- Removed systemic barriers, for example, police aversion to having to care for recovered endangered species

Dener Giovanini
Brazil, 1999

Figure 11.7   Examples of Ashoka Fellows' impact

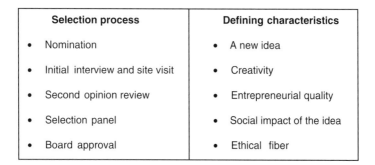

Selection process	Defining characteristics
• Nomination	• A new idea
• Initial interview and site visit	• Creativity
• Second opinion review	• Entrepreneurial quality
• Selection panel	• Social impact of the idea
• Board approval	• Ethical fiber

Figure 11.8   Selecting an Ashoka Fellow

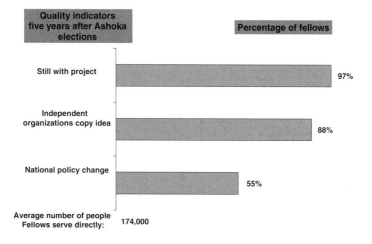

Quality indicators five years after Ashoka elections — Percentage of fellows

- Still with project: **97%**
- Independent organizations copy idea: **88%**
- National policy change: **55%**
- Average number of people Fellows serve directly: **174,000**

Source: Ashoka's "Measuring Effectiveness" studies. (Average results over two years)

Figure 11.9   Effectiveness of Ashoka Fellows

institutions they do not control copy their idea, another measure of success. Fifty-nine percent have impacted national policy. On average, each Fellow is directly serving 174,000 people. So our process is able to find the people who were not just local changemakers, who were really major patterns-changers.

And the point of showing this is twofold. First, these people exist in large numbers; and, second, disciplined judgment works. Now, the legal system figured out a long time ago that very rarely are the facts clear. If the facts are clear, then people do not litigate. When you end up in court, you have to make judgments about who is telling the truth. That is why we have juries. The judge is there to make sure that the evidence going to the jury is presented in a nontricky, honest way, and that the laws are explained. But ultimately the whole system is built around the idea that judgment has to be made about who is telling the truth. It is a system that is designed to build in disciplined judgment. I cannot tell you how frightened it makes me every time all the bureaucrats keep saying, "We've got to be like business . . . . There are more quantitative measures . . . ," et cetera, et cetera.

Financial Services for the Citizen Sector

Fourth, we need a new financial-services sector. What has changed in government grant agencies and foundations in the last 25 years? Well, when your client changes radically and you do not change, it is probably an indication that there is not a very good relationship–a listening relationship–with the client. Contrast that with the financial-services industry serving business. The banks have basically lost most of the lending to business because new actors came in who were more efficient. We invented angel investors in the last 15 years. There is billions of dollars of angel investment going on. We have got angel investments, merchant bankers, commercial banks, leasers, brokers—specialization by one type of function. We in the citizen sector did not have that. This is an area where there is tremendous need for a whole wave of innovation.

Certainly, around the world, we have a very alarming situation. Outside the United States and a few other places, financing from the citizen sector has not grown; a broad citizen base of support is not there. I just talked recently with one of our Fellows from Brazil, and his organization is about 30 percent citizen supported and 10 percent internationally supported; the rest of the support is from government. He is dealing with HIV. It is the largest HIV organization in the country. His statistics were that 92 percent of HIV organizations get money only from government.

What has happened is an explosive growth in the citizen operating side, but no change in institutional finance. So it is absolutely critical to try to encourage a new financial-services sector and clearly a facilitating tax policy. That would make a big difference. Having said that, I do not think it is going to happen until our sector gets organized and we figure out that it is in our self-interest, and we have the savvy and the energy to go after it. Then the tax laws will change.

Careers for Change

The fifth feature of this agenda concerns you. There is tremendous career opportunity. This is an area that is growing faster than any other part of society. The previous figures show it. It is no longer a lagging sector.

Salaries have improved and are actually beginning to gain on business, because citizen-sector productivity is gaining on business. This is an area where you can have a big impact and serve your values. People are now beginning to understand what this is and will be more interested in you at a dinner party than the investment banker sitting there. There are no glass ceilings. And it does not require brilliance. The biggest problem is getting beyond the "you can't" syndrome. But, anyone who can't see the problems out there is utterly blind. All the problems sitting there are invitations to be creative, to make use of your skills and the resources out there and find a solution. The barriers are in the mindset, not in the objective world. It is just a matter of giving yourself permission and then being persistent in seeing the problem or opportunity and in thinking about it until you come up with interesting ideas that might change the pattern.

Furthermore, it is not just entrepreneurs. We need professionals, we need managers. We are huge organizations. The supply and demand is very favorable. People do not even see this is here. The demand is enormous. You want to be part of a limited supply during a big expansion. This is a very attractive field. So there is a huge opportunity here if you can just see it; if you give yourself permission to do it.

Institutional Implications

The next level and final feature I want to discuss is institutional. Anyone who is running a business needs to understand that there are new major forces at work. By working together with large, sophisticated citizen groups in the slums of Mexico City and Guadalajara and the company Cemex (in the Patrimonio Hoy program), thousands of families are getting a way to finance and build better housing. It takes a family in Mexico four or five years to build one room. But with this program they can build the same room, with better quality, in just nine months, and with a savings of 30 percent, of higher quality and much less hassle. Ashoka is partnering with Cemex to leverage social-distribution networks to accelerate the expansion of Patrimonio Hoy. The company involved is going to make $100 million net profit, within the next two years. The citizen groups involved are getting a 30 percent markup on a very large sales volume. What have we done? You combine the strengths of what businesses are good at with what the citizen sector is good at. Well, if you do not happen to be that business—if you are one of the competitors and you do not wake up fast—you are going to lose a big market.

And I can use many other examples. If you are running a health agency in the government and you do not understand what this force is at work, how can you possibly be effective? Whether you are a scholar or you are a

- Launch a big pattern-change idea

- Launch the entrepreneur's long career

- Launch the needed institution

- Create highly contagious (because so empowering) role models

- Strengthen democratic decentralization

- Speed social problem solving

Figure 11.10   Pattern-change social entrepreneurs: No higher leverage

journalist—all the issues I have raised apply. There is a tremendous need and an opportunity.

Government still has a role. No one elected Bill Gates or Florence Nightingale. They are not representative. They can't be; it is inherently not logical in a competitive setting. So a democratic government is uniquely strong and it is the only element in society that represents everyone. It has to set the rules of the game; it has to define the incentives; it has to put the safeguards in, and it has to constantly change them and be aware that that is its job—I think it is very weak at that. And it has to do that with the purpose, on the one hand, of trying to encourage the maximum autonomy of individual and small-group management, and, on the other hand, channeling initiative in socially constructive ways.

Final Remarks

I have just one last thought. I think you have all seen figure 11.10 before, but I still recommend taking 15 seconds in silence to contemplate it.

I am enormously optimistic, *and* we have very serious problems to overcome. We have a backlog of problems that have built up. The reason to be optimistic, I think, is that everyone is becoming a changemaker. We are going to have more changemakers than problems. And we are wiring ourselves together. We are organizing so it is not just one changemaker. It is not just the individual. It is teams. It is coalitions of teams. It is us working together at the global level as well as at the local level. This is completely new, and it ultimately depends on all of us.

Index